CRITICAL ISSUES
IN SPECIAL AND
REMEDIAL EDUCATION

CRITICAL ISSUES IN SPECIAL AND REMEDIAL EDUCATION

James E. Ysseldyke
University of Minnesota

Bob Algozzine
University of Florida

HOUGHTON MIFFLIN COMPANY   BOSTON
Dallas   Geneva, Illinois   Hopewell, New Jersey   Palo Alto   London

To our children: Amy, Heather, Kathy, and Mike

Excerpts from the following publications have been reprinted by permission of the publishers:

E. P. Cubberley. *Readings in Public Education in the United States.* Boston: Houghton Mifflin Company, 1934. Reprinted by permission.

Paul Copperman. *The Literacy Hoax.* New York: William Morrow & Company, 1978. Copyright © 1978 by Paul Copperman. By permission of William Morrow & Company.

Seymour B. Sarason and John Doris. *Educational Handicap, Public Policy, and Social History: A Broadened Perspective on Mental Retardation.* New York: The Free Press, 1979. Copyright © 1979 by The Free Press, a Division of Macmillan Publishing Company, Inc. Reprinted by permission.

L. Mann. *On the Trail of Process.* New York: Grune & Stratton, Inc., 1979. Reprinted by permission.

B. Algozzine and C. D. Mercer. "Labels and Expectancies for Handicapped Children and Youth." In L. Mann and D. Sabatino (Eds.), *Fourth Review of Special Education.* New York: Grune & Stratton, Inc., 1980. Reprinted by permission.

D. N. Bersoff. "Regarding Psychologists Testily: Legal Regulation of Psychological Assessment in the Public Schools." *Maryland Law Review,* 1979, *39,* 27-120. Reprinted by permission.

R. Lynn. *Learning Disabilities.* New York: The Free Press, 1979. Copyright © 1979 by The Free Press, a Division of Macmillan Publishing Company, Inc. Reprinted by permission.

PRINTED IN THE U.S.A.

Library of Congress Catalog Card Number: 81-82560

ISBN: 0-395-31712-6

Contents

Preface

PURPOSE

Periodically, the state of the art in any area should be evaluated. American public education has received little systematic critical analysis in its hundred-year history; special and remedial education has received virtually none. *Critical Issues in Special and Remedial Education* presents a straightforward, objective analysis of the major conceptual and practical issues that face professionals involved in special and remedial education.

Each chapter comprehensively examines issues that need to be debated by individuals concerned with education. Specifically, the text addresses major issues in personnel preparation; identification and classification; assessment; intervention; research; and legislation and litigation. Additionally, the text includes a historical perspective on the mission of schooling in America as well as an analysis of the future of special and remedial education.

The text does not offer solutions to the many problems confronting those who are attempting to serve America's public school children. In examining the development and status of special and remedial education, our purpose is to identify current issues in a thought-provoking fashion that will stimulate debate and discussion. We believe we have at least identified the kinds of questions asked about special and remedial education. Jean Piaget has taught us that the kinds of questions children ask reveal much about their cognitive development; similarly, we believe that the kinds of questions professionals ask tell much about the development of their field.

AUDIENCE

This text is designed for use in many college and university courses. Because the issues discussed cut across specific courses and disciplines concerned with special and remedial education, the text is appropriate for a variety of education-related courses (for example, education, special education, educational administration, school psychology, counseling, and school social work).

ACKNOWLEDGMENTS

The initial impetus for this book came while we were sitting in a diner in Dinkytown, Minnesota. Behind the counter was a new broom in a cellophane wrapper on which was written, "This broom sweeps four times better." We wondered, "Better than what?" and "Why not 3.5 times better?" The claim provoked a discussion about claims currently made for much of special and remedial education. We thank the manufacturers of that broom.

We also thank the many persons who helped us throughout the development of this text. Nettie Bartel, Temple University; Barbara Bateman, University of Oregon; Allan Beane, Murray State University; Ronald Eaves, Auburn University; Anita Hermann, University of Wisconsin, Milwaukee; Gayle McBride, University of Florida; Catherine Morsink, University of Florida; and Wayne Otto, University of Wisconsin, Madison provided constructive criticism on early drafts of the manuscript. Audrey Thurlow, Leila Cantara, and Marilyn Hyatt offered their professional assistance in preparation of the manuscript. Sylvia Rosen was an invaluable resource as technical editor.

This book is a collaborative effort in the fullest sense, and speaks for both of us.

James E. Ysseldyke

Bob Algozzine

CRITICAL ISSUES
IN SPECIAL AND
REMEDIAL EDUCATION

Chapter 1

On the Mission of Schooling and the Failure to Teach Significant Numbers of Students

What does education in America consist of? Why are schools organized as they are, and why do they try to educate students as they do? What are the fundamental purposes of education in America? What are the schools trying to accomplish? To what extent are students meeting the goals that schools and society have set for them? Are schools influenced by the society in which they function, or is education the same everywhere? Is the mission of schooling different for different kinds of students? If so, to what extent?

These questions provide the context for the current critical issues in special and remedial education that are examined in this book. These issues emerged when schools (or society through its schools) were perceived as failing in their purposes and obligations to the nation's children and youth. Because the failures cut across all of education, we must start by scrutinizing the fundamental purposes of schooling and the extent to which schools do what they purport to do.

Let us examine, in this first chapter, the mission of schooling in America and, assuming that the mission differs for different kinds of students, the extent of the difference. To do so, we must review the social, political, and legal bases for both general and special education. Inasmuch as the current mission of schooling has evolved over the decades, a

1

brief history of important educational events will help us to acquire a perspective. Society has always had ideals about education, and thus it is important to know how those ideals have shaped current beliefs about the purpose and nature of schooling. Given our focus on schooling in America, we also should understand the social and economic influences on American society's perception of education.

It is a fact that large numbers of students are failing to accomplish the objectives of America's schools. Thus this chapter ends with an examination of both the objectives of American education and the failure to achieve them. We offer current estimates of the magnitude of failure and information on the kinds of students who are failing to accomplish the objectives set for them.

A HISTORICAL PERSPECTIVE ON EDUCATION IN AMERICA

Schools were established for a very specific reason: to prepare the young to assume society's responsibilities. Although the conceptions of the responsibilities have changed with time and place, the reason is still considered to be valid. A text on the history of education typically traces education's roots to Greek society, but in this book we begin with the establishment of schools in America, although not without recognizing and examining, when appropriate, the influences of earlier societies.

The very first schools in this country were secondary schools, which were established in Massachusetts in the early seventeenth century. Called Latin grammar schools, largely because of their curricula, the first one was established in Boston, Massachusetts, in 1635. The sole purpose of the Latin grammar schools was to prepare students to enter Harvard College, America's first institution of higher education, which was established in 1636. The pattern of schooling followed that established in Europe, where higher education in general was reserved for the top two classes in society—the landed nobility and the landed gentry. When John Adams attended Harvard, the students were ranked according to social standing, not academic achievement. He was near the bottom. The curricula of the Latin grammar schools consisted almost entirely of the study of Latin and Greek, an emphasis that had its historical roots in the early religious basis of education: to train youth to read the Old and New Testaments. The purpose of schooling was reflected in Harvard's initial entrance requirements. Eligibility for admission required a student to demonstrate the following skills:

When any scholar is able to read Tully, or such like classical Latin author *extempore,* and make and speak true Latin in Verse and Prose, and decline perfectly the paradigms of nouns and verbs in the Greek tongue, then he may be admitted into the college, nor shall any claim admission before such qualifications. (Knight & Hall, 1951, p. 4)

Between 1634 and 1638, the first laws were enacted for the public support of education in America—laws enabling the Commonwealth of Massachusetts to tax its populace and to assume responsibility for schooling. It is important to recognize that the Commonwealth took on the responsibility of public education because parents were allegedly doing an inadequate job of educating their children. The Massachusetts Law of 1642 reads as follows:

This court, taking into consideration the great neglect of many parents and masters in training up their children in learning, and labor, and other implyments which may be proffitable to the common wealth, do hereupon order and decree, that in every towne ye chosen men appointed for managing prudentiall affaires of the same shall henceforth stand charged with the care of the redresse of this evil, so as they shalbee sufficiently punished by fines for the neglect thereof, upon presentment of the grand jury, or other information or complaint in any Court within this jurisdiction; And for this and they, or the greater number of them, shall have power to take account from time to time of all parents and masters, and of their children, concerning their calling and implyment of their children, especially of their ability to read and understand the principles of religion and the capitall lawes of this country, and to impose fines upon such as shall refuse to render such accounts to them when they shall be required; and they shall have power, with consent of any Court or the magistrate, to put forth apprentices the children of such as they shall [find] not to be able and fitt to imploy and bring them up. (Cubberley, 1934, pp. 16–17)

The first laws establishing public support of education had a religious basis, as evidenced in the Massachusetts Law of 1647, often called "the old deluder, Satan, Act." This law reads, in part, as follows:

It being one chiefe project of that old deluder, Satan, to keepe men from the knowledge of the Scriptures, as in former times by keeping them in an unknown tongue, so in these latter times by persuading from the use of tongues, that so at least the true sence and meaning of the originall might be clouded by false glosses of saint seeming deceivers, that learning may not be buried in the grave of our fathers in church and commonwealth, the Lord assisting our endeavors.—
    It is therefore ordered that every township in this jurisdiction, after the Lord hath increased their number to 50 householders, shall then forthwith appoint one within their towne to teach all such children as shall resort to him to write and reade, whose wages shall be paid either by the parents or

masters of such children, or by the inhabitants in general, . . . and it is further ordered that where any towne shall increase to the number of 100 families or householders they shall set up a grammar schoole, the Master thereof being able to instruct youth so farr as they shall be fitted for the University, provided that if any town neglect the performance hereof above one year, that every such town shall pay five pounds to the next school till they shall perform this order. (Cubberley, 1934, pp. 18–19)

Virtually the only kind of public secondary school in America until the middle of the eighteenth century was the Latin grammar school. A significant change occurred in 1750 when Benjamin Franklin opened his academy (later the University of Pennsylvania). Franklin believed that students should be educated in modern languages, especially English, and in practical subject matter like navigation, surveying, and kite flying. Franklin's school also included instruction in history, geography, rhetoric, logic, astronomy, geometry, and algebra.

In the past, laws establishing education were enacted by the state, and education in America continues to be the responsibility of the states. It is important to recognize that no provision in the United States Constitution establishes federal responsibility for education, and therefore the Tenth Amendment allocated responsibility for education to the states. Objectives for education thus may vary from state to state, as do regulations specifying the kinds of educational services to be provided. The fact that education is the responsibility of the states becomes especially interesting and important when we look at litigation and legislation relevant to the education of handicapped children and youth. Federal courts have intervened in the affairs of schools when constitutional or legal rights have been at issue, and the federal government has intervened by providing funds, contingent on the states' ensuring specific educational services for specific populations of students (for example, the handicapped).

By law, education is also compulsory. In 1840 Rhode Island passed the first compulsory education law, and in 1852 Massachusetts passed the second such law. By 1918 compulsory education was legally effective in all states.

THE IDEALS OF EDUCATION

To study education in America is to study American society and culture (Silberman, 1970). Inasmuch as schools reflect the culture of their society, it is not surprising to find educational ideals reflecting societal ideals. Three ideals have guided the development of education in America and are evident in all aspects of schooling. In analyzing these ideals, it is important to recognize that as such, they are generalizations to which exceptions can be found readily.

One of the outstanding characteristics of American society is that it is democratic. Volumes have been written on the meaning of democracy, but it can be described quite simply as a system in which the individual is perceived as central and in which all political, social, and economic institutions serve the individual's well-being. We readily repeat Abraham Lincoln's words in the Gettysburg Address—"government of the people, by the people, and for the people"—to define democracy. Corollaries of the democratic ideal include beliefs in the individual's worth, equality of opportunity, freedom of thought, and faith in reason. Based on this societal ideal, "We are committed to the democratic proposition that each child—genius or moron, black or white, rich or poor—should be educated to bring out the best that is in him [or her]" (Callahan, 1961, p. 145). As we shall see, in this chapter as well as in other chapters, the democratic ideal that *all* should be appropriately educated has directed much educational thinking, especially that related to the schooling of minority and handicapped students.

A second ideal, one that characterizes American society and through it American education, is nationalism. Americans regard this nation as the center of the universe, and this strong loyalty is symbolized by the American flag and the national anthem, heroes, myths, and legends. Nationalism is developed and nurtured through the process of education, both in and out of schools. When children learn to read English, they encounter national symbols in their earliest readers, and teachers tell them the stories of George Washington and the cherry tree, Paul Bunyan and his Blue Ox, and Thanksgiving. Children learn the pledge of allegiance and the national anthem, and they study the lives of American presidents. Yet, American education teeters between fostering nationalism and developing respect for and concern with other nations, understanding their rights, and recognizing their contributions.

The third characteristic of American society is individualism. The schools' emphasis on individualism has led to an emphasis on achievement or success. Because individual success is a dominant value in American society, we see it nurtured in the schools, and we see evaluations of schools using the "success" of graduates (for example, admission to colleges or universities) as a criterion.

SOCIAL AND ECONOMIC CHARACTERISTICS OF SOCIETY

Not only is the nature of American education guided by the American ideals of democracy, nationalism, and individualism, but also the specific social and economic characteristics of American society direct and constrain the purposes of schooling (Callahan, 1964).

American society is scientific and technical, and the curricula of its schools reflect the role of science and technology in the development of modern America. Although in principle it is a classless society, in fact it is also a class society in which class membership is dictated by vocation, income and source of income, family background, and type of house or residential area. America is said to be a "land of equal opportunity," but class membership often determines the amount of schooling a person receives and membership in a particular class, in turn, is influenced by the amount of one's schooling.

America is also segregated by race, despite the belief in equality and equal opportunity. In most sections of the country, cities are divided into neighborhoods on the basis of ethnicity and race. Although segregation in schools has been declared unconstitutional, it still exists to a considerable extent.

American society is also industrial. Industrialization has encouraged increases in population because more people can be fed and clothed, created high-density population centers around industries with large work forces, and led to the organization of labor unions. Schools are patterned after industry and often have adopted such industrial goals as operational efficiency, increasing productivity, and inservice training.

American society is also a mass society characterized by mass education. Conformity and uniform standards for education are emphasized, and only recently have individual differences and efforts to plan individualized educational programs (IEPs) been recognized.

Finally, American society is characterized by capitalism. Competition is a basic characteristic of our society, and commercialism flourishes. Schools no longer exist solely to prepare students for the next level of education, but are also expected to prepare students for different roles in the world of work. In most secondary schools the offerings include business, commercial, and vocational curricula.

WHAT IS SCHOOL?

Simply stated, schools are social institutions. Schools are established when informal learning is no longer sufficient to induct the young into the culture, when there is a body of knowledge and skill to be taught formally. (Broudy, 1978, p. 25)

The presumption for the establishment of schools is that humans lack general knowledge, morals, and intellect but are capable of learning and attending to the presentation of knowledge and are desirous of learning. Wallace (1973) defined *school* as follows:

School is an institution which deliberately and systematically, by the presentation of symbols in reading matter, lectures, or ritual, attempts to transform from a condition of ignorance to one of enlightenment the intellect, the morality, and the technical knowledge and skills of an attentive group of persons in a definite place at a definite time. (p. 231)

A number of implications can be inferred from the preceding definition of schools: school is defined as an institution; we can infer that it is a social institution established by society to instill in children its beliefs and knowledge base and that school instruction is both systematic and deliberate.

Organized much like society, schools give evidence of a class system, segregation, and competition; and the administrative model parallels that of industry. Schools conform to sets of standards that are set by local, state, and federal governments to ensure uniformity, productivity, and efficiency, and they model the social values they are designed to inculcate.

THE GOALS AND OBJECTIVES OF EDUCATION

The ideals of American society (democracy, nationalism, and individualism) and its social and economic characteristics have interacted to shape and influence the nature of American education. What, then, are the goals or objectives of American education?

Stated broadly and in nonoperational terms (like most statements about school-system philosophy or objectives), schools in America exist for the purpose of educating all the children in the society; inculcating in them an appreciation of democratic principles, a sense of nationalism, and a belief in the worth of the individual; and educating them to their utmost capacity. There is little disagreement over this general goal. But because objectives are statements of preferences, choices, or values, we expect changes over time and differences among individuals and groups in their objectives for their children's education. The *public*, according to Broudy (1978), is not singular: "It is no longer possible to speak meaningfully of *a* public school serving *a* public good. For there are as many publics as there are constituencies vocal enough to make their expectations—often conflicting—known to local, state, and federal educational agencies" (p. 24).

Because there may be considerable debate over the specific objectives of schooling and considerable variance in the objectives among the states and among local education agencies, it is useful to look at the educational goals of representative national groups. In the past, the first formally stated educational goals or objectives were the seven cardinal principles of education identified in 1918 by the Commission on Reorganization of Secondary Education of the National Education Association: (1) health,

(2) command of the fundamental processes, (3) worthy home membership, (4) vocation, (5) citizenship, (6) worthy of leisure, and (7) ethical
character.

In 1922 the Department of Superintendence of the National Education
Association of the United States passed a number of resolutions on
schooling in America, one of which is the following:

We believe that a system of public education to meet thoroughly and effectively the needs and demands of a free and self-governing people with universal suffrage, must offer a program of free educational opportunity extend-
ing from kindergarten through the university, that the courses offered should
be responsive to the growing thought and needs of society and should prepare for complete living in the social, intellectual, and industrial life of a
democratic community. (p. 31)

In 1938 the Educational Policies Commission of the National Education Association proposed a new classification of educational objectives,
based on the following four endeavors: (1) development of the individual;
(2) home, family, and community life; (3) economic demands; and (4)
civic and social duties. They formulated four groups of objectives, each
with subdivisions (see Table 1.1).

According to the belief that education should prepare people for life-
long learning, in 1963 the National Committee of the Project on Instruction of the National Education Association identified five educational
priorities. The committee report, entitled *Deciding What to Teach,* stated in
part:

It is the view of the National Committee of the Project on Instruction that
identification of the essential objectives of the school program must be pre-
mised on a recognition that education is a process of changing behavior and
that a changing society requires that its members acquire the capacity for
self-teaching and self-adaptation. Therefore, priorities in educational objectives need to be placed upon such ends as (a) learning how to learn, how to
attack new problems, how to acquire new knowledge; (b) using rational
processes and developing an abiding interest in learning; (c) exploring values
in new experiences; (d) understanding concepts and generalizations; (e) competence in basic skills. The Committee recommends these objectives for
schools in every community in every part of the United States. They might
be considered the national objectives of the schools. (p. 92)

Goodlad (1980) made the following statement on the status of schooling
in America:

Data from our Study of Schooling support my contention that parents still
want their schools to educate comprehensively for the intellectual, voca-

Table **1.1**   Objectives of Education as Identified in 1938 by the Educational Policies Commission of the National Education Association

---

THE OBJECTIVES OF SELF-REALIZATION

The Inquiring Mind. The educated person has an appetite for learning.

Speech. The educated person can speak the mother tongue clearly.

Reading. The educated person reads the mother tongue efficiently.

Writing. The educated person writes the mother tongue effectively.

Number. The educated person solves his problems of counting and calculating.

Sight and Hearing. The educated person is skilled in listening and observing.

Health Knowledge. The educated person understands the basic facts concerning health and disease.

Health Habits. The educated person protects his own health and that of his dependents.

Public Health. The educated person works to improve the health of the community.

Recreation. The educated person is a participant and spectator in many sports and other pastimes.

Intellectual Interests. The educated person has mental resources for the use of leisure.

Esthetic Interests. The educated person appreciates beauty.

Character. The educated person gives responsible direction to his own life.

THE OBJECTIVES OF HUMAN RELATIONSHIPS

Respect for Humanity. The educated person puts human relationships first.

Friendships. The educated person enjoys a rich, sincere, and varied social life.

Cooperation. The educated person can work and play with others.

Courtesy. The educated person observes the amenities of social behavior.

Appreciation of the Home. The educated person appreciates the family as a social institution.

Conservation of the Home. The educated person conserves family ideals.

Homemaking. The educated person is skilled in homemaking.

Democracy in the Home. The educated person maintains democratic family relationships.

THE OBJECTIVES OF ECONOMIC EFFICIENCY

Work. The educated producer knows the satisfaction of good workmanship.

Occupational Information. The educated producer understands the requirements and opportunities for various jobs.

Occupational Choice. The educated producer has selected his occupation.

Occupational Efficiency. The educated producer succeeds in his chosen vocation.

Occupational Adjustment. The educated producer maintains and improves his efficiency.

Occupational Appreciation. The educated producer appreciates the social value of his work.

Table **1.1**   Objectives of Education (cont.)

Personal Economics. The educated consumer plans the economics of his own life.

Consumer Judgment. The educated consumer develops standards for guiding his expenditures.

Efficiency in Buying. The educated consumer is an informed and skillful buyer.

Consumer Protection. The educated consumer takes appropriate measures to safeguard his interests.

THE OBJECTIVES OF CIVIC RESPONSIBILITY

Social Justice. The educated citizen is sensitive to the disparities of human circumstance.

Social Activity. The educated citizen acts to correct unsatisfactory conditions.

Social Understanding. The educated citizen seeks to understand social structures and social processes.

Critical Judgment. The educated citizen has defenses against propaganda.

Tolerance. The educated citizen respects honest differences of opinion.

Conservation. The educated citizen has a regard for the nations' resources.

Social Applications of Science. The educated citizen measures scientific advance by its contribution to the general welfare.

World Citizenship. The educated citizen is a cooperating member of the world community.

Law Observance. The educated citizen respects the law.

Economic Literacy. The educated citizen is economically literate.

Political Citizenship. The educated citizen accepts his civic duties.

Devotion to Democracy. The educated citizen acts upon an unswerving loyalty to democratic ideas.

SOURCE: Educational Policies Commission, *The purposes of education in American democracy.* Washington, D.C.: National Education Association of the United States and the American Association of School Administrators, 1938, pp. 50, 72, 90, 108.

tional, social, and personal development of their children. Of course, they want their offspring to be able to read, write, spell, and manipulate numbers with some proficiency, but they also want them to be knowledgeable about science, social studies, literature, and the arts. (p. 37)

Schools may function in accordance with specific educational objectives, but they clearly take on more than education. In *What Schools Are For* (1979), Goodlad observed:

Our school system, a huge enterprise, operates as though its social purpose is exclusively educational; it sets goals that are educational, and it is evaluated as though what it does is educational. Meanwhile, it serves purposes appearing to be other than educational, performs functions other than educational, but is generally not evaluated by criteria that are other than educational. (p. 8)

Within a broad context, society formally or informally calls on schools to help solve such societal problems as racism, unemployment, poverty, and war. Yet these goals are seldom, if ever, formally articulated. Goodlad (1979) described the multiple functions of the schools as follows:

They have served to socialize immigrants; to prepare the young for jobs; to keep young people off the labor market; to foster patriotism; to relieve and free mothers from chores of child rearing and supervision; to develop individual talents; to teach certain facts, concepts, and processes; and on and on. Some who would rewrite American educational history say that they also have served to select winners and losers on the basis of circumstances of birth; to increase the gap between the haves and the have-nots in our economic system; to turn off certain kinds of talent while fostering others; and to lower the self-concept of those who do not adjust easily to the expectations and regimens of schooling. What schools have done is not necessarily what they should have done. (p. 2)

THE FAILURE OF SCHOOLS TO EDUCATE SIGNIFICANT NUMBERS OF STUDENTS

A fundamental mission of American schools is the education of all students, regardless of race, religion, sex, national origin, or creed. Yet it is apparent that either schools fail to educate significant numbers of students, or significant numbers of students fail to profit sufficiently from schooling. The double-edged meaning of the preceding sentence is intentional because, obviously, we are dealing with a two-sided, or maybe a many-sided, problem: many American children are not in school; many who are in school fail to acquire basic skills; and many adults are functionally illiterate. Two questions are addressed in this section: (1) the magnitude of failure in this nation's schools and (2) the matter of who is failing.

THE MAGNITUDE OF FAILURE

Criticism of schools and schooling is not new. In both the professional literature and the popular press, schools have been blamed repeatedly for their alleged failures to accomplish their socially determined missions.

During the last twenty years we have seen both numerous challenges to the missions of schooling and the organization of several governmental commissions or studies to investigate the magnitude of failure in America's schools. Indeed, the schools are said to be in trouble because large numbers of students drop out and do not achieve at expected levels. Entire volumes have been devoted to the study of national literacy. Popular books like *Why Johnny Can't Read* (Flesch, 1955), *How Children Fail* (Holt, 1964), and *Death at an Early Age* (Kozol, 1967) quickly catch the attention of the American public.

Several studies over the past decade have focused on dropout rates, achievement levels, and literacy rates, which reveal the magnitude of failure in America's schools. In the early 1970s the Children's Defense Fund sponsored a project to study the number of children who were not in school. In its summary report, the fund's researchers noted that in part:

According to our analysis of the 1970 U.S. Bureau of Census data on non-enrollment, nearly two million children 7 to 17 years of age were not enrolled in school. Over one million were between 7 and 15 years of age. More than three-quarters of a million were between the ages of 7 and 13. (Washington Research Project, 1978, p. 1)

The Children's Defense Fund's investigators viewed their findings as a minimal estimate. They indicated that, based on their survey of more than 8,500 households, the estimated figure of two million did not include all American children actually not in school: census numbers do not reflect students who are enrolled but who have been suspended or expelled, students whose parents do not understand English and thus have difficulty completing census forms, and many handicapped and pregnant students who receive instruction at home. The study did include children who were physically not in school, but the children who are functionally not in school may have a greater problem:

The only children included in the Census data and in our school survey were those who were *physically* out. Not counted are the far greater number of children who are technically in school but who benefit little or not at all. They are the *functionally* or *partially* excluded children. They may remain in schools and learn little or nothing. (p. 2)

Whereas the dropout rate has been used as an index of the magnitude of failure, declining achievement also has been studied as a symptom of the schools' problems. Silberman (1970) observed that anyone who studies American education during the last third of the twentieth century is struck by a paradox:

On the one hand, the system would appear to be in grave trouble, with the very concept of public education coming under question, from critics on the left as well as the right. In most large cities and a good many smaller ones, for example, the public schools are in disarray, torn apart by conflicts over integration, desegregation, decentralization, and community control. . . . And yet from another perspective, the United States educational system appears to be superbly successful—on almost any measure, performing better than it did ten, twenty, fifty, or a hundred years ago. (pp. 12–14)

In *The Literacy Hoax* (1978), Copperman reported that since the mid-1960s, academic performance and academic standards have shown a sharp and widespread decline:

Today's eighth grader reads approximately as well as the average seventh grader just ten years ago and computes about as well as the average sixth grader of that period. On college admissions tests only about a quarter of our current high-school graduates attain the level recorded by the average high school graduate in the early 1960's. (Copperman, 1978, p. 15)

The graph in Figure 1.1 (from Copperman, 1978) shows the decline in college entrance examination (Scholastic Aptitude Test) scores from 1952 to 1977. Copperman not only decried the decline in achievement but also pointed to a generalized decline in academic standards:

The decline in academic standards is as sharp as the decline in basic academic skills. The amount and quality of academic work demanded of public-school students has been cut sharply. For one thing, students are simply not taking as many academic courses as they did in the 1960's. As a percentage of high school enrollment, enrollments in English, history, science, and math are sharply lower. Even the enrollment figures underestimate the reduction in the academic courseload of the average student. Many traditional and rigorous courses have been replaced with fare best described as educational entertainment. Courses in film literature and science fiction are replacing English composition; courses in contemporary world issues and comparative revolutions are replacing world history. In these courses the amount of work assigned and the standard to which it is held are considerably lower than in the courses they replace. (Copperman, 1978, p. 16)

Copperman reported that educational achievement had increased steadily until the "post-sputnik era" but began to decrease steadily in the 1960s and continued into the 1970s. Although achievement in the early primary grades has risen, thereafter it has dropped sharply:

The past ten years have witnessed a sharp and widespread decline in the primary academic skills of America's students. An historical profile of academic achievement in the United States since the early 1960s shows a startling pattern: the reading-readiness skills of preschool children have improved substantially; the academic skills of primary-grade (first to third) students have

Figure **1.1**   Decline in Scholastic Aptitude Test (College Entrance Examination) Scores Between 1952 and 1977.

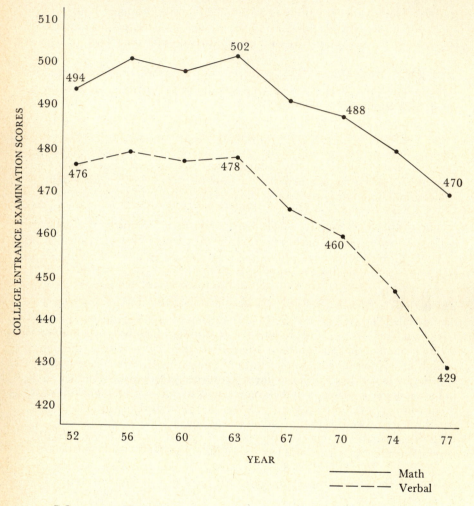

SOURCE: P. Copperman, *The literacy hoax: The decline of reading, writing, and learning in the public schools and what we can do about it.* New York: Morrow, 1978, p. 38. Copyright © 1978 by Paul Copperman. By permission of William Morrow & Company.

increased slightly; the reading, writing, and computing skills of late-elementary and secondary students have deteriorated sharply. (Copperman, 1978, p. 29)

During the same period, federal, state, and local spending for public education tripled (from $559 per pupil in 1963 to $1,580 per pupil in 1975–1976); teachers' salaries more than doubled (from an average $5,995 in 1963 to an average $12,524 in 1975–1976); and the ratio of pupils to teacher decreased about 20 percent (from 26 to 1 in 1963 to 20 to 1 in 1975–1976) (Copperman, 1978).

A variety of reasons can and have been offered to "explain" the observed decline in achievement during the 1960s and 1970s, and we discuss these explanations in greater detail in Chapter 2. They include the belief that the late 1960s was a period of revolt by youth against the banalities of education and that schooling was perceived as unrelated to "real" life. Other reasons offered for the observed decline are that the post-World War II population boom strained the intellectual resources of schools and that the schools failed to teach people how to learn. Still others attribute the observed decline in achievement test scores to the retention in school of a broader and more diverse population base which includes more handicapped and minority students, who allegedly bring average scores down.

Discussions of the literacy rate in the United States often appear in the popular press. Estimates of the rate of functional illiteracy vary greatly, largely because investigators use different criteria to decide whether an individual is functionally literate or illiterate. One reasonably accurate index of literacy is the number of adults who have completed various levels of education. Figure 1.2 shows the educational attainment by adults over 25 years of age between 1910 and 1975: educational attainment increased steadily during this period, although in 1975 close to 40 percent of adults had completed less than 11 years of schooling.

WHO IS FAILING?

General statements and data on failure are enlightening, but they provide only a partial picture of the nature and magnitude of the problem in America's schools. More revealing are analyses of the kinds of students who do not meet the objectives of public education. In Chapter 2, we examine the alternative attributions for blame in instances of failure.

Section 402 of the Civil Rights Act of 1964 instructed the commissioner of education to conduct a survey of equality in educational opportunity in U.S. public schools and to report the results to both the president and

Figure **1.2**   Percentage Distribution of Formal Schooling Completed by
Persons 25 Years Old and Over Between 1910 and 1975.

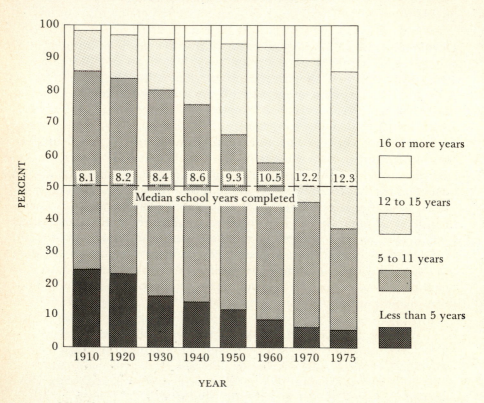

SOURCE: M. A. Golladay, *The condition of education.* Washington, D.C.: National Center for Education
Statistics, 1977, p. 103.

Congress. The report of that survey, published in 1966 and entitled *Equality of Educational Opportunity,* is commonly called the Coleman Report, after James Coleman, director of the survey.

The Coleman Report addressed four questions: (1) the extent to which racial and ethnic groups are segregated from one another in the public schools; (2) whether the schools offer equal educational opportunities according to other criteria that are regarded as good indicators of educational quality; (3) how much the students learn as measured by their performance on standardized achievement tests; and (4) possible relationships between students' achievement and the kinds of schools they attend. The summary of the findings includes an analysis of the extent to which pupils profit from education and the extent to which educational attainment differs according to race, sex, ethnicity, and socioeconomic status.

Coleman (1966) reported that public education for Blacks and Whites was unequal. "In its desegregation decision of 1954, the Supreme Court held that separate schools for Negro and white children are inherently unequal. This survey finds that, when measured by that yardstick, American public education remains largely unequal in most regions of the country" (p. 3). White pupils attended schools in which the number of pupils per room was smaller than that for Blacks; and black pupils had fewer books and less access to scientific and language libraries, academically oriented curricula, and extracurricular programs than Whites did.

In examining pupil achievement on standardized tests, the survey results indicated that with the exception of Asian Americans, minority students (Puerto Ricans, Indian Americans, Mexican Americans, and Blacks) scored distinctly lower on standardized achievement tests than the average white pupil did. In first grade, minority pupils scored one standard deviation below that for white pupils, and in twelfth grade the minority pupils scored even farther behind white pupils. In short, minority pupils' deficiencies in achievement grew with the grade level.

When Coleman and his colleagues controlled for socioeconomic status in their data analyses, they found that the differences among schools accounted for only a small fraction of the differences in pupil achievement:

One implication stands out above all: that schools bring little influence to bear on a child's achievement that is independent of his background and general social context; and that this very lack of independent effect means that the inequalities imposed on children by their home, neighborhood, and peer environment are carried along to become the inequalities with which they confront adult life at the end of school. (1966, p. 325)

An independent study of large-city high schools conducted by Burkhead, Fox, and Holland (1967) reached largely the same conclusions:

Variations in educational outcomes in large-city high schools, measured in terms of test scores, are almost wholly conditioned by the socioeconomic environment of the neighborhood. The income class of the neighborhood, housing conditions, occupations of parents, ethnic status—these are the important determinants of educational outcomes. (p. 12)

Coleman (1966) also reported that the schools do not overcome nonschool debilitating factors:

Whatever the combination of nonschool factors—poverty, community attitudes, low educational levels of parents—which put minority pupils at a disadvantage in verbal and nonverbal skills when they enter the first grade, the fact is the schools have not overcome it. (p. 20)

The surveys by Coleman and by Burkhead and his colleagues were conducted during the mid-1960s when, as Copperman (1978) noted, educational attainment was just beginning to decline. Recent data (1977–1979) from the National Center for Education Statistics indicate that the low achievement by poor and minority students has not improved and perhaps is even worse. Figure 1.3 presents the relationship of performance on achievement tests in social studies, science, mathematics, career and occupational development, and reading to a national mean for black, white, and Hispanic students, aged 9, 13, and 17 years. Whereas the white students consistently scored above the national mean, the black and Hispanic students consistently scored 10 to 20 and 10 to 15 points, respectively, below the national mean. These are group data and should not be read to mean that all Blacks and Hispanics score lower than all Whites do, but, rather, black and Hispanic students as groups score 13 to 23 percentage points, on the average, below white students as a group. To some extent, this observation and its implication were the basis for the development of the many remedial (alternative) education programs (see Chapter 2).

Similar data are available for the performances of male and female students in mathematics, science, social studies, and career and occupational development. Considerable disparity exists between the scores of boys and girls on mathematics measures (the difference increased from two percentage points at age 9 to about five percentage points at age 17) and on science measures (differences increased from about two percentage points at age 9 to about six percentage points at age 17). As a group, boys generally perform better than girls do on measures of mathematics, science, and social studies. There was very little difference in the performance of the two groups on measures of career and occupational development.

Given the differences in achievement among racial and ethnic groups in school, one also might expect differences among students not in school. Indeed, the statistics are parallel. Coleman (1966) reported that 17 percent of all black adolescents and 9 percent of all white adolescents dropped out of school, but the racial differences in the dropout rate were drastically reduced when socioeconomic status (SES) was taken into account.

The Children's Defense Fund (Washington Research Project, 1978), in their study of American children out of school, reported that:

Children are out of school all over America and come from every racial and income group. But low income children and those from unemployed house-

Figure **1.3**   Achievement in Five Subject Areas by Age and Racial-Ethnic Group.

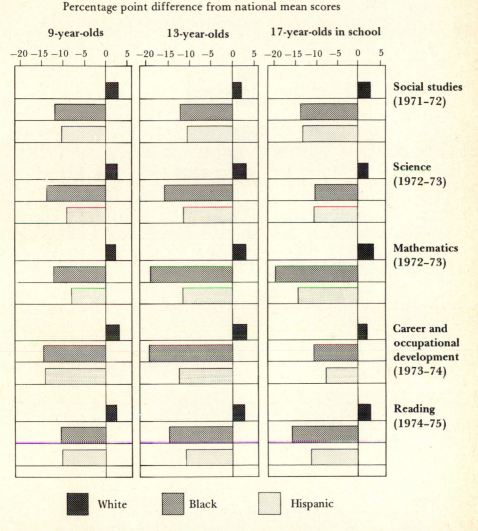

Percentage point difference from national mean scores

9-year-olds   13-year-olds   17-year-olds in school

Social studies
(1971–72)

Science
(1972–73)

Mathematics
(1972–73)

Career and
occupational
development
(1973–74)

Reading
(1974–75)

■ White   ▨ Black   ☐ Hispanic

SOURCE: M. A. Golladay & J. Noell, *The condition of education.* Washington, D.C.: National Center for Education Statistics, 1978, p. 95.

Figure **1.4**   Achievement in Four Subject Areas by Males and Females at 9, 13, and 17 Years of Age Showing Differences from National Means.

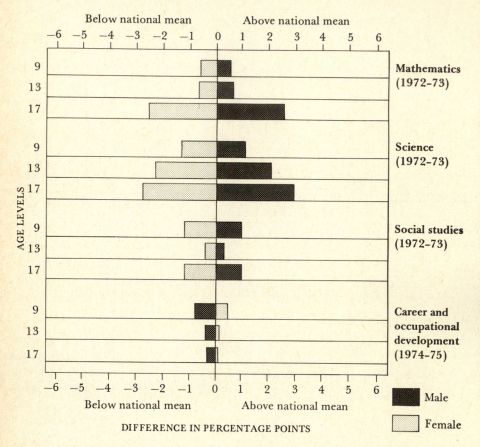

SOURCE: M. A. Golladay, *The condition of education.* Washington, D.C.: National Center for Education Statistics, 1977, p. 112.

holds are disproportionately nonenrolled. Children from families with less education are out of school more than children whose families have more education. Minority children are out of school more than white children. And rural children are nonenrolled more than urban children. (p. 3)

Data from the National Center for Education Statistics support the observations of the Children's Defense Fund. Figure 1.5 shows, by five-year age intervals, the number of black, white, and Hispanic males and females who completed high school. An increase is evident in the number of adults of both sexes who completed high school, but the percentages of

Figure **1.5**   High School Graduates by Sex, Age, and Racial-Ethnic Origin for Three Groups.

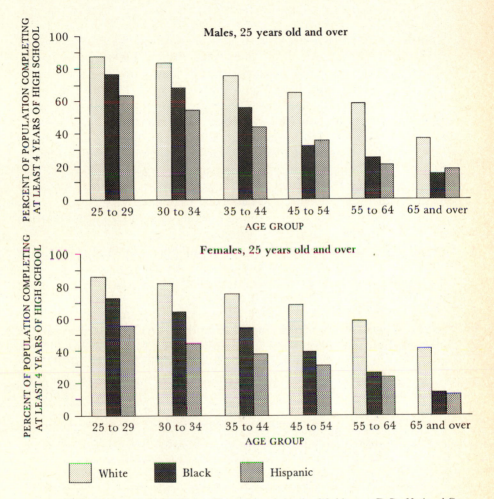

SOURCE: N. B. Dearman & V. W. Plisko, *The condition of education.* Washington, D.C.: National Center for Education Statistics, 1979, p. 225.

completion among the three groups differ markedly. Far more Whites than Blacks, and significantly more Blacks than Hispanics, completed high school.

Data compiled by the National Center for Education Statistics on young adults not enrolled in school also support the observations of the Children's Defense Fund Research Group. In 1977 one-third of all young Hispanic adults and one-fifth of all young black adults had not completed high school. The dropout rate for Blacks fell appreciably in the early 1970s but leveled off in later years, whereas the dropout rate for Whites remained consistent at about 15 percent to 18 percent over a ten-year period.

Another group of children viewed as being out of school are those regarded as handicapped. How many students are identified as handicapped? What proportion attends school? And how are they being served? Prior to the implementation of Public Law 94–142, the Education for All Handicapped Children Act of 1975, approximately 7 percent of the school-age population was identified as handicapped, and most of these students under age 17 were enrolled in school. Figure 1.6 shows the percentage of individuals between 5 and 25 years of age identified as handicapped. About 98 percent of those aged 5 to 13 and about 85 percent to 90 percent of those aged 14 to 17 were enrolled in school. About 25 percent to 30 percent of those aged 18 to 25 were enrolled in school. Note that for students aged 5 to 13, a greater percentage of handicapped than nonhandicapped were enrolled in schools.

In its 1980 report to Congress on the implementation of Public Law 94–142, the Office of Special Education and Rehabilitative Services (OSERS) reported that during the 1979–1980 school year, about 3.8 million handicapped children were served under Public Law 94–142, and about 230,000 handicapped children were served under Public Law 89–313. Together, the states classified and served 8.2 percent of the nation's school-age population as handicapped, but individually, the states varied in their percentages served from 6.75 percent to 13.87 percent. OSERS reported that most students who were identified as handicapped were served in regular classrooms with auxiliary services and that more options for the delivery of services to handicapped students were needed. During the 1979–1980 school year, the following (approximate) percentages of students were served, according to their categorical labels:

Speech impaired—30%
Learning disabled—32%
Mentally retarded—22%
Emotionally disturbed—8%
Other health impaired—3%
Orthopedically impaired—2%
Deaf and hard of hearing—2%
Visually handicapped—1%

OSERS indicated that about 12 percent of the school-age population is handicapped, though there is considerable disagreement over the actual number. In its 1980 report to Congress, OSERS identified the percentage

Figure **1.6**   Estimated Population Percentage and School Enrollment of Handicapped Persons.

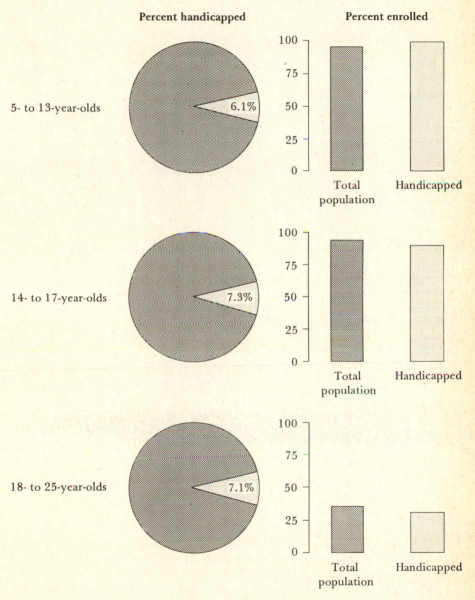

SOURCE: M. A. Golladay & J. Noell, *The condition of education.*   Washington, D.C.: National Center for Education Statistics, 1978, p. 39.

Figure **1.7**   Percent of Children Ages 3–21 Served[1] Under PL 94-142 and
PL 89-313, School Year 1979–80.

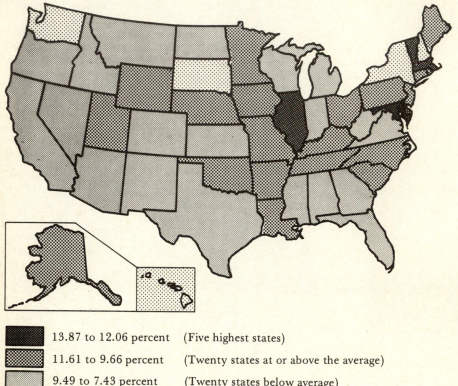

	13.87 to 12.06 percent	(Five highest states)
	11.61 to 9.66 percent	(Twenty states at or above the average)
	9.49 to 7.43 percent	(Twenty states below average)
	7.42 to 6.75 percent	(Five lowest states)

The average for the states and territories is 9.54 percent.

1. Handicapped children ages 3–21 served as a percentage of school enrollment.

SOURCE: U.S. Department of Education, *To assure the free appropriate public education of all handicapped children. Second annual report to Congress on the implementation of Public Law 94-142, the Education for All Handicapped Children Act.* Washington, D.C.: U.S. Department of Education, 1980.

of children served in each state. Estimates are that as many as 250,000 students may not be served in some states. The percentage of children served in each state is shown in Figure 1.7.

The Children's Defense Fund's investigators described the kinds of students who were not enrolled in school at the time of their study:

We found that if a child is not white, or is white but not middle class, does not speak English, is poor, needs special help with seeing, hearing, walking, reading, learning, adjusting, growing up, is pregnant or married at age 15, is not smart enough or is too smart, then, in too many places, school officials decide school is not the place for that child. In sum, out of school children share a common characteristic of *differentness* by virtue of race, income, physical, mental, or emotional "handicap," and age. They are, for the most part, out of school not by choice, but because they have been *excluded.* It is as if many school officials have decided that certain groups of children are beyond their responsibility and are expendable. Not only do they exclude these children, they frequently do so arbitrarily, discriminantly, and with impunity. (1978, p. 4)

The problem of school failure is not easily solved. American society is complex, and its objectives for schooling are many and equally complex. In the next chapter we discuss the ways in which the schools have coped with the failure to educate significant numbers of students.

Chapter 2

The Schools Cope with Failure to Educate a Significant Number of America's Children

Educators have not failed to recognize that significant numbers of students discontinue their education before completing high school, that minority and low socioeconomic status students generally profit less from schooling than do other students, and that achievement levels among today's students are lower than they were ten years ago. The past quarter-century has seen the dedication of many educators to resolving the issues and problems identified in Chapter 1. In Chapter 2 we look at how schools have tried to cope with the failure of significant numbers of students.

ATTRIBUTIONS FOR FAILURE

The actions taken by educators to address the problem of student failure reflect their views on the causes of failure. Typically, when educators find a problem, they search for its causes, and there are three views of these causes:

1. Many educators have argued that the schools are doing an inadequate, perhaps deplorable, job of educating students and, indeed, that the schools are not designed to teach (Baer & Bushell, 1981). Baer and Bushell developed this premise after taking a careful look at why poor students do not do well in school. American public schools, they stated, direct considerable time, effort, and energy toward the following societal functions: providing day care for young children; delaying the entrance of adolescents into the labor market; posing different kinds of problems that children must learn to solve for themselves; and sorting and sifting children into different social positions according to how well they teach themselves to solve academic problems (Baer & Bushell, 1981, p. 262).

2. Other educators argue that the schools are designed to teach, that teachers are prepared to do an adequate job of teaching students, but that many students simply have too many defects, deficiencies, or disabilities to profit from instruction. These educators argue that students enter school with so many deficiencies that the schools hardly can be expected to overcome them. They maintain that the home situations from which such students come are so problematic that they make it impossible for the students to learn.

3. Still another group of educators attributes student failure to achieve educational objectives to a combination of internal constraints, external pressures, and unattainable objectives; in other words, the schools are being asked to do too much. Given the nonoperational nature of many

educational goals (for example, to develop self-realization) and society's unwritten goals (for example, to eradicate poverty), the argument says that it is impossible to demonstrate how many, if any, students achieve them. Broudy (1978), for example, noted that education cannot possibly eradicate poverty, unemployment, and war.

Despite the identification of these three reasons as the causes of failure, it is clear that most educators attribute failure to deficiencies in the students and/or their home environment. In 1979 the research staff of the National Education Association conducted a poll that asked teachers why children do poorly in school. Of the responses, 81 percent blamed the students' home lives, and 14 percent blamed the students themselves; only 1 percent attributed the cause to teachers, and 4 percent blamed the schools (NEA, 1979). A total of 95 percent of the teachers blamed the students' poor performance on either the students themselves or the students' home lives.

Quay (1973), in a survey of assessment and intervention practices for handicapped students, said that the particular kinds of assessment and intervention strategies varied according to the educators' views regarding the causes of exceptionality, and he identified four perspectives or viewpoints on the causes of handicapping conditions: (1) process dysfunctions, (2) experiential defects, (3) experiential deficits, and (4) interaction.

PROCESS DYSFUNCTIONS

The many educators who believe that the causes of failure reside within the students themselves generally attribute school problems and failure to either process dysfunctions or experiential defects. Quay (1973) described the process dysfunction view as the belief that problems in sensory acuity (for example, deafness), response capability (for example, motoric responses), or internal processes (for example, short attention span, poor visual sequential memory) are the reason for students' academic difficulties. Process dysfunctions are seen as either expressed (for example, deafness or blindness) or implied (for example, minimal brain dysfunction). Until recently, it was generally believed that process dysfunctions were unremediable and that they must be either compensated for or bypassed (for example, teaching deaf students to use manual communication). Since the early 1950s there have been extensive efforts in special education to remediate certain process dysfunctions (for example, perceptual-motor or psycholinguistic) or symptoms of process dysfunctions (for example, inadequate eye-hand coordination).

Mann (1979) traced early views about processes and process dysfunction to the early writings of the Greeks, who attributed specific kinds of functions, or appetites (for example, practical, vegetative, speculative, mechanical, and intellectual), to the soul. These functions or appetites were believed to guide behavior. Mann (1979) stated:

Behavioral or psychological processes are, whatever their validity, hypothetical "inner" events or entity constructs. They are usually used to explain behavior, i.e., presumed to cause behavior. While there is nothing that precludes process theorists from identifying their processes with numerical codes, say 45D, they have usually chosen to name their constructs in a commonsense way—as would the man on the street; the name of a process is usually assigned to it on the basis of the behavior it is presumed to generate. "Intelligent behavior" is the result of intelligence. "Remembering" is brought about by memory; we "perceive" with our perceptual abilities. The famed Roman medical authority Galen (130–200) noted a given faculty "exists only in relation to its own effect" (Riese, 1959, p. 22). Earlier, Aristotle had attempted a similar operational definition: "Mind must be related to what is thinkable as sense is to what is sensible." Frostig similarly defined perceptual processes, centuries later.

During the decade leading up to America's bicentennial, there was a process explosion as new areas of psychological investigation proliferated. Witness Neisser's list of cognitive processes. In the visual area, we find transient iconic memory, verbal coding, perceptual set, span of apprehension, displacement and rotation in pattern recognition, backward masking, template matching, decision time, visual search, feature analysis, focal attention, preattentive control figural synthesis, figural synthesis, perceptual defense, etc. In the auditory area, Neisser lists segmentation, echoic memory, filtering, auditory synthesis, recoding, slotting, decay, linguistics, gestalts, and grammatical structure (Neisser, 1967).

Processes come and go; they are evoked or evolved to explain phenomena of interest and then discarded to die or disappear if no one any longer cares about the phenomena they "explain." They are often absorbed into other, newer processes or assume new names according to the changing times or fashions. Frequently they are reinterpreted and given new meanings. Many of the old processes are no longer with us. Where have they gone? Where were the newest of today's processes when we needed *them* years ago. (Mann, 1979, p. 14)

Although in the past, deviant behavior was seen as stemming from demon possession, even then there were some people (for example, Hippocrates, 460–377 B.C.) who viewed deviant behavior as a natural phenomenon that could be understood by rational laws. Ullmann and Krasner (1969) noted that:

[Hippocrates] . . . made astute *observations* about mental disorders, arguing that disorders such as epilepsy and melancholia arose from natural causes similar to those of physical diseases and that the seat of such disorders was the brain. His recommendations to his patients included marriage as a treatment for hysteria (then seen as a disorder of the uterus, and consequently restricted to women) and that of a peaceful, sober, sexless, mildly athletic, vegetarian life for mental disorders. (p. 110)

Early thinking about the causes of conditions now associated with special education can be seen in Samuel Howe's (1848) attribution of idiocy to the violation of natural laws:

Idiocy is found in all civilized countries, but it is not an evil necessarily inherent in society; it is not an accident; and much less it is a special dispensation of Providence; to suppose it can be so, is an insult to the Majesty of Heaven. No! It is merely the result of a violation of natural laws, which are simple, clear, and beautiful; which require only to be seen and known, in order to be loved; and which, if strictly observed for two or three generations, would totally remove any family, however strongly predisposed to insanity or idiocy, all possibility of its recurrence. (p. 2)

Howe went on to cite data from 359 cases of "congenital idiocy" which he had studied and concluded that:

The immediate progenitors of the unfortunate sufferers had, in some way, widely departed from the normal condition of health, and violated the natural laws. That is to say, one or the other, or both of them, were very unhealthy or scrofulous; or they were hereditarily predisposed to affections of the brain, causing occasional insanity; or they had intermarried with blood relatives; or they had been intemperate, or had been guilty of sensual excesses which impaired their constitutions. (p. 2)

People who believe that exceptionality is caused by process dysfunctions search for the causes of disorders by studying heredity, nutrition, biochemistry, brain function, and so on (Ullmann & Krasner, 1969). To them, remediation is dependent on advances in biochemistry, physiology, pharmacology, and genetic engineering.

Educators have spent a considerable amount of time, effort, and money developing instructional interventions to remediate process dysfunctions (see Chapter 6). They designed remedial programs to alleviate or ameliorate visual-perceptual, auditory-perceptual, and psycholinguistic deficits, believing that such deficits caused academic difficulties and that children would not (indeed, could not) learn to read, write, and compute until such presumed deficits were overcome.

Educators often rely on medical findings to create still other interventions. Evidence suggesting the importance of nutrition to development and learning led to the establishment of school lunch programs, breakfast programs, and vitamin therapy. An entire industry has grown up and prospered in response to the belief and evidence that some conditions of behavioral deviance result from abnormal levels of specific body chemicals.

The idea that academic problems are caused by process dysfunctions leads educators either to give up efforts to resolve problems (as when educators abandon the education of children who demonstrate cognitive deficits, in the belief that intelligence is innate) or to design and implement remedial interventions to alleviate unseen but assumed dysfunctions (for example, visual-sequential memory deficits).

EXPERIENTIAL DEFECTS

The second view of the causes of exceptionality (Quay, 1973) is that it is caused by defective experience or adverse life experiences. The investigation of emotional disturbance is replete with examples of situations in which it is hypothesized that "deleterious early experiences (e.g., overinhibition of a child's behavior) produce conditions within the child (e.g., fear and anxiety) which interfere with learning" (Quay, 1973, p. 166). People who ascribe to this view do recognize that certain process dysfunctions or defects (for example, minimal brain dysfunction) exist but they regard these dysfunctions as the result of experiential defects. Entire special education remedial programs have been developed on the presumption that defective experience (for example, failing to creep and crawl appropriately) causes brain dysfunction and results in academic difficulties. The programs thus are designed to undo the harm caused by the defective experience.

EXPERIENTIAL DEFICITS

Quay (1973) named the third view of the causes of exceptionality the experiential deficit view, that is, the belief that although students have intact learning apparatuses, they have limited behavioral repertoires which create difficulties for them. Educational difficulties are seen as resulting from deficient rather than defective (adverse) experience. Much has been written on the "disadvantaged," or the "deprived," child and the effects of deficient early experience on later intellectual, academic, and social development. Educators today believe that deficient experience is a major cause of school difficulties. Whiteman and Deutsch (1968) described this view well:

The child from a disadvantaged environment may have missed some of the experiences necessary for developing verbal, conceptual, attentional, and learning skills requisite to school success. These skills play a vital role for the child in his understanding of the language of the school and the teacher, in his adapting to school routines, and in his mastery of such a fundamental tool subject as reading. (p. 87)

The locus of the problem in this view is outside the child: teachers may view the problem as within the child but caused by outside factors. The child is seen as displaying deviant social behavior and having a limited vocabulary and limited reading skills which are caused by deficient experience and environmental disadvantages. This view is often called the sociological perspective because various social explanations for the development and existence of deviant behavior have been proposed. Each explanation points to rules of social conditions as the source of the problems. For example, social disorganization theory emphasizes differences among communities as the basis for differing levels of abnormal behavior. Levy and Rowitz (1973) reported that the highest rates of mental illness are found in cities' central sections and that the crime rate is likely to be higher in disorganized than in organized communities. Other sociological theorists believe that deviance or dullness is learned by association with deviant or dull individuals. Proponents of such cultural transmission theories were influential in the early history of American education. Recently, a similar hypothesis was formulated by Jensen (1969a). His report that Blacks, because of inherent inferiority, performed significantly lower than Whites did on tests of intelligence stirred up considerable controversy. The finding and analysis of differences in intelligence for different racial and ethnic groups of people are not new:

Some would hold that this difference between [IQs of] 87 and 102 represents roughly the difference in the mentality of the two races. The writer would contend that this difference is probably exaggerated because of the predominance of verbal tests used. Wherever we have non-language and language tests given to the same groups we find the Italians drawing close to the Americans on the non-language tests. The results of Young, Pintner, and Kirkpatrick show this. Nevertheless, even on these tests, the Italian groups are below the Americans. If the median IQ of American children in general is 100, then that of the Italians is undoubtedly below this. In all probability it is not as low as 87. A rough estimate might place it between 90 and 95. (Pintner, 1932, p. 451)

Similar findings were reported by Hirsch (1926) and Goodenough (1926). Goodenough (1926) blamed the differences on innate differences and environmental factors:

Two theories have been offered to account for these differences. The first ascribes the inferior showing made by the South Europeans and the negroes to such postnatal factors as inferior environment, poor physical condition and linguistic handicaps. The second point of view, while it recognizes that the factors named may to some degree affect the test-results, nevertheless holds that it is impossible to account for all the facts which have been observed upon any other hypothesis than that of innate differences among the groups under consideration.

It is unquestionably true that the home surroundings of certain racial groups, notably the Italians and negroes are, as a rule, far less favorable than those of the average American children. Not only is this true of the foreign-born Italians, but their American-born descendents frequently continued to live in the same neighborhoods and with little or no improvements in social or hygienic conditions. In this respect a notable difference may be observed between the Italian and the Jew. Both find a home in the slum on first coming to this country; but while the Italian remains there, the Jew soon moves to a better neighborhood.

It seems probable, upon the whole that inferior environments is an effect at least as much as it is a cause of inferior ability, as the latter is indicated by intelligence tests. The person of low intelligence tends to gravitate to those neighborhoods where the economic requirement is minimal, and, once there, he reacts toward his surroundings along the line of least resistance. His children inherit his mental characteristics. (Goodenough, 1926, pp. 388–391)

It is clear that Goodenough, a prominent, influential psychologist in her day, attributed most of the perceived problems of Italians and blacks to environmental factors. The parallels today are obvious in our interest in culturally disadvantaged, culturally diverse, underprivileged, and bilingual children.

When academic and social problems, school failure, declining achievement, and high dropout rates are viewed as the result of deficient experience, the people holding this view too often limit their explanations to out-of-school environments. As we observed earlier, 95 percent of the teachers who responded in a recent survey attributed problems to home environments and to the children themselves (NEA, 1979). Nevertheless, more and more blame is now being placed on the schools.

Hall, Greenwood, and Delquadri (1979) quoted a statement by the Reverend Jesse Jackson:

We keep saying that Johnny can't read because he's deprived, because he's hungry, because he's discriminated against. We say that Johnny can't read because his daddy's not in the home. Well, Johnny learns to play basketball without daddy.

We do best what we do most, and for many of our children that is playing ball. One of the reasons Johnny doesn't read well is that Johnny doesn't practice reading. (p. 14)

Baer and Bushell (1981) asserted that for students, public school is a series of hurdles, and those who figure out for themselves how to get over and around the hurdles are the ones who advance. The school provides a few resources, such as books and adults, which can help students get over the hurdles if they learn how to use them.

Baer and Bushell (1981) noted that when the school gives problems to children, they often carry them out of the school in the form of homework, along with textbooks that contain examples of these problems and illustrations of step-by-step solutions for a few of them. From these examples, the children who know how to induce may acquire the recipe for solving similar problems. At home there may be other books, parents who may, and older brothers and sisters who probably do, remember how to solve such problems and a telephone with which to call friends who may have figured out the method of solution. If the children do have access to these resources, and are successful in using one or some combination of them, they will return the solution of that problem to the school and pick up another problem.

But Baer and Bushell observed (1981) that other children, even some in the same classrooms, are not good at inducing, perhaps because they can barely decipher the textbook's example or because they are not skilled at induction per se. They do not have out-of-school resources or, perhaps, have not learned how to use them well enough to return to school with solutions. They move from a school that does not teach them (or anyone else) how to solve problems to a home and neighborhood that do not know how to teach them. Because the children fail to deliver many solutions, they clear very few hurdles and soon are designated as candidates for remedial, compensatory, or special programs that try to make the hurdles smaller. According to Baer and Bushell (1981):

> Children who live in environments that do not help them to teach themselves, and attend schools that do not help them to teach themselves, do not learn how to teach themselves. Children who live in more instructive environments learn to teach themselves *regardless of what their schools do.* (p. 263)

INTERACTIVE VIEW

The fourth view regarding the nature of exceptionality was named by Quay (1973) as the interactive view. It recognizes that handicaps, disorders, or disabilities may result from process dysfunctions, experiential defects, and experiential deficits in interaction. Problems are seen as arising from an interaction among within-student dysfunctions, experiential defects, and experiential deficiencies (including inadequate teaching).

It is easy to observe the selective rather than the general effects of both nature and environment. Sarason and Doris (1979), for example, stated, "Not all abusive parents abuse *all* of their children, and not all parents with characteristics of abusive parents have abused their children" (p. 21). Similarly, we have seen that referrals for psychological evaluations occur at varying rates for children with similar and different characteristics; children who exhibit the same behaviors often do not receive the same school experiences: problem behaviors occur in normal as well as deviant children. Sarason and Doris (1979) suggest that a "transactional approach" (Sameroff & Zax, 1973) might be useful in explaining such outcomes:

[From the transactional perspective,] heredity and environment are never dichotomous. It can even be misleading to say they "interact" because that is more often than not interpreted in terms of effects of heredity on environment just as for so long we have paid attention to the effects of parents on children and virtually ignored the influence of children on parents. The transactional approach is always a two-way street. There is nothing in the transactional formulation that denies the existence and influence of genetic processes or the existence of a socially structured context populated by diverse people (Sarason & Doris, 1979, p. 25).

A similar perspective, that is, an ecological theory, has been suggested by Rhodes (1967, 1970) to explain emotional disturbance. This theory was described by Algozzine, Schmid, and Mercer (1981) as follows:

Ecological theorists believe that deviance is as much a function of where and *with whom* a child interacts as it is the nature of the interaction in terms of behaviors which are exhibited by the child (cf., Rhodes, 1967, 1970); to these theorists emotional disturbance is in the "eye of the beholder" and is generated or develops when an individual's behavior is viewed as *disturbing* or bothersome by others with whom interaction occurs. Deviance, then, is as much a function of *reactions to behavior* as it is the behavior in and of itself. (p. 168)

An interesting application of the ecological, or transactional, theory was suggested by Sarason and Doris (1979) in their discussion of iatrogenic retardation:

To the extent that it is appropriate to view the common school as a prescribed cure for the ills of society, we maintain that a considerable proportion of mental retardation encompassed by the term "educably retarded" can be viewed as an iatrogenic disease. By that we mean, just as the administration of certain medications in the treatment of physical disease can cause the appearance of new disease related to the nature of the medication and to the patient's idiopathic response to it, irrespective of its effect upon the original disorder for which it was prescribed, so, in like manner, a considerable part of the problem of educably retarded children derives from the way in which we have devised our educational system. To the extent that we have ignored cultural differences, differences in patterns and tempos of learning, social and affective differences in the temperaments of children, to the extent that we have set goals of achievement for individual children that are either unrealistically high or low, we have ensured the development of that educationally disordered child, with cognitive and social handicaps, that we relegate to the special classroom.

This is not to deny a continuum of competence that may be based on genetic and environmental factors acting together and independent of the educational environment in which society attempts to develop and measure competence. It is to state that the continuum of competence, cognitive and social, existing prior to entry into school becomes distorted by the very system that society has devised for the development and measurement of competence. And that the distortion is of such a nature that individual social and ethnic class differences interact with the categorical rigidities of curriculum, methods of instruction, and administrative organization to sort out the children not solely in terms of the constitutional and environmentally determined differences existing prior to school entry, but to a large extent independently of such preschool individual differences. (Sarason & Doris, 1979, pp. 154–155)

From this point of view, retardation is not simply the consequence of the child's nature or the school's environment; rather, it is the product of transactions among the child's characteristics and school environments, each in response to the other.

COPING WITH FAILURE

INACTION

One way that the schools have coped with the failure of certain students to acquire educational objectives is by simply doing nothing about it. The Children's Defense Fund (Washington Research Project, 1978), in their extensive study of American children not in school, identified 13 factors which they labeled "bureaucratic excuses for inaction":

1. *We're the experts.* Parents are often told that they (parents) do not understand the complexity of the problem and that they (educators) know best.
2. *Agency Denial.* Many state and local education agencies deny that students are not being served, that students are being excluded from school, or that they may be inappropriately classifying students.
3. *The Exception.* When school officials are confronted with evidences of failure to educate students, they often label these as exceptions to the normal state of affairs.

4. *Priorities*. Those who call attention to the problem are told that the problem just is not as important as others.
5. *Confession and Avoidance*. School officials often admit to the facts but claim that "overriding considerations" keep them from acting.
6. *Improper Jurisdiction*. School officials often claim that it is not their responsibility to deal with instances of academic and/or social deviance, but the responsibility of the family and other institutions.
7. *Prematurity of Request*. Those who confront the school with evidence of failure are told that the school has "a plan to correct the situation."
8. *Generalized Guilt*. Those who confront the school are told that "other school systems have similar problems."
9. *Improper Forum*. School officials often claim that the problem is in the hands of local, state, and/or federal government agencies, and that there is little they can do to alleviate the problem.
10. *Recrimination*. School officials often simply recognize that there are students who are excluded and who have problems, but simply state "It's their own fault."
11. *Further Study*. School officials often say that they have referred the problem for further study.
12. *Community Resistance*. Schools often fail to take action under the guise that the attitudes of the community are such that they (the community) won't support action.
13. *Funding*. Parents and others who confront school officials are told there is no money. (Washington Research Project, 1978, pp. 12–14)

EXCLUSION

Another way that schools cope with the failure of certain students to acquire academic skills, especially when those students also evidence disturbing social behaviors, is by excluding them from school. Early educational efforts in America relied almost exclusively on exclusion as a way to deal with children and youth who did not learn and/or who caused noticeable difficulty in the system. Exclusion has run the gamut from expelling students who are disruptive, who do not have short hair, who wear armbands protesting the Vietnam War (see the discussion of *Tinker* v. *Des Moines Community School District* in Chapter 8), or who are pregnant, to institutionalizing those students who are considered to be too "sick" to learn or incapable of learning. The history of intelligence testing is especially enlightening on this last point. Intelligence tests were first developed by Alfred Binet for the express purpose of identifying children who would not or could not profit from schooling.

ABILITY GROUPING

One way that schools have tried to cope with individual differences is to group students for instruction on the basis of ability. At its simplest level, the practice is still seen in the organization of reading groups in the lower elementary, regular classrooms. In its systematic application, students are assigned to ability tracks that are designed to prepare them for certain life roles. According to Goodlad (1980):

Partly in the name of individual differences in students' learning abilities, we frequently place secondary students in different learning tracks. It seems reasonable to assume that the levels of these tracks represent different levels of complexity or difficulty in a sequential, cohesive body of subject matter. Those in the lower tracks presumably will encounter the subject matter covered in the upper tracks in succeeding semesters or years. I doubt that such assumptions are reflected in practice. (p. 38)

Schools have used ability grouping on the assumption that it was a way of more effectively meeting students' needs. But, it can be and has been argued that education in the lower track(s) is distinctly inferior to education in the upper track(s). Goodlad (1980) reported his research observations:

It was frequently observed that the content and materials taught in the upper and lower tracks differed so much that they appeared to be different subjects rather than different levels of the same subject. (p. 38)

When ability grouping is followed, different educational tracks are established with different goals in mind for the students who are assigned to the tracks. Yet, there are many questions as to the extent to which students in the lower tracks achieve the goals set for those tracks. Goodlad (1980) found:

Apparently assuming that some students are incapable of progressing in academic subjects beyond the bare minimums, we take comfort in the assumption that they are being prepared for jobs. But what jobs? The record on placing students in jobs for which the schools prepared them should elicit no cheers. Moreover, the prospect that many vocational trainees will have limited job mobility and will be unemployed is downright depressing. (p. 39)

In 1967, Judge Skelly Wright, in the landmark decision in *Hobson* v. *Hansen,* declared unconstitutional the use of intelligence tests to assign pupils to ability groups.

SPECIAL EDUCATION

Regardless of one's perspective on the blame or causes for children's school failures or other forms of "differentness," one cannot deny that these failures are the foundations for the development of special education. In searching the literature to develop a "historical perspective on the development of special education," Sarason and Doris (1979) found public policies on schools and society to be particularly revealing:

We noted that in the latter half of the 19th century, the schools, endeavoring to provide for the efficient and economically feasible instruction of ever growing numbers of pupils, were forced to adopt class-graded instruction in which schooling was provided in sequential yearly units for children grouped approximately by age and degree of academic achievement. In that same era, for a number of reasons involving child welfare, the politics of labor and industrial relations, and the presumed curative effects of education for social problems, the various states also adopted and enforced ever more stringent compulsory education laws. Such laws kept within the educational system those children who for one or another reason were apparently unable to pass through the newly developed class-graded schools with normal rates of progress.

These two educational developments that called for a lock-step progression of pupils through class-graded schools, and forced attendance of all children within a given age range, immediately confronted the educator with the problem that not all children were capable of maintaining the necessary rate of progress required by the lockstep instructional system. And yet all children had to attend school. Various adjustments in the class graded system were called for. Obvious remedies for the less severe problems were retention in grade or demotion for children not keeping up with their class, and the development of various tracking systems. For those children unable to keep pace even with such adjustments on the part of the system it was necessary to set up special classes where the requirement of lockstep progression could be completely suspended. At first, all children who fell too far behind their age mates were placed into such classes regardless of the cause, be it behavioral adjustment or scholastic ability. Eventually different kinds of special classes evolved. Truants and behavior problems were sorted into correlational classes and the ungraded classes were reserved for what we would now classify as the educably retarded child. (p. 137)

The stage for special education was set, then, by the requirement that all children attend school and the recognition that schools (as conceived currently or historically) were not for everybody. Around the turn of the century, James Van Sickle (1908–1909), superintendent of schools in Baltimore, wrote, "Before the attendance laws were effectively enforced there were as many of these special cases in the community as there are now; few of them, however, remained long enough in school to attract serious attention or to hinder the instruction of the more tractable and capable" (p. 102). The "deviant" children were always (and always will be) with us. When they are absent or excluded from school, they do not attract attention. Perhaps by mistake, social policy has forced them to become more visible in school, and society and school personnel have reasoned that their presence interfered with the proper training of "capable" children.

For all practical purposes, the early educational programs of our country were dichotomous: a student either received and profited from instruction in lock-step graded classes or was educated in a special class. One view was that these early education programs were way stations or clearing-houses for children who were en route to the prevailing treatment facilities (that is, institutions) for the physically, mentally, or morally "deviant" members of our society. In a speech to the National Education Association, E. R. Johnstone (1908) openly stated that the special class

must become a clearing-house. To it will not only be sent the slightly blind and partially deaf, but also the incorrigibles, the mental deficients, and cripples. . . . The only thing to do is to give them the best of care and training possible. Keep them in the special classes until they become too old for further care in school, and then they must be sent to the institutions for safety. . . . (p. 1115)

Although some early programs and schools were set up for children and youth with specific disabilities (for example, in 1817 the American Asylum for the Education and Instruction of the Deaf was founded; in 1829, the New England Asylum for the Blind; and in 1859, the Massachusetts School for Idiotic and Feebleminded Youth), many early public school classes were the repositories for all kinds of children who simply did not fit into the regular classroom:

The special classes in the public schools of the city of New York had their beginning in Public School, 1, Manhattan, in 1889. It is interesting to know that this class, which was to demonstrate the need for further classification of children in public schools was not the result of any theory. It grew out of conditions in a neighborhood which furnished many and serious problems in truancy and discipline. This first class was made up of the odds and ends of a large school. There were over-age children, so-called naughty children, and the dull and stupid children. They were taken from any and every school grade. The ages ranged from eight to sixteen years. They were the children who could not get along in school. They were typical of a large number of children who even today are forced directly or indirectly out of school; they were the children who were interested in street life; many of them earned a good deal of money in one way or another. While some of them had been in trouble with the police, as a class they could not be characterized as criminal. They had varied interests but the school, as they had found it, had little or nothing for them. If these boys were to be kept in school they had to be interested. They had to be shown that school could be more than mere study of books in which they had no interest. They had to be convinced that to attend school was a privilege not a punishment. This "about face" on the part of these boys was accomplished after many months. (Farrell, 1908–1909, pp. 91–92)

With time, the size of the problem increased. In his *Fourth Annual Report of the City Superintendent of Schools,* New York City's first chief school administrator noted that when principals were asked to identify the number of "defective, backward or dull" children, they "reported about 8,000." However, "more careful scrutiny of their answers indicated that the actual number of such children was "not more than a fourth of that reported" (Maxwell, 1902, p. 108). Maxwell pointed out that it was important, when dealing with "abnormal" or "atypical" children, to distinguish the various types. He offered the following subdivisions as inclusive of "almost all children of the atypical class"

(a) Dull children; those who are behind in any or all studies; those who exhibit precocity in one or more studies; those who have lost time because of irregular attendance or frequent transfer; those who are deficient in English because of foreign birth and residence.
(b) Defective children, whose minds may be clouded; those whose defects are partial; those whose defects may be cured; those who, because of some abnormal growth, such as adenoids in the throat and deafness, are behind the other members of their class.
(c) Idiotic or permanently defective children. (1902, pp. 108–109)

Maxwell left the severe category undefined, perhaps because about 54 years earlier Samuel Gridley Howe (1848), quoting Seguin, wrote:

An idiot is an individual who *"knows nothing, can do nothing, cannot even desire to do anything."* This is the maximum of idiocy; the minimum of intelligence; and but very few cases can be found (we were inclined to think that none could) in which a being in human shape is so much below even insects, and so little above a sensitive plant. (p. 6)

Howe went one step further to differentiate these people from "fools" and "simpletons," or "imbeciles":

Idiots of the lowest class are mere organisms, masses of flesh and bone in human shape, in which the brain and nervous system have no command over the system of voluntary muscles; and which consequently are without power of locomotion, without speech, without any manifestation of intellectual or affective faculties.
    Fools are a higher class of idiots, in whom the brain and nervous system are so far developed as to give partial command of the voluntary muscles;

who have consequently considerable power of locomotion and animal action; partial development of the affective and intellectual faculties, but only the faintest glimmer of reason, and very imperfect speech.

   Simpletons are the highest class of idiots, in whom the harmony between the nervous and muscular system is nearly perfect; who consequently have normal powers of locomotion and animal action; considerable activity of the perceptive and affective faculties; and reason enough for their simple individual guidance, but not enough for their social relations. (1848, pp. 6–7)

   Howe included "specimen case studies" in which he described the characteristics (for example, parentage, appetite for food, instinct of reproduction, self-esteem) of the "unfortunate beings." He also stated:

As a class of fools is much larger than that of idiots, so that of simpletons is much larger than that of fools. Indeed, it is very difficult to estimate their number, or to say what persons shall be included in it, for they can only be measured by a sort of sliding scale, with a standard adapted to different localities and conditions of society. (p. 13)

   It seems that Superintendent Maxwell was exercising the flexibility suggested by Howe when he attempted, at the local education agency level, to differentiate among the "atypical," "abnormal" children of New York City. Interestingly, many current definitions, although perhaps superficially less offensive, are equally vulnerable with regard to the numbers of children identified and equally flexible to permit (or force) local education agencies to find and serve exactly the numbers of children they want.

DEFINITIONS, DILEMMAS, AND DISAPPOINTMENTS

The function of definitions in special and remedial education is to provide a conceptual model for understanding the condition(s) created by the act of defining. In addition, definitions provide the bases from which identification practices evolve. When we know what we are looking for, we have some indication of how to look for it. It is important to note, however, that no one thing represents the categories or names we assign to the observed differences in other people. The meanings of the terms we use to refer to these categories (for example, idiocy, mental retardation, learning disability, blindness) depend on the people who use the terms. Bogdan and Taylor (1976) offered the following examples:

. . . some have argued, mental retardation is a social construction or a concept which exists in the minds of the "judges" rather than in the minds of the "judged". . . . A mentally retarded person is one who has been labeled as such according to rather arbitrarily created and applied criteria.

Retardate, and other such clinical labels, suggests generalizations about the nature of men and women to whom the term has been applied. . . . We assume that the mentally retarded possess common characteristics that allow them to be unambiguously distinguished from all others. We explain their behavior by special theories. It is as though humanity can be divided into two groups, the "normal" and the "retarded." (p. 47)

Sarason and Doris (1979) put it this way:

Mental retardation is not a thing you can see or touch or define in terms of shape and substance. It is a *concept* serving two major purposes: to separate a group of people; and to justify social action in regard to those who set apart. (p. 11; emphasis added)

The position we take is that learning disability, emotional disturbance or handicap, underachievement, blindness, deafness, and other similar categories are simply terms we use to refer to concepts that we have constructed in order to confirm that individuals in our society differ from each other. They are theoretical attributes we assign to justify our belief that an individual is different.

The definitions we have created to describe the people that we believe are different fall into two groups: (1) those that have an objective, sensory basis (that is, blindness, deafness) for the concept they represent; and (2) those in which differences (that is, learning disabilities, mental retardation) are completely subjectively derived.

OBJECTIVE DEFINITIONS

Blindness

Blindness was first legally defined in 1935 by the Social Security Act (Hatlin, Hall, & Tuttle, 1980). The National Society for the Prevention of Blindness (1966) offers the following definitions of blindness and partially seeing persons:

Blindness is generally defined in the United States as visual acuity for distance vision of 20/200 or less in the better eye, with acuity of more than 20/200 if the widest diameter of field of vision subtends an angle no greater than 20 degrees.

The partially seeing are defined as persons with a visual acuity greater than 20/200 but not greater than 20/70 in the better eye with correction. (p. 10)

The exact criterion (20/200 rather than 20/100) for blindness or partially seeing is subjective but is founded on objective standards that reflect similar functional difficulties among individuals who are similarly defined.

Deafness

Moores (1978) gave two definitions of individuals with sensory problems that are related to hearing. Each differs from the other on the extent of hearing loss:

A "deaf person" is one whose hearing is disabled to an extent (usually 70 dB ISO or greater) that precludes the understanding of speech through the ear alone, without or with the use of a hearing aid.
   A "hard of hearing" person is one whose hearing is disabled to an extent (usually 35 to 69 dB ISO) that makes difficult, but does not preclude, the understanding of speech through the ear alone, without or with a hearing aid. (p. 5)

SUBJECTIVE DEFINITIONS

Learning Disability

According to the most recent definition by the U. S. Office of Education, the term *specific learning disability*

means a disorder in one or more of the basic psychological processes involved in understanding or in using language, spoken or written, which may manifest itself in an imperfect ability to listen, think, read, write, spell, or to do mathematical calculations. The term includes such conditions as perceptual handicaps, brain injury, minimal brain dysfunction, dyslexia, and developmental aphasia. The term does not include children who have learning problems which are primarily the result of visual, hearing, or motor handicaps, of mental retardation, or emotional disturbance, or of environmental, cultural, or economic disadvantage. (USOE, 1977b, p. 65083)

Although the primary manifestation of learning disability (LD) is imperfect ability in important school-related areas, the definition itself offers no basis for differentiating an LD child from a school underachiever. The criteria for determining the condition of learning disability, which are outlined in the same *Federal Register* (USOE, 1977b, p. 65083), add very little to the specifics necessary to distinguish imperfect abilities and/or to quantify achievement that is not commensurate with assumed ability. In fact, although these guidelines for applying the federal definition of learning disability suggest that the discrepancy between ability and achievement should be severe, no standards are given; thus local or state education agencies must flesh out the skeletal structure offered by the federal agency. So, like early educators faced with carrying out decisions relating to the nation's "simpletons," contemporary educators dealing with other, more subjective, highly prevalent, and popular notions of disability or deviance also must rely on a standard that can be "adapted to different localities and conditions of society" (see Howe, 1848, p. 13).

Emotional Disturbance

In the current government definition, the term *seriously emotionally disturbed* is defined as follows:

(i) The term means a condition exhibiting one or more of the following characteristics over a long period of time and to a marked degree, which adversely affects educational performance: (a) an inability to learn which cannot be explained by intellectual, sensory, or health factors; (b) an inability to build or maintain satisfactory interpersonal relationships with peers and teachers; (c) inappropriate types of behavior or feelings under normal circumstances; (d) a general pervasive mood of unhappiness or depression; or (e) a tendency to develop physical symptoms or fears associated with personal or school problems. (ii) The term includes children who are schizophrenic or autistic. The term does not include children who are socially maladjusted, unless it is determined that they are seriously emotionally disturbed. (U. S. Office of Education, *Federal Register,* Section 121a. 5, 1977b).

Interestingly, this definition is very similar to that used in the early 1960s and more recently to describe children who are less severely emotionally handicapped or have behavior problems (cf. Bower, 1969; Kauffman, 1980; Reinert, 1967; Shea, 1978). Since the professionals make up the definitions, they can decide whether the definitions match serious or regular versions of the disorders.

Mental Retardation

The *Manual on Terminology and Classification in Mental Retardation,* published by the American Association of Mental Deficiency (Grossman, 1973), provides a succinct definition: *"Mental retardation refers to significantly subaverage general intellectual functioning existing concurrently with deficits in adaptive behavior, and manifested during the developmental period"* (p. 11). The manual also describes the key elements of the definition: "intellectual functioning" "may be assessed by one or more of the standardized tests developed for that purpose," and "significantly subaverage" is "performance which is more than two standard deviations from the mean or average of the tests" (p. 11).

This definition is similar to others that have been devised since the development of intelligence tests: mental retardation is a condition characterized by abnormal intellectual functioning. The basis for this conception was the work of Binet and Simon (1916) who recognized the need for a *"precise basis for differential diagnosis"* (p. 335): "We do not think that we are going too far in saying that at the present time very few physicians would be able to cite with absolute precision the objective and invariable sign, or signs, by which they distinguish the degrees of inferior mentality" (p. 335). What would probably come as a surprise to Binet and Simon is that there is no absolute, objective, and invariable sign of mental retardation; in fact, that which comes the closest and is the most frequently used (that is, intelligence) is also a construct that has defied definition and remains the center of controversy (cf. Sarason & Doris, 1979).

When Binet discovered a way to measure a construct that was thought to reflect an important social issue, his work became the basis for the subsequent conceptualizations of mental retardation.

DILEMMAS

Objective definitions are founded, at least, in measurable phenomena; that is, the distance one can see or the level at which one can hear surely can be measured more objectively than the information one knows or the intelligence level one demonstrates. Even so, it still is difficult to define them. For example, what does one call an individual whose measured hearing is 68 dB ISO (within the hard-of-hearing range of 35-69 dB ISO) but whose ability to hear is disabled to the extent that it precludes understanding speech through the ear alone? More pervasive problems are evident in the use of highly subjective definitions such as those for learning disabilities, emotional disturbance, and mental retardation.

One important reason for defining our categories of disabilities is that we are then able to evaluate the extent or pervasiveness of the problem. For example, having defined blindness, we can count the number of individuals who fall within that definition and therefore are blind, and we then can determine the course and direction of the social policies for these disabled persons. Similarly, having defined mental retardation, we can estimate the extent of the problem and construct programs to remedy it. When we realize that our definitions at best are arbitrary attempts to objectify social, political, and moral constructs, we know we have a problem.

The history of special education is replete with controversy over *the* definition of mental retardation, *the* definition of learning disabilities, and *the* definition of all other types and kinds of special children. It seems that as soon as someone comes out with *a* definition, it is the stimulus for other persons to criticize, convene, propose a new definition, and take their turn on the defensive. The main implication of this continuing discussion among professionals is that these definitions do not exist in a vacuum: each change in definition directly or indirectly affects the identification and treatment of children with learning problems. At a round-table conference on the assessment of learning-disabled students, Lovitt (1978) captured the dilemma of professionals when he said:

I believe that if we continue trying to define learning disabilities by using ill-defined concepts, we will forever be frustrated, for it is an illusive concept. We are being bamboozled. It is as though someone started a great hoax by inventing the term then tempting others to define it. And lo and behold scores of task forces and others have taken the bait. (p. 3)

Robinson and Robinson (1976) pointed out:

The most significant change in 1973 as compared with the 1959 definition [of mental retardation] is a return to a *more traditional cutoff score,* two standard deviations below the mean. The 1959 definition had defined "borderline retardation" as intelligence only one standard deviation below the mean and thereby had tended to shift the emphasis from the severely retarded to the much larger group with mild and borderline retardation. (p. 31)

From 1959–1973, a child with subaverage general intellectual functioning that was one standard deviation below the mean was likely to be classified as *retarded;* after 1973, that same child was not considered retarded. The label applied only to children whose intellectual functioning was at least two standard deviations below the mean. Thus, many children ceased to be retarded simply by a pen stroke of the American Association for Mental Deficiency.

Similar problems are surfacing with regard to emotional disturbance. "Definition provides the basis for prevalence" (Kauffman, 1980, p. 524). We would add that definition is the basis for the existence of some conditions and for the interest in them; without definition, for all practical purposes, there is no category or problem! Lambert (1981) recounts an example of the way in which labeling a condition creates interest in it. She states that during the early 1960s, she and Eli Bower were writing a summary of research in California on emotionally handicapped students in preparation for legislation to be introduced in the state legislature in the winter of 1961. They described different levels of intervention for students based on the degree of their handicap:

Inasmuch as the children we had studied who needed the small group instruction most, and benefitted most from it, were those who were significantly behind in their academic subjects, we called them "learning disability groups.'' When this name appeared in California special education parlance, the search was on to find the deficit responsible for the failure rather than the method to teach the child.

It was only a matter of time before the discovery would be made that explanations for significant discrepancies between ability and achievement were many, chief among them failure of the instructional program to provide an appropriate level of tasks for the child as well as appropriately modified regular class learning situations. (Lambert, 1981, p. 200)

Once defined, the importance of the category becomes a function of the number of children assigned to it. For years, the U. S. government estimated that 2 percent of the school population was "disturbed" (Kauffman, 1980); in fact, recent "child counts" indicated that the figure is actually 0.5 percent (*Report to Congress,* 1979). Kauffman (1980) argued that the reported difference in prevalence stems from the differences in identification practices brought about by federal rule making:

If federal law has had and will continue to have a suppressing effect on identification of most disturbed children, then it is obvious that legal precedent is supplanting, or at least is being used to define, clinical judgment in our society's view of deviance. Bureaucratic-legal domination of our thinking about disordered behavior and the tacit assumption that extralegal considerations are the least pressing issues in special education today may represent advancement or regression, depending on one's view of what forces should move the field forward. To the extent that extralegal judgment is trusted, one could argue that the bureaucratic-legal approach will result in the unfortunate denial of services to many mildly and moderately disturbed children who would benefit from identification and intervention. To the extent that legislation, bureaucratic control, and litigation are trusted as the best means for defining children's deviance, one could rejoice in the fact that social institutions such as schools will be required to tolerate behavioral difference unless it violates standards of conduct that are unassailable in court. (p. 526)

Definition *is* the basis for prevalence; we would argue that definition is the basis for the *existence* of the condition. Without definition, for all practical purposes, there is no category! If the federal government or any other group of professionals for whatever reason decides that it is time to serve the *severely handicapped* and, either through outright changes in definitions or more subtly through financial grants and contract bargaining, establishes an interest in severely handicapped children, the interest in identifying and serving the more moderately or mildly handicapped youngsters will diminish. In an editorial entitled "What Happened to Mild and Moderate Mental Retardation?" in the *American Journal of Mental Deficiency,* Carl Haywood (1979) noted that despite the plans and good intentions that must have been the basis for the shift in the emphasis of research and service from mildly to severely retarded individuals, the outcome has been unfavorable:

It is practically certain that the individuals who pleaded for increased attention to severely and profoundly retarded persons hoped that the increased attention would represent a total increase in scholarly interest, public funds, and services for the entire field of mental retardation, i. e., that additional funds, research, and services directed toward severely and profoundly retarded persons would be "added on" to the existing levels of support for the entire field. What has happened instead has been a shift of resources away from mildly and moderately retarded persons, to such a marked degree that it is frequently quite impossible to obtain public funds to support both research and services in this important area unless one promises to give primary emphasis to those individuals who are severely or profoundly handicapped. (p. 429)

The dilemma that psychologists and educators face is one of their own making: should they provide special services for more children by expanding the definitions of disabilities and court the risks of labeling, or should they provide fewer formal special services by narrowing the definitions of disabilities and hazard denying some children the special supports they need? It is obvious that there are plenty of students failing in school (see Chapter 1) and it is equally obvious that we can create definitions that characterize many of them. The problem is that the definitions are simply conceptual models: they are necessary, but we cannot specify their effects. We can say what mental retardation is (for example, subaverage intellectual functioning), but we cannot say what effect will be produced when our definition is applied (for example, special classes enrolling 80 percent boys). In fact, the current definition of mental retardation is a product of the social, political, and moral history of a particular country, state, or other locality, and in this regard, we agree with Sarason and Doris (1979):

We are not opposed to definitions in principle, but we are opposed to the lack of recognition that definitions tell us what to exclude as well as what to include. The thrust of this discussion is that by virtue of what definitions of intelligence and mental retardation have excluded, they have contributed to confusion and fruitless controversy. One can live with confusion and fruitless controversy were it not for the fact that these definitions give rise to techniques for measurement which in turn are used to determine policies that will affect the lives of people. In the areas with which we are concerned definitions have not been empty exercises. The quest for clear and rigorous definition was a consequence of society's need to act and deal with what it had come to see as a problem. And if the definitions changed over time, it was less because of new knowledge and more because societal attitudes toward the problem had changed. (p. 29)

DISAPPOINTMENTS

Recently, there has been considerable interest in the similarities and differences among children who are classified as learning disabled, mentally retarded, and emotionally disturbed. Hallahan and Kauffman (1977) discussed the difficulty of identifying differences among mildly handicapped children. Neisworth and Greer (1975) pointed out that there is much overlap among the characteristics of some mentally retarded, learning-disabled, and emotionally disturbed children, and indicated that the "degree and nature of such overlap depends, in part, upon the measures employed to describe performance" (p. 19). In this sense, differences among children may be psychometric contrivances rather than characteristics that have diagnostic or practical importance.

Psychological diagnosis has always been regarded with some suspicion; and as far back as 1924 one observer described the situation as follows:

Clinical psychology today is more an art than it is a science. In spite of the very marked improvement in clinical technique, one cannot escape the conclusion that mental diagnosis is more subjective than it is objective, and that accuracy of diagnosis is largely a matter of expertness and skill rather than of exact measurement. One of the most important needs of clinical psychology, in view of its wide-spread application and the great social importance of its findings, is greater objectivity. (Doll, 1924, p. 26)

This need for objectivity was expressed also by Rutter (1978) in regard to the diagnosis of autism. This quotation is relevant here because it brings up the question of universal and specific characteristics:

By suggesting autism constituted a syndrome, [Leo] Kanner meant two things: first, that there were certain behaviors which tended to group together, and second, that these behaviors differed from those found in other psychiatric conditions. Accordingly, the first step was to determine by comparative studies how far this was true in order to clarify the diagnostic criteria. There was a need to find out which symptoms were both universal and specific — that is, those which were present in all or nearly all autistic children and also which were relatively infrequent in children who did not have the syndrome. A differentiation had to be made between behaviors which could occur in autism (but which also occurred in other conditions) and those behaviors which were specifically characteristic of autism. (p. 4)

The search for both the universal and specific characteristics of the conditions (for example, mental retardation, learning disability, and education disability) we have observed and defined has been largely fruitless. Those features that overlap the least (for example, intelligence scores) are themselves constructions; those that overlap the most (for example, overt behaviors) have the least diagnostic or practical value. The search for universal and specific features of various conditions is dependent on society's need to deal with what it sees as problems. If the definitions we create are not adequate, we change them or create new ones; and the defining of, searching for, and treating of problems continue.

THE INVENTION OF ALTERNATIVE EDUCATION

If the current system of education were satisfactory, there would be no need for special education. Similarly, if the current system of education (that is, regular and special) were adequate, there would be no need for head starts, alternative education, or any other form of modified compulsory education. In fact, many such alternatives periodically surface and become popular.

EARLY CHILDHOOD EDUCATION

The history of preschool and early childhood education has been characterized by considerable fluctuation in community interests, public funding, and educational improvement. The 1960s marked a major turning point in early childhood education: to Frost (1968) it was a "rediscovery," and to Shane (1969) it was a "renaissance." This increased interest grew out of a concern for the disadvantaged, as many educators hoped that compensatory education could begin to counterbalance the negative effects of poverty on the development of young children. Remember that in the early days of American education, compulsory attendance was thought to be the solution to the problems presented by parents who were "indifferent to the public good" and who refused to send their children to school. According to Bourne (1870):

In a Government like ours, "founded on the principle that the only true sovereignty is the will of the people," universal education is acknowledged by all to be not only of the first importance, but necessary to the permanency of our free institutions. If, then, persons are found so reckless of the best interests of their children, and so indifferent to the public good, as to withhold from them that instruction without which they cannot beneficially discharge those civil and political duties which devolve on them in afterlife, it becomes a serious and important question whether so much of the natural right of controlling their children may not be alienated as is necessary to qualify them for usefulness, and render them safe and consistent members of the political body. The expediency of such a measure would be confined pretty much—perhaps entirely—to large seaport towns, and, in its practical operation, would be found to affect but a few native citizens. The number of families arriving in this city almost daily from Europe is so great as to require some measure of the kind; for the means heretofore used to induce the attendance of their children at the public schools have proved insufficient. (p.153–154)

Now, about 100 years later, responding to evidence of the scope and effects of poverty (Harrington, 1962, Hurley, 1969) and to the pleas of civil rights leaders for quality education for all Americans, educators once again have undertaken to force-feed the likely-to-be-failing youngsters.

Head Start

In 1964, the Economic Opportunity Act provided massive funding for educational programs for preschool children. During the summer of 1965, 550,000 youngsters (about 10 percent of all children in preschool programs) were enrolled in school programs which were set up as part of Project Head Start. Over 40,000 teachers (many with no experience with preschool children) were hired, and a total of 100,000 adults participated in the programs to "compensate" for the negative effects of poverty likely to hamper some of America's youth. The curriculum in many programs was intense, and it was thought that the best way to overcome economic, cultural, and social disadvantage was to start school early. Copperman (1978) noted that prior to Head Start, "the primary goal of preschool child care was the normal and healthy psychosocial development of young children, to be achieved through peer-group play and other guided play activities" (p. 57). To counteract the likely effects of social and economic disadvantages, early childhood education specialists recommended that accelerated academic development be adopted as the primary goal of preschool programs.

   The major effect of this early instruction seems to have been increases in readiness abilities; however, "the preponderance of recent research indicates that most of the gains experienced by preschool children in group educational programs disappear by the end of first or second grade" (Copperman, 1978, p. 58).

Early intervention produces substantial gains in IQ as long as the program lasts. But the experimental groups do not continue to make gains when intervention continues beyond one year, and, what is more critical, the effects tend to "wash out" after intervention is terminated. The longer the follow-up, the more obvious the latter trend becomes (Copperman, 1978, p. 59).

Follow Through

When the effects of Head Start "washed out," it seemed logical to provide follow-up compensatory education programs. In 1969, Congress established the Follow Through program to try to compensate for the failings of the compensatory Head Start efforts. Copperman (1978) reported that the effects of this program were similar to those of its predecessor; in fact, some evidence indicates that Follow Through produced more negative than positive effects (Stebbins et al., 1977).

Handicapped Early Childhood Education

From the beginning of his study of intelligence, Binet saw the concept "not as a thing, or an amount, or something 'inside' a person, but an active transaction between individual and external stimuli" (Sarason & Doris, 1979). He saw intelligence as educable and wrote in 1911 that the educability of intelligence was the basis for pioneering early intervention work. Early interventionists believe that "we can ameliorate, that we can alter, that we can prevent further deterioration of mental function if we start young" (Kirk, 1977, p. 4). Hirshoren and Umansky (1977) agreed:

Early education for children with handicaps offers a number of benefits that warrant serious consideration by school systems. Early intervention with children who have some handicaps may alleviate many of the manifestations of the handicaps that could inhibit development and learning. Furthermore, provision of services in the early years could substantially reduce costs of later education (p. 191)

With the passage of Public Law 90–538 (Handicapped Children's Early Education Assistance Act) in 1968, Congress set the stage for the Handicapped Children's Early Education Program (HCEEP). The purpose of the program was to assist in the development of demonstration models for the provision of comprehensive services to all handicapped preschool-aged (birth to eight years) children and their families (DeWeerd & Cole, 1976; Swan, 1980). The HCEEP was originally funded in 1969–1970 with an appropriation of $1 million, which supported 25 grants. The program grew over its first 10 years, and in 1978–1979 the HCEEP received an appropriation of $22 million, which supported 214 grants and contracts.

DeWeerd and Cole (1976) reported that the initial evaluation results of the program's effectiveness (conducted by Stock et al., 1976) were favorable (see also Swan, 1980). Swan (1980) conducted a subsequent study to measure the extent of continuation (that is, local and state) funding support which the initial HCEEP projects had obtained seven years after the completion of their "seed" grants. Of the 21 projects studied, 86 percent had received continuation funding and were still operating.

In 1972, the Head Start program was expanded by Public Law 92–424, which provided that not less than 10 percent of the national enrollment opportunities available through Head Start were to be designated for handicapped children (LaVor, 1972; LaVor & Harvey, 1976). Legislation in 1975 (Head Start, Economic Opportunity, Community Partnership Act of 1974) altered the initial 10 percent enrollment opportunities from a national base to state bases. The change had the "net effect of forcing each state to focus on and meet the needs of handicapped children within the state" and guaranteed that states would "no longer be able to disregard the minimum 10% requirement by averaging their totals with overall national or regional enrollments" (LaVor & Harvey, 1976, p. 227).

Education for preschool handicapped children has arrived. The first major legislative support came from Public Law 90–538 in 1968 and the establishment of model demonstration programs. Public Law 93–380 required that the state plans submitted to the Bureau of Education for the Handicapped include timetables and plans for providing services to all handicapped children from birth through age 21. Similarly, the law mandated states to "establish and maintain efforts to *find* all handicapped children from birth through age 21" (see discussion of law in Cohen et al., 1979). Public Law 94–142 (the Education for All Handicapped Children Act of 1975) provides two sources of funds for preschool handicapped children's programs. States are entitled to funding according to the numbers of handicapped children in their populations, which may include the number of children in the 3 to 5-year-old range; similarly, incentive grants are available to states who have approved plans to serve children in this age range (Cohen et al., 1976). Hirshoren and Umansky (1977) reported that 12 states offered certification for teachers of preschool handicapped children; and Lessen and Rose (1980) found that 7 of 45 state consultants who responded to their survey indicated that their states had specific definitions for preschool handicapped youngsters.

The rise of preschool education for handicapped children has not occurred without problems. Karnes and Zehrbach (1977) discussed key issues related to preschool education of handicapped students, citing difficulties in identifying students to be served, service models, and staffing patterns. Cohen, Semmes, and Guralnick (1979) expressed concern with the effects of labeling young children as handicapped, determining who shall provide services, and the lack of specific timetables in Public Law 94–142 regarding mandatory "free appropriate" public education for all three- through five-year olds (currently, education is a state's right, and federal directives cannot require that which state law or court order "expressly prohibits or does not authorize"). Lessen and Rose (1980) concluded that "it would behoove state departments of education to provide a definition or specific guidelines for early identification so that every child has the opportunity to begin his or her school experience with as few interfering problems as possible" (p. 469).

BILINGUAL EDUCATION

During the 1970s, a new option began to receive support in the search for ways to provide equal educational opportunities for America's school children. John-Steiner and Souberman (1977) reported that during the 1972–1973 school year, only 5 percent of the minority children who could benefit from bilingual instruction were actually receiving it. They then discussed several problems (for example, parental concerns, biased testing, and cultural deprivation) and concluded as follows:

The overwhelming hope that bilingual education will prove to be an important solution for the implementation of equal education opportunity cannot help but lead to disappointment and failure without a broader approach to learning. Such an approach would have to include environmental and nutritional, as well as linguistic and cultural, factors that contribute to and shape the effective education of each child. (p. 69)

Although the problem and its parameters have been defined, the ensuing difficulties and solutions are anything but simple:

Providing an appropriate and effective education for minority group students who are both exceptional and come from culturally and/or linguistically diverse backgrounds is without a doubt one of the greatest challenges facing special educators as we enter the 1980s. (Baca, 1980, p. 583)

The magnitude of cultural diversity in our schools is apparent in the data presented by Almanza and Mosley (1980), who cited Hazard and Stent (1973) as follows:

Some data on school populations may give needed perspective to the reality of cultural diversity. In the fall of 1970, over 51 million children were enrolled in public and private elementary and secondary schools. The most recent (1968) data indicate that 14.5 percent (6,282,200) pupils were Black, 4.6 percent (2,003,000) were Spanish Americans, and 143,630 (less than .05 percent) were American Indians. Predictably, the twenty-one largest school systems reported substantially different racial-cultural "mixes" in their school districts for the same year (1968). Of the total pupil population of 4,728,886, Black pupils numbered 1,921,465 (40.6 percent); 502,528 (10.6 percent) were Spanish American; 7,912 (0.2 percent) were American Indians, and 68,680 (1.5 percent) were Oriental . . . to postulate our education on bases other than cultural diversity and pluralistic notions seems to ignore the realities of our schools' population. (pp. 17–18)

The existence of diverse cultural backgrounds of America's schoolchildren is certainly not new, nor are the problems related to the education of minority children. Sarason and Doris (1979) described the challenge to special education and the problem of minority discrimition and concluded:

Given a society of varied groups—of ethnic, religious, racial, social, and economic differences—to what extent can we devise a common education capable of transmitting intellectual skills and moral values that does not have built into it the potential for becoming a procrustean bed to terrify or deform the children of one minority group or another? We suspect, as we recall the Amish children being chased through the cornfields of Iowa and the stoning of bus loads of black children, that the potential will always be there. The best we may be able to do is to maintain the sensitivity to identify those instances when the potentiality threatens to become reality, and to respond with firm commitment and balanced judgment to adjust not the child to the school but to adjust the interaction of the school, the subculture, and the family for the benefit of the child (p. 354).

Hilliard (1980) argued that:

Special education will succeed with diverse cultural groups only when certain conditions prevail.
1. Culturally sensitive diagnostic validity must exist.
2. Professional practices must work significantly better than chance.
3. A valid link between special education assessment/diagnosis and teaching strategies must be present. (p. 585)

We would argue that the need for the above conditions has always existed but that the conditions never have been (and probably never will be) met by American education, special education, or remedial education. Our discussion of issues related to assessment (Chapter 5) and intervention (Chapter 6) is germane.

CAREER AND VOCATIONAL EDUCATION

The traditional school curriculum includes emphasis on college preparatory course work. Vocational training is often viewed as a less respected alternative to higher-level academic subjects, and career education is assumed simply to be a part of going to school. Supporters of career and vocational education insist that the traditional schools and their course work fail to provide appropriate direction for many young people and that as society advances technologically, specialized training and preparation become necessary components of a complete education.

Brolin and D'Alonzo (1979) noted that:

The career development of handicapped students has been an area of concern among many special educators for a great number of years. In the 1950s and 1960s work-study programs were initated in many schools because it was apparent that academically oriented curricula were not adequately meeting the vocational and community adjustment needs of most handicapped students leaving the school system. (p. 246)

Again, a special program is created to fill the need created by a special program in which the federal government is deeply involved. In 1975, the Bureau of Education for the Handicapped sponsored a special conference to help it decide on the funding of research and demonstration projects in career education. Many legislative actions have brought career and vocational education into the mainstream. Miller, Ewing, and Phelps (1980) nicely summarized these trends as follows:

In the early and mid-1970s, additional federal legislation generated a new impetus for improved vocational opportunities for the handicapped. This new legislation demonstrated the federal government's commitment to end exclusion and discrimination against handicapped persons. Societal barriers which had continued to limit the participation of the handicapped in vocational education were dealt a critical blow by passage of four pieces of legislation and accompanying sets of regulations which relate in whole, or in part, to the vocational education of the handicapped. Section 504 of the Rehabilitation Act of 1973 (PL 93–112), the 1973 Comprehensive Employment and Training Act (PL 93–203), the Education for All Handicapped Children Act of 1975 (PL 94–142), and the Vocational Education Amendments of 1976 (PL 94–482) each provided increased fiscal considerations, which, as expected, stimulated vocational preparation of the handicapped. Section 504 of the Rehabilitation Act of 1973 prohibited discrimination on the basis of handicap in any private or public program receiving federal assistance. Section 503, a companion set of regulations, required businesses having more than $50,000 per year in federal contracts to initiate an affirmative action plan to recruit, train, and promote qualified handicapped persons. (pp. 450–451)

The issues that face career and vocational educators are good examples of those facing special and remedial educators in general. Brolin and D'Alonzo (1979) urged that "it is time for consensus to be reached about

a universal and operational definition of career education so that programs can be developed and constructed in a systematic manner" (p.
249). There are problems with definitions in all areas of special and remedial education. Similarly, the extent to which career (or any special) education should be delivered as a separate but equal or integrated part of the
school curriculum is an issue of continuing professional interest. Finally,
the nature of career education interventions and their impact on the preparation of professional personnel are critical to determining the influence
of this specialized form of additional education on regular or special students. These and other issues are addressed in other sections of this book
(see Chapters 3 and 6).

EDUCATIONAL ALTERNATIVES

There are alternatives to traditional or contemporary education. Because
society has agreed to educate all its children and youth and makes some
portion of that education mandatory, the need for alternatives is clear.
According to Glatthorn (1975):

The challenge is even more important: we have committed ourselves to educating all youth in the established schools; it is incumbent on us to find ways
of making those schools more responsive to the diverse needs of the students
they serve. The reasonable person, therefore, rejects the cry of the radical
that the burning question is how to destroy the school. He or she also rejects
the complaint of the cynical critic that no change is possible. The only
important question left is: in a time when change is sanctioned, in a context
where the experience of schooling is more important than its product, what
changes do we implement in the conventional school?
    The author does not intend to offer one more panacea, one more instant
solution to the problems these schools face. Instead, he would argue, for several reasons, that the only reasonable answer is to provide for teacher, student, and parent, a wide range of options and alternatives: alternative organ-
izational patterns, alternative curricula, alternative teaching styles,
alternative learning strategies. (p. 5)

Glatthorn discussed 12 examples of 3 different types of alternative
schools, the categories and examples of which are presented in Table 2.1.
He also presented a scheme clarifying the "twenty most significant characteristics of alternative schools" (Table 2.2). Other similar schema have
been discussed by Goodlad (1973) and Smith, Barr, and Burke (1976).
    For the most part, the alternatives to traditional or current education
are outside the programs and are generated by dissatisfaction either with
the progress (or lack of it) being made by the students or with the inadequacies of the system's administrative or instructional arrangements.

Table **2.1**   Selected Types of Alternative Schools

TYPE OF ALTERNATIVE	EXAMPLE
Student centered	Schools for students out of school
	Schools for disruptive students
	Schools for special ethnic groups
	Schools for gifted and talented
Program centered	Career schools
	Performing arts schools
	Skills-training schools
	Open learning schools
Place centered	Schools without walls
	Community schools
	Multidistrict schools
	Wilderness schools

SOURCE: Adapted from A. A. Glatthorn, *Alternatives in education.* New York: Harper & Row, 1975.

Many educators would argue that alternatives within the current education system can also be useful and necessary. As Reisler (1981) states:

Public schools are failing in significant ways to provide the high quality education the American public desires. . . . The current crisis of confidence in public schooling—more widespread, persistent, and intense than at any previous point in history—is precisely the time to reaffirm the legacy and potential of public education (p. 413).

That public education provides alternative programs with the potential to reaffirm its own support is documented: for example, Florida has an Alternative Education Law (Thrasher, 1981). In regard to the first decade of public school alternatives; Raywid (1981) wrote:

A number of schools have been credited as the first public alternatives—Philadelphia's Parkway, which opened in 1969 after two years of dreaming and planning; Wilson Open Campus School in Mankato, Minnesota, which dates from 1968; and Murray Road in Newton, Massachusetts, and Harlem Prep, both of which got under way in 1967. Since then all these programs have experienced many changes, and countless others have followed in their wake. The aggregate, after 10 years of steady growth and sharing, is a distinctive and fairly healthy movement (p. 551).

Table **2.2**   A Taxonomy for Alternatives

FACTORS	OPTION I	OPTION 2	OPTION 3
1. Funding	Public tax funds	Federal, state, foundations	Tuition and contributions
2. Control	Public school system	Church, university, or other institution	Parents, community
3. Students	Heterogeneous	Basically homogeneous by virtue of interest	Intentionally homogeneous on basis of predetermined criteria
4. Board	Inactive board	Moderately active board	Dominating board
5. Daily governance	Teachers	Teachers and students	Students
6. Leadership	Single strong leader	Single democratic leader or team of leaders	No single leader, decision by consensus
7. Relationships with conventional school	Housed in same building	Annex	Completely separate
8. Facilities	School building	Nonschool facility	No single building
9. Full-time or part-time program	Part of day or part of year	Chiefly full-time, with some movement back to main school	All education in alternative
10. Staff	Certificated	Chiefly certificated, with some noncertificated	Noncertificated

11. Staff organization	Differentiated	Some differentiation	No differentiation or specialization
12. Student selection	"Forced" assignment	Lottery from among applicants	Open admissions
13. Exclusion	Pupils excluded if they break rules	Only a few pupils excluded for very serious infractions	No one ever asked to leave
14. Program evaluation	Comprehensive	Minimal	None
15. Degree of structure	Highly structured and controlled	Students and staff develop minimal structure	Openly permissive
16. Nature of program	Conventional school offerings	Mixture of conventional and esoteric	Chiefly esoteric offerings
17. Grade organization	Graded	Nongraded within limits	Wide range of ages intentionally mixed
18. Schedule	College schedule	College schedule with variations	No schedule
19. Pupil grading	Letter grades with options	Noncompetitive evaluation	No evaluation at all
20. Crediting	Carnegie unit	Carnegie unit with variations	No credit

SOURCE: From pp. 28–29 of *Alternatives in education* by Allan A. Glatthorn. Copyright © 1975 by Harper & Row, Publishers, Inc. Reprinted by permission of the publisher.

One wonders, if the alternative education system continues to grow, whether the traditional system will soon be the alternative. Similarly, if the number of children who need and can profit from special education continues to grow, it may be that the entire system will soon be special, and then there will likely be a need for special classes in which regular students will be taught.

The current system appears to be failing. Much time, money and personnel have been allocated to the creation and conduction of special education. The issues related to training personnel to serve special children, as well as those related to identifying, evaluating, teaching and researching those children, are important to their future. When problems surface, the tradition in education is to come up with new answers to old questions. It is time for some new questions, and we believe that a straightforward analysis of contemporary issues can serve as the basis for generating these new questions.

Chapter 3

Issues in Personnel Preparation

The idea of special education teacher training evolved from the obvious failure of apprenticeship to meet the needs of children when compulsory education became a reality. Prior to that time, teachers had learned by working with teachers, and to a large extent, supply and demand were in balance. When schools were forced to accept more and more children, changes in the training of teachers became necessary. Mayer (1961) commented:

If the state insisted that the child go to school, the state also had to insist that the teacher in whose hands the child would be placed possessed at least a minimal level of competence. State "certification" of teachers was a political and ethical necessity. (pp. 47–48)

Howsam (1980) added:

Teacher education was introduced to America in 1839 when the first normal school was established in Massachusetts to improve the quality of teachers. In the first half of the 20th century teacher preparation was gradually transferred to the universities, even as preparation for the other professions was moved to the campuses. The difference, in the case of education, was the retention of direct control of teacher education by the state through program approval and teacher certification. (p. 95)

Before the systematic development of normal schools and requirements for teaching certificates, formal education for teachers consisted of institutes or teacher-training classes with "instruction in the subject matter and the methods of teaching appropriate for the common schools" (Sarason & Doris, 1979).

With the opening of the first normal school, teacher training became institutionalized; that is, curricula were established and questions on the appropriate content of teacher-training programs were raised. By 1860, 18 public and private normal schools were training teachers. Their curriculum consisted of liberal arts courses (for example, English, mathematics, philosophy) and instruction in teaching methods (Sarason & Doris, 1979). In 1874, 121 normal schools were serving prospective teachers, and in 1898, 331 were in operation (Connor, 1976). Today, nearly 1,400 institutions provide "pedagogical education," and "only the state in which they reside has jurisdiction over their programs" (Smith, 1980, p. 87). Many of the courses offered satisfy the instructor's interests rather than a teacher's job requirements (Smith, 1980). The problem in teacher education has not been so much the establishment of training programs as the content of the training programs.

SPECIAL EDUCATION TEACHER TRAINING

For the most part, the education and training of both the special education teachers and the children used to take place at the institutions and training schools for youngsters with various handicaps. Lincoln (1903) reported:

The original plan was very simple. The best possible teachers were selected—women of experience in their profession, acquainted with kindergarten methods, some of whom had been trained by regular service at Barre and Mrs. Seguin's school, while others had been sent by the Board to spend three months in residence at [the Pennsylvania State School at] Elwyn previous to taking classes in Boston. The teachers thus chosen were practically allowed to act as their own judgment dictated. There was no requirement, scarcely even a suggestion, as to the results to be sought, or the methods to be used; the work to be done is very much the same as in state schools for feeble-minded, and such differences as may be observed between individual classes are chiefly matters of detail and personal preference. (p. 84)

Other institutions besides the Pennsylvania State School at Elwyn participated in teacher training; Sarason and Doris (1979) reported that Vineland Training School (in New Jersey) was active in training teachers
through a series of summer school programs begun in 1903. The course of
study consisted of lectures and laboratory work conducted by Henry Goddard (Johnstone, 1909–1910). Although initially only 5 students enrolled,
by 1914 the Vineland summer school was restricting participation to 60
students (Sarason & Doris, 1979).

Some teachers were trained in other institutions (those of higher learning). Gallaudet College established a teacher-training program in 1891
(Craig, 1942). Connor (1976) found:

According to Wallen (1914), the University of Pennsylvania offered a three
course sequence in 1897 in the Education of the Mentally Retarded. Soon
after, New York University initiated a course, "Education of Defectives,"
and Teachers College, Columbia University offered "The Psychology and
Education of Exceptional Children" in 1906 and 1908 respectively. (p. 369)

Citing work by Schleier (1931), Connor also found that by 1929,

37 teachers colleges and eight normal schools in 22 states and an additional
54 colleges and universities in 38 states and the District of Columbia offered
from 1 to 12 courses for the preparation of teachers and supervisors of
retarded children. Schleier recommended that, except in unusual situations,
only one training center be established in each state in order to (a) prevent
unnecessary duplication of courses in a state, (b) eliminate the need to conduct programs for small groups of students, (c) eliminate duplication of
equipment and special facilities, and (d) keep the cost at a minimum. (p.
369)

This was a shallow warning, for the mechanism for the proliferation of
programs was set in motion and running full steam. But the major impetus came in 1958, when the Eighty-fifth Congress enacted Public Law
85–926 which "authorized grants to universities and colleges for training
leadership personnel in mental retardation and grants to state education
agencies for training teachers of the mentally retarded" (Burke, 1976, p.
144). In 1963, the law was amended by Public Law 88–164 to include
support for the training of personnel in other disability areas (for example, hard of hearing, deaf, seriously emotionally disturbed). The first
Education of the Handicapped Act (EHA) of 1970 (Public Law 91–230)
established the federal commitment to training personnel in special education as did the amendments to EHA—Public Law 93–380—enacted in
1974 (Burke, 1976). In fact, the Education for All Handicapped Children
Act of 1975 (Public Law 94–142) Amendments

Table **3.1**   Federal Funding Pattern for Personnel Preparation 1960–1976

FISCAL YEAR	FUNDS[a]	FISCAL YEAR	FUNDS[a]
1960	985,222	1969	29,699,920
1961	993,433	1970	29,910,000
1962	2,492,238	1971	32,550,000
1963	2,486,755	1972	33,945,000
1964	12,992,758	1973	38,960,000
1965	14,499,444	1974	39,615,000
1966	19,500,000	1975	37,700,000
1967	24,500,000	1976	40,375,000
1968	24,499,974		

[a] Based on Division of Personnel Preparation records of obligated funds 1960–1971 and appropriations allocated to the Division of Personnel Preparation 1972–1976.

SOURCE: From Personnel preparation: Historical perspective by P. J. Burke, *Exceptional Children*, 1976, *43*, 144–147. Copyright 1976 by The Council for Exceptional Children. Reprinted with permission.

did not change Part D (the training section) of P. L. 93–380 though it is clear that the training provisions called for in the new law will have far reaching impact on personnel preparation relationships among state education agencies, colleges and universities, local education agencies, and the Bureau of Education for the Handicapped (BEH). (Burke, 1976, pp. 144–145)

Since the federal government became involved in the preparation of teachers of special education, the amount of money made available by the Division of Personnel Preparation has increased by a factor of over 50; in 1960, obligated funds were $985,222 (see Table 3.1), and in 1979 the government planned to disburse $55,375,000 (Harvey, 1978b). The steady increase in program funding for personnel preparation is evident in the data presented in Table 3.1.

Of course, the federal government does not just give away money; with each bit of aid goes the requirement for compliance with guidelines and directives. Current funding patterns are based on proposals for 12 priority areas (Harvey, 1978b). The projected distribution of federal funds for fiscal 1979 is presented in Table 3.2. There is some concern that in responding to the shifting, transient federal priorities, many populations may no longer be served. The proliferation of programs has made federal assistance necessary, and it includes directives, guidelines, and consequences that we must follow. Drummond and Andrews (1980), however, consider the federal approach to leadership to be straightforward:

A problem or concern is identified, legislation is passed, the federal bureaucracy prepares rules and regulations, and the program is launched. Not only

Table 3.2 Projected Distribution of Federal Funds for Personnel Preparation 1979

	PRESERVICE AMOUNT	NUMBERS TRAINED*	INSERVICE AMOUNT	NUMBERS TRAINED*	TOTAL AMOUNT	NUMBERS TRAINED*
PREPARATION OF SPECIAL EDUCATORS						
Early childhood	$ 3,698,000	1,155	$ 2,465,000	6,117	$ 6,163,000	7,272
Severely handicapped	5,024,000	1,571	2,951,000	7,787	7,975,000	9,358
General special education	4,496,000	1,363	2,754,000	7,227	7,250,000	8,590
Subtotal	$13,218,000	4,089	$ 8,170,000	21,131	$21,388,000	25,220
PREPARATION OF SUPPORT PERSONNEL FOR REGULAR AND SPECIAL EDUCATION						
Paraprofessional	$ 1,051,000	744	$ 762,000	1,799	$ 1,813,000	2,543
Physical education	957,000	299	493,000	1,109	1,450,000	1,408
Recreation	728,000	227	359,000	886	1,087,000	1,113
Interdisciplinary	971,00	303	479,000	1,076	1,450,000	1,379
Vocational/career education	1,523,000	475	652,000	1,662	2,175,000	2,137
Volunteer program	434,000	292	653,000	1,661	1,087,000	1,953
Subtotal	$ 5,664,000	2,340	$ 3,398,000	8,193	$ 9,062,000	10,533
SPECIAL EDUCATION TRAINING FOR REGULAR EDUCATION TEACHERS**	$ 7,250,000	—	$11,875,000	46,929	$19,125,000	46,929
Subtotal	$ 7,250,000	—	$11,875,000	46,929	$19,125,000	46,929
INSTRUCTIONAL MODELS						
Developmental assistance	—	—	$ 725,000	1,782	$ 725,000	1,782
Model implementation	2,385,000	745	2,690,000	6,780	5,075,000	7,525
Subtotal	$ 2,385,000	745	$ 3,415,000	8,562	$ 5,800,000	9,307
TOTAL	$28,517,000	7,174	$26,858,000	84,815	$55,375,000	91,989

* Estimated to receive financial support from this source.

** Direct financial assistance related to preservice training of regular classroom teachers is not provided. (Preservice is for Deans' Grants.)

SOURCE: J. Harvey, Regional collaboration. In J. Smith (Ed.), *Personnel preparation and Public Law 94–142: The map, the mission and the mandate* (2nd ed.). Boothwyn, Pa.: Educational Resources Center, 1978, p. 13.

do these programs exert influence through the available federal funds, but they also enlarge state influence by making funds available to the state departments of education. (pp. 98–99)

Who shall determine who will be trained is but a minor concern in personnel preparation. The more salient issues are teacher burnout, the nature of training, the nature of teaching, and educational professionalism.

TEACHER BURNOUT

Four weeks into the school year, a first year teacher in a class for behaviorally disordered junior high students had quit, too physically and emotionally exhausted to continue. By all accounts, she was well prepared for her job, having completed teacher preparation programs in both regular and special education. She had been a good student in her classes, had had successful experiences in student teaching, and had worked as a teacher aide in a state hospital school during two previous summers. She was enthusiastic, appeared to have realistic expectations of what she was getting into, and wanted to teach behaviorally disordered children. In short, she showed considerable promise. Even so, she could not cope with the situation in which she found herself. (Zabel & Zabel, 1980, p. 23)

Approximately 250,000 teachers are working special education in this country today, and their rate of attrition is around 6 percent. (Siantz & Moore, 1978, p. 27)

At present no data exist on exactly how many teachers burn out each year, or how many continue to teach while burned out. (Weiskopf, 1980, p. 18)

Teacher burnout, like burnout among other professionals, is a reality (Freudenberger, 1977; Landsman, 1979; Maslach, 1976; Maslach & Pines, 1977; McGuire, 1979; Weiskopf, 1980; Zabel & Zabel, 1980). Although the exact number of burned-out teachers may not be known, a recent survey by McGuire (1979) indicated that many teachers are frustrated with their jobs and would prefer not to be teaching.

BURNOUT SYMPTOMS

Maslach (1976) defined *burnout* as "emotional exhaustion resulting from the stress of interpersonal contact" (p. 56). A variety of terms have been used to describe the emotional exhaustion that may result from stressful interactions with children and young adults in educational settings. For example, negativism and cynicism regarding students and one's job in general, feelings and complaints of overwork, mild depression, boredom, or reduced interest in work and physical symptoms (for example, fatigue, irritability, excessive smoking) have been used to describe burnout (Freudenberger, 1977; Mattingly, 1977; Maslach,1976; Zabel & Zabel, 1980). Weiskopf (1980) also indicated that often burnout victims will limit social interaction with their peers; they "may miss faculty meetings, eat lunch alone in the classroom, skip coffee breaks, and leave school early or very late, thereby avoiding other teachers" (p. 21). Often, excessive hours at work will result in less and less productivity in work. Absenteeism is also a noticeable characteristic of burned-out teachers.

WHY TEACHERS?

Stress and job satisfaction are inversely related (Cooper & Marshall, 1976; Mattingly, 1977; Weiskopf, 1980), and there are a number of stressful factors in teaching that may increase the likelihood of burnout. Teachers are expected to do something with the children in their classrooms. A teacher's perception or extent of belief that his or her behavior results in student performance may be defined as a sense of efficacy. Many factors defeat teachers' sense of efficacy. Education is a "loose-coupled" system, and it is not easy to ascertain the effects of one's efforts. More often than not, attention is focused on the things that go wrong. Learning requires motivation, but students often are discouraged by school, and their lack of interest works against their teachers' efforts to bring about change. Pupil-teacher ratios also hide the progress made by many youngsters; small changes in school behavior go unnoticed amid the hustle and bustle of a typical classroom. Teachers tend not to keep records that could be useful in measuring and documenting teaching-related change; and in fact, most of the typical measurement activities (for example, standardized tests) may do more harm than good in this respect.

There are many social, political, and practical factors that cause stress in teachers. Often, administrators provide only minimal supports for teachers, who are expected to do the job (generally loosely defined) alone. Similarly, much of a teacher's work is not specifically teaching; that is, paperwork and other "administrivia" occupy more and more instructional time. Parents pressure the educational system in general and the teachers in particular. And recently, the schools have become battlegounds for the legal determinations of appropriate education and discipline. Teachers are low-paid professionals who have a loosely defined, highly important job to do. Working under such conditions certainly must be stressful.

Finally, a teacher's training is misleading. Undergraduate and graduate teachers-in-training often reveal (near the end of their programs) their apprehension of work in the real world; many become depressed by how little they know about teaching, and others simply never enter the profession. Sarason, Davidson, and Blatt (1962) observed that "teachers are more painfully aware than any other professional group about the inadequacies and irrelevancies of their training" (p. 12). Teachers also assert that much of what a teacher is taught in school is unrelated to what he or she actually must do.

NATURE OF TRAINING

What is done to students to make them teachers? In the United States, there are approximately 1,400 "institutions of higher learning" that train teachers (Smith, 1980). Nearly 800 train special education personnel (Irvin, 1978). What do the faculties of these institutions do to "train" teachers? Fuller and Bown (1975) offered an interesting view:

The empirical literature yields a disturbing conclusion about the experience of learning to teach. Becoming a teacher is complex, stressful, intimate, and largely covert, but in accomplishing this demanding task teachers do not feel helped by teacher education. What laymen, legislators, and education students have been claiming for decades may be true: teacher education is orthogonal to the teacher. (p. 25)

PRESERVICE TRAINING

For the most part, education is considered an academic rather than a clinical area of study, and education students take courses in, about, and related to it. Smith (1980) reported that some "colleges offer more than 600 courses" (p. 88). Typical college catalogues list courses in social foundations of education, history of education, educational research, secondary education, elementary education, special education, open education, humanistic education, competency-based education, and methods in social studies, science, mathematics, and language arts education (this list is by no means exhaustive). Despite all the time students spend in class, education "has the lowest proportion of credit hours allocated to the specifically professional aspects of the program of any of the professions or semi-professions" (Howsam, 1980, p. 94). Smith and Street (1980) reported that from 1939 to 1979 secondary education students majoring in English at the University of Florida took between 16 percent and 24 percent of their courses at the professional school; elementary education majors during the same period took 28 percent to 48 percent of their courses there. For the whole university, the number of professional courses ranged from 44 percent to 50 percent for the College of Pharmacy, 40 percent to 57 percent for the College of Law, and 45 percent to 55 percent for the College of Engineering's Department of Civil Engineering. The Florida Barbers' Board requires more hours of schooling than that required of the secondary education major (Smith & Street, 1980). Clark and Marker (1975) present similar figures for the percent of instruction offered to teachers in schools, colleges, and departments of education.

For the most part, the content of this professional program is quite similar across the country. Prospective elementary school teachers take foundations and general methods courses (for example, introduction to education, social and/or psychological foundations of education, elementary school curriculum) and specific methods courses (for example, teaching reading, mathematics, social studies) and spend some time student teaching. Special education teachers take background courses in the foundations of education (for example, history of education, social foundations of education) and then specialize in exceptional child education. Their professional program includes foundations and general methods courses (for example, introduction to special education, assessment in special education, teaching special children), specific methods courses for particular types of children (for example, teaching the mentally retarded, learning disabled, emotionally disturbed) and student teaching. Interestingly, training programs for school psychologists offer courses in the same general areas (cf. Brown, 1979). Clark and Marker (1975) noted:

> State certification and/or national accreditation standards are usually given the credit or charged with the blame, for this uniformity. It is probably more reasonable to assume, however, that the pattern represents the *best current and conventional wisdom* about the education of teachers (and support personnel), which is then reflected in certification and accreditation standards and in the content and structure of higher education programs. (p. 56)

Regardless of whether the chicken (that is, the courses) or the egg (that is, the standards) comes first, there are problems in the omelet's (that is, the teacher's) ability to pass as appropriately prepared. Sarason, Davidson, and Blatt (1962) put it directly: "It is obvious to all who have attended college that knowledge of subject matter bears no simple relationship to the effectiveness of teaching" (p. 2). They added; "The learned or scholarly teacher—regardless of the age of the pupils being taught—is not necessarily the effective teacher" (p. 75). Smith (1980) pointed out that "many if not most courses are added to the college curriculum to satisfy the interests of instructors, although their value to teachers is often rationalized by objectives to which the courses do not lead" (p. 88) but which the instructor carefully chooses for their "content validity." He added: "The criterion of instructor interest is appropriate for academic departments, but leads in a professional school to a multiplicity of courses having *little content or relevance* to the work of the professional" (p. 89) (that is, the teacher). The response to the lack of relationship between course work and practice has been a developing interest in competency-based or performance-based instruction. Unfortunately, the achievement of this noble goal has remained largely a dream rather than becoming a reality. Our knowledge of what a teacher does is limited; and our attempts to identify competencies are weak.

COMPETENCIES OF SPECIAL EDUCATION TEACHERS

Blackhurst and Hofmeister (1980) reviewed the literature and noted that "considerable efforts have been expended to identify and specify competencies for various special education professions" (p. 216). Included under special education professions were the following: teachers of educable mentally retarded students, special education curriculum consultants, teachers of secondary-level educable mentally retarded students, special education supervisors, directors of special education, directors of special education resource centers, clinical teachers, special education professors, teachers of children with learning and behavior disorders, teachers of the gifted, teachers of the severely handicapped, and elementary teachers involved in mainstreaming.

There are numerous lists of competencies for special teachers which generally are developed from and based on expert opinion (that is, special educators, state department personnel) and/or verified against the judgments of practitioners (Blackhurst & Hofmeister, 1980; Shores et al., 1973). Table 3.3 presents examples of areas of study and competencies considered essential to individuals who participate in making classification and placement decisions. According to Cegelka (1978), they represent the work of an interagency meeting.

Those functions and specific competencies reported by regular elementary classroom teachers to be necessary to mainstream handicapped children effectively were identified by Redden and Blackhurst (1978) and are presented in Table 3.4. Even with extensive validation, competencies such as these, developed by reviewing the literature or by surveying teachers, represent little more than statements of what someone should do; often the competence is not observable, and/or the desirable standards for performance are not specified or known. Shores, Cegelka, and Nelson (1973) asserted that, "before a competency statement is considered valid, it should be demonstrated that successful teachers actually

Table **3.3**   Selected Areas of Study and Competencies for Persons Responsible for Classification Decisions

RECOMMENDED AREAS OF STUDY	EXPECTED COMPETENCIES
Individual Assessment	

Nature of intelligence	Is familiar with and can critically evaluate a wide range of intelligence and other assessment instruments
Developmental milestones	
Behavioral observation	
Test selection	Selects appropriate battery of tests or scales to answer specific questions for various ages, functioning levels, and disability groups
Administration of individual scales, tests, or other measures of intelligence, social adaption, perceptual motor performance, academic achievement, language development, or personality	
	Makes reliable and pertinent behavioral observations and can report observations clearly
Scoring and test profile interpretation	Can assess the functioning level of infants and of mute, blind, deaf, or physically handicapped persons with various levels of intellectual functioning
Integration of test results with developmental, behavioral, and other data	
Relation of measurement to individual programing	Can integrate measurement results, developmental data, and information from other disciplines into a meaningful report that is useful for program development
Written and oral communication of results	
Consultation and followup	Reports results of assessment clearly in written and oral form to parents and professionals
Cross-cultural studies, including the effects of linguistic background on test results	
	Is aware of the effects of situational factors and cultural background on test results
	Can accurately administer scales, tests, or other measures under a variety of working conditions
	Can formulate a plan for monitoring the efficacy of recommendations derived from test results
	Is familiar with subcultural and ethnic group vocabularies

(continued)

Table **3.3**   *(cont.)*

Individual Differences	
Theories of development	Has knowledge of major theories of development
Developmental sequence	
Learning and development	Knows the possible effects of maturation upon test behavior at different ages
Maturation and test behavior	
	Is familiar with and can readily identify developmental sequences, milestones, and behaviors that are found through the life range

The Exceptional Child	
Survey of disability groups	Is knowledgeable about the characteristics, differential assessment, and learning needs of a variety of disability groups and can relate learning needs to specific educational alternatives.
General and specific learning disabilities	
Differential assessment	
Educational alternatives	

SOURCE: From Competencies of persons responsible for the classification of mentally retarded individuals by W. J. Cegelka, *Exceptional Children*, 1978, *45*, 26–31. Copyright 1978 by The Council for Exceptional Children. Reprinted with permission.

engage in the behavior or skill described, that the skill discriminates between successful teachers, and that it has the desired effect on children's classroom performance'' p. 193). There is very little evidence that this form of validation has occurred (cf. Schofer & Lilly, 1980). Perhaps a more important question concerns the extent to which a trained teacher (with or without competencies) is ready to teach.

THE STUDY OF PROFESSIONAL READINESS

A reasonable place to start when considering the readiness of teachers seems to be with the concept of effective teaching. If we use the qualities, characteristics, and behaviors of successful teachers as criteria, then we can decide on a new teacher's readiness to enter the profession. The only drawback to this logically valid approach is that we have no such criteria for our knowledge regarding effective teachers and/or their characteristics. Menges (1975) listed several methods for defining effective profes-

Table **3.4**   Functioning Areas and Competencies Necessary to Mainstream
Handicapped Children

FUNCTION I.0: DEVELOP ORIENTATION STRATEGIES FOR MAINSTREAM ENTRY

1.1 Participate in schoolwide planning for mainstreaming activities.

1.2 Set up a training plan that will provide supplementary instruction in areas necessary to teach effectively in a mainstream setting.

1.3 Participate in parent and community orientation programs on mainstreaming.

1.4 Seek out consultative relationships with specialists or school staff.

1.5 When appropriate, develop a program to prepare the special student for entry into a regular class.

1.6 Prepare members of the regular class for the entry of special students into the class.

FUNCTION 2.0: ASSESS NEEDS AND SET GOALS

2.1 Gather information to determine the educational needs of each student.

2.2 Evaluate each student's present level of functioning.

2.3 Determine for each student in the class individual goals that are appropriate, realistic, and measurable.

2.4 Determine group goals for the class as a whole and for subsets within the class.

2.5 Involve parents in setting goals for their child and for the class as a whole.

FUNCTION 3.0: PLAN TEACHING STRATEGIES AND USE OF RESOURCES

3.1 Design a system of teaching procedures that provides for individual differences in students.

3.2 Specify and prepare a variety of activities that will involve the entire class in grouping patterns that are varied and flexible.

3.3 Develop and design a variety of alternate teaching strategies.

3.4 Develop a plan for use of human and material resources.

3.5 Develop a flexible time schedule that provides for the learning, physical, and social needs of each student.

3.6 Provide an optimal classroom climate through appropriate arrangement and adaptation of the physical properties of the classroom.

FUNCTION 4.0: IMPLEMENT TEACHING STRATEGIES AND USE RESOURCES

4.1 Select and use a variety of individualized teaching methods to instruct each student within the student's level or capability of functioning.

4.2 Develop, schedule, and maintain on a regular basis a variety of grouping patterns that provide opportunities for students to reach class goals, both social and academic.

4.3 Use the efforts of the special education resource staff with the special students' classroom activities.

4.4 Acquire, adapt, and develop materials necessary to achieve learning goals.

4.5 Plan and maintain a system to use the assistance of volunteers (other students, parents, etc.) to reinforce and supplement classroom activities.   (continued)

Table **3.4**   *(cont.)*

4.6 Develop a plan to use the talents of parents in supporting the learning activities of their child and those of other students in the class.

FUNCTION 5.0: FACILITATE LEARNING

5.1 Identify and differentiate between a variety of behavior management techniques and develop skills in selecting appropriate techniques to manage individual and/or group behavior.

5.2 Select and apply adequate behavior management techniques and measures to meet the learning goals set for the class and each individual student.

5.3 Acknowledge appropriate behaviors in each student in order to stimulate continued effort.

5.4 Conduct class activities in a way to encourage interaction between and among students.

5.5 Provide ample instruction and practice for each child to develop and refine adequate coping strategies.

5.6 Plan with class for systematic appraisal and improvement of the psychological climate of the class.

FUNCTION 6.0: EVALUATE LEARNING

6.1 Organize a system to collect and record data by which to evaluate student progress toward goal attainment.

6.2 Develop a feedback system that will furnish continuous data to student, teacher, and parents on goal attainment.

6.3 Use evaluation data to assess goal attainment in order to measure terminal outcomes and set new goals.

SOURCE: From Mainstreaming competency specifications for elementary teachers by M. R. Redden & A. E. Blackhurst, *Exceptional Children*, 1978, *45*, 615–617. Copyright 1978 by The Council for Exceptional Children. Reprinted with permission.

sional practice and discussed surveys, observations, and correlational research as state-of-the-art techniques. Rosenshine and Furst (1971), reviewing "research on teacher performance criteria," included the following, listed in the order of importance, in their discussion of the "most promising of the variables studied": (1) clarity, (2) variability, (3) enthusiasm, (4) task-oriented and/or businesslike behaviors, (5) student opportunity to learn criterion material, (6) use of student ideas and general indirectness, (7) criticism, (8) use of structuring comments, (9) types of questions. (10) probing, and (11) level of difficulty of instruction. It should be pointed out that usually correlational research, rather than experimental studies, established these variables as important teacher behaviors and that at least two behaviors actually could be student controlled (items 5 and 6) and one could be curriculum controlled (item 11).

We have not been able to define very well the behaviors of effective teachers. As a substitute strategy, we have investigated and defined effectiveness in other ways. Menges (1975) proposed that studies of personality characteristics or knowledge of subject matter has been of limited value but that assessing simulated and actual job performance is a more promising alternative. Besides analyzing work samples and the use of noninterpersonal and interpersonal simulation activities, he discussed performance-based teacher education (PBTE) as a solution to teacher competence and readiness. In PBTE, "the teacher is asked to demonstrate his ability to perform certain *critical teaching acts* or to enable students to demonstrate certain specified abilities which they could not do before instruction" (Roth, 1973, p. 287). Heath and Nielson (1974) reviewed the research basis for performance-based teacher education and reached the following three conclusions:

First, the research literature on the relation between teacher behavior and student achievement does not offer an empirical basis for the prescription of teacher-training objectives.

Second, this literature fails to provide such a basis, not because of minor flaws in the statistical analyses, but because of sterile operational definitions of both teaching and achievement, and because of fundamentally weak research designs.

Last, given the well-documented, strong association between student achievement and variables such as socioeconomic status and ethnic status, the effects of techniques of teaching on achievement (as these variables are defined in the PBTE research) are likely to be inherently trivial. (p. 481)

We find curious the possibility of evaluating readiness to teach by using essentially nonexistent or, at best, loosely defined criteria. The decision of who enters teaching when must be made according to some other standards. In fact, it seems that those criteria that Menges (1975) considered more limited (for example, knowledge of subject matter and personality characteristics) are more often than not the basis for decisions about readiness to teach. Based on his review, Menges (1975) concluded:

First, definitions of effective practice should emphasize many discrete behaviors and characteristics rather than global definitions. Second, measures of these characteristics (predictors) should be as similar to the criterion itself as possible. Third, multiple assessment devices should be used so that no single type is over-emphasized. Measures of subject matter knowledge, in particular, should be less heavily weighted. Fourth, data should not be used for decision making until longitudinal studies demonstrate adequate predictive validity. (p. 201)

In practice, however, decisions on readiness to teach are based simply on the extent to which a prospective teacher has met certification requirements.

CERTIFICATION IN REGULAR AND SPECIAL EDUCATION

Bush and Enemark (1975) found that in regard to education, "the *de jure* control and responsibility are, of course, in state hands, that is, they are vested in elected and appointed state officials, state legislators, state boards of education, chief state school officers, and governors" (p. 266). Additionally, they acknowledged, as we do, the influence of federal legislators and the U. S. Office of Education (see Chapter 2). The state is the guardian of quality control primarily by determining the rules of teaching certification. One widely accepted purpose of certification is to "establish and maintain standards for the preparation and employment of persons who teach or render certain nonteaching services in the schools" (Kinney, 1964, p. 3). State officials, of course, do not exercise this power without guidelines:

Almost from the beginning of the exercising of centralized state responsibilities for teacher education and certification, state departments of education, in one degree or another, in one manner or another, sought to involve the teaching profession in the public schools and teacher education institutions in deriving fair and effective standards. (Stinnett, 1969, pp. 388–400)

It is no wonder that current state certification requirements pertain mainly to course work. In the preface to the 1974 *Manual on Standards Affecting School Personnel in the United States* (Stinnett, 1974), John D. Sullivan, then director of instruction and professional development for the National Education Association, proclaimed "the 'good news' that now the bachelor's degree is clearly the minimum standard for teaching in elementary and secondary schools" (p. iii). Each state's minimum requirements, in 1974, for the lowest regular teaching certificates are presented in Table 3.5. Although teacher certification is based mostly on course work, all states have other requirements as well (see Table 3.6).

An analysis of the certification standards for special education personnel suggests that most states require certifiability in an area of regular education plus professional study in special education. This professional study generally includes various amounts of time spent in special education courses and practicum experience. The information listed by Woellner (1979) for several states is illustrative. For example, to be a certified special education teacher in Illinois, appropriate courses in characteristics, methods, and diagnosis and a survey of exceptional children courses are required, in addition to having completed a bachelor's degree and satisfied general and professional education requirements. Similarly, in Missouri, Virginia, and most other states, degrees and/or course work in education or psychology of exceptional children, curricular methods, diagnostics, and practicum will certify a special education teacher.

INSERVICE TRAINING

Inasmuch as the competencies and qualities of a good teacher are virtually unknown, the methods of training good teachers are based more on past practices than on knowledge. Thus, we find that preservice training programs are largely academic and that entrance requirements typically depend on the simple counts of courses taken. It is no wonder that, at present, inservice training is the major "growth industry" (Howsam, 1980) in education. Regular teachers are the needy consumers (Siantz & Moore, 1978):

Approximately 250,000 teachers are working in special education in this country today, and their rate of attrition is around 6 percent. A few more than 25,000 new people enter the field each year after completing preservice training, but, when the attrition rate is considered, this leaves only about 10,000 additional teachers who enter the manpower pool annually. However, to serve between 7 and 8 million children, we know that we need 500,000 teachers and support personnel. Since we also know that many of these children must be served in the least restrictive environment of the regular classroom for at least part of the school day, it becomes clear that a large group of the 250,000 additional personnel we need must be recruited and retrained from the ranks of regular educators. It will not be possible to give these youngsters the best education unless regular teachers understand exceptional children and how to work with them. Thus, a major area of development, both now and in the future, will be the comprehensive inservice training of regular educators. (p. 27)

Howsam (1980) pointed out that the American Association of Colleges for Teacher Education (AACTE) recognizes three levels of teacher education: preservice, inservice, and continuing. Preservice training, of course, takes place prior to entrance in the field; inservice and continuing education are necessary to help the teacher adjust to the particular requirements of the work place or to keep up with changes in the field. He added:

In practice, because of inadequacies of initial preparation, inservice education has had to address those initial inadequacies. This unfortunate circumstance simply recognizes and reinforces the semi-professional status of teachers. Since there is never an opportunity for the teacher to catch up, let alone keep up, the teaching force never escapes the stigma of inadequacy or dependence on the administrative system. (p. 96)

Inservice training for regular and special teachers is a big business: of the more than $55 million disbursed by the personnel preparation division of the Bureau of Education for the Handicapped, $10 million was for inservice only (Harvey, 1978b). The requirements of Public Law 94–142

Table 3.5 Minimum Requirements for Lowest Regular Teaching Certificates*

	ELEMENTARY SCHOOL					SECONDARY SCHOOL				
STATE	Degree	General Education (Semester Hours)	Professional Education (Total Semester Hours)	Student Teaching (Included in Col. 4)	Educational Philosophy-Psychology-Sociology (Included in Col. 4)	Degree	General Education (Semester Hours)	Professional Education (Total Semester Hours)	Student Teaching (Included in Col. 9)	Educational Philosophy-Psychology-Sociology (Included in Col. 9)
1	2	3	4	5	6	7	8	9	10	11
Alabama	B	59	27	6	—	B	44	21	6	—
Alaska	B	AC	AC	AC	AC	B	AC	AC	AC	AC
Arizona	B[a]	40	24	6	3	B[a]	40	22	6	3
Arkansas	B	48	18	6	3	B	48	18	6	3
California	B[b]	AC	AC[†]	AC[†]	AC[†]	B[b]	AC	AC[†]	AC[†]	AC[†]
Colorado	B	AC	AC	AC	AC	B	AC	AC	AC	AC
Connecticut	B[c]	75	30	6	6	B[c]	45	18	6	6
Delaware	B	60	30	6	6	B	60	18	6	9
District of Col.	B[d]	AC	AC	AC	AC	M[d]	AC	AC	AC	AC
Florida	B	45	20	6	6	B	45	20	6	6
Georgia	B[e]	40	18	6	—	B[e]	40	18	6	—
Hawaii	B	AC	18	AC[f]	—	B	AC	18	AC[f]	—
Idaho	B	42	24	6	6[g]	B	—	20	6	6[g]
Illinois	B	78	16	5	2	B	42	16	5	2
Indiana	B[h]	97	27	8	10	B[h]	50	18	6	6
Iowa	B	40	20	5	—	B	40	20	5	—

80

State										
Kansas	B	50	24	5	12	B	50	20	5	12
Kentucky	B[i]	45	24	8	—	B[i]	45	17	8	—
Louisiana	B	46	24	4	9	B	46	18	4	9
Maine	B	60	30	6	3	B	60	18	6	3
Maryland	B[k]	80	26	8	6	B[k]	—	18	6	6
Massachusetts	B[l]	—	18	2[m]	—	B[l]	—	12	2[m]	—
Michigan	B[n]	40	20	6	6[o]	B[n]	40	20	6	6[o]
Minnesota	B	AC	AC	AC	AC	B	—	27[p]	6[p]	—
Mississippi	B	48	36	6	6	B	48	18	6	6
Missouri	B	AC	18	5	7	B	40	18	5	7
Montana	B	AC	AC	AC	AC	B	AC	16	AC	AC

LEGEND: —means not reported. AC means approved curriculum; B means completion of the bachelor's degree; M means completion of the master's degree; C means a course; NS means not specified; NCATE means standards of the National Council for Accreditation of Teacher Education.

* Requirements listed are those which are basic for lowest regular certificates. Some variations may be found in the requirements for specific certificates listed for the respective states in chapter 2.

a For the temporary certificate, valid for six years only. Teachers must qualify for the standard certificate by completing a fifth year of preparation.

b For the initial standard credential. Teachers must qualify for the permanent credential by completing a planned fifth year program of 30 semester hours (s.h.) postbaccalaureate work (or whatever constitutes a year of work in the preparing institution)—within seven years for elementary teachers, five years for secondary teachers.

† For elementary teachers. California standards apparently call for 20 s.h. of professional studies (8 student teaching, 8 educational psychology/sociology/philosophy, 4 curriculum and methods); for secondary teachers 15 s.h. (6, 6, and 3).

c For the provisional certificate, valid for five years and renewable once for five years. Teachers must qualify for the standard certificate by completing a fifth year of preparation.

d Bachelor's degree for elementary and junior high schools; master's degree for senior and vocational high schools.

e Effective July 1, 1974, the initial certificate, based on the bachelor's degree, will be nonrenewable; completion of a fifth year of preparation will be required for continuing certification.

f Not included in total professional education.

g Three s.h. in educational psychology, 3 in principles of education.

h For the provisional certificate, valid for five years only; teachers must qualify for the professional certificate by obtaining a master's degree.

i For the provisional certificate, valid for ten years and extendable only on completion of a fifth year of preparation. A master's degree is required for the standard certificate.

j Recommended but not required.

k For the initial certificate, valid three years and renewable for seven; teachers must qualify for the professional certificate, based on the master's degree or equivalent, after ten years of service.

l Or graduation from a four-year normal school approved by the State Board of Education.

m The requirement is 6 s.h. for the bilingual education certificate.

n For the provisional certificate, valid for six years and renewable for three; teachers must complete an additional 18 s.h. for continuing certification.

o Or equivalent

p Quarter hours.

(continued)

Table 3.5 *(cont.)*

STATE	Degree	ELEMENTARY SCHOOL				Degree	SECONDARY SCHOOL			
		General Education (Semester Hours)	Professional Education (Total Semester Hours)	Student Teaching (Included in Col. 4)	Educational Philosophy-Psychology-Sociology (Included in Col. 4)		General Education (Semester Hours)	Professional Education (Total Semester Hours)	Student Teaching (Included in Col. 9)	Educational Philosophy-Psychology-Sociology (Included in Col. 9)
1	2	3	4	5	6	7	8	9	10	11
Nebraska	B[q]	AC	AC	AC	AC	B	AC	AC	AC	AC
Nevada	B	—	18[r]	6	—	B	—	20	6	—
New Hampshire	B[s]	AC	AC	AC	AC	B[s]	AC	AC	AC	AC
New Jersey	B	45	24	—[t]	—[u]	B	45	15	—[t]	—[u]
New Mexico	B[v]	48	24	6	—	B[v]	48	18	6	—
New York	B[w]	NS	24	NS[f]	—	B[w]	NS	12	NS[f]	—
North Carolina	B	35–40%	15–20%	—	—	B	35–40%	15–20%	—	—
North Dakota	B	NCATE	16	5	—	B	NCATE	16	5	—
Ohio	B[x]	60	29	6	6	B[x]	30	21	6	6
Oklahoma	B	50	21	9	—	B	50	21	9	—
Oregon	B	—	24	6	—	B[y]	—	20	6	—
Pennsylvania	B[z]	AC	AC	AC	AC	B[z]	AC	AC	AC	AC
Rhode Island	B[aa]	—	30	6	—	B[aa]	—	18	6	—
South Carolina	B	42–45	21	6	3	B	42–45	18	6	3

State										
South Dakota	B[bb]	30	26	6	—	B	—	20	6	—
Tennessee	B	40	24	4	—	B	40	24	4	—
Texas	B	60	18	6	—	B	60	18	6	—
Utah	B	AC	25	8	6	B	AC	21	8	6
Vermont	B	AC	18	9	3	B	AC	18	9	3
Virginia	B	60	18	6	3	B	48	15	6	3
Washington	B[ee]	70%[dd]	20%[dd]	—	—	B[ee]	70%[dd]	20%[dd]	—	—
West Virginia	B	40	20	6	AC	B	40	20	6	—
Wisconsin	B	AC	26	5	AC	B	AC	18	5	AC
Wyoming	B	40	23	C	C	B	40	20	C	—

q Elementary teachers in accredited schools must hold a certificate based on the degree. Nebraska does issue provisional rural elementary and commitment certificates on a minimum of 60 s.h., valid only for specifically endorsed grades or subjects in designated classes of school districts for a limited time.

r For the five-year nonrenewable certificate: teachers must qualify for the regular certificate, which requires 30 s.h.

s A provisional conversion license may be issued to the holder of a bachelor's degree from a regionally accredited institution but not in a program approved by New Hampshire. A certificate will be issued on completion of the conversion program and recommendation of the superintendent attesting to competent performance and satisfactory professional growth.

t College requirement; not included in total professional education column.

u Educational psychology; included in total professional education.

v For the provisional certificate, valid for four years and renewable once for four years. Teachers must complete a fifth year of preparation for continuing certification.

w For the provisional certificate, valid for five years only. Teachers must qualify for permanent certification by completing a fifth year of preparation.

x Total s.h. —124.

y For the initial certificate, valid for three years and renewable once for three years. Secondary teachers must complete a fifth year of preparation for continuing certification.

z For the provisional certificate, valid for three years and renewable once for three years. Teachers must qualify for the permanent certificate by completing 24 s.h. of postbaccalaureate work.

aa For the provisional certificate, valid for six years only. Teachers must qualify for the professional certificate by completing a fifth year of preparation (36 s.h. or a master's degree).

bb South Dakota still lists a nondegree elementary certificate, valid for teaching grades K-9, except in K-12 school systems. The 1970 edition noted that this certificate was to be discontinued in 1972.

ee For the provisional certificate, valid for three years and renewable once for three years. Teachers must qualify for the standard certificate by completing a fifth year of preparation.

dd Ten percent electives.

SOURCE: T. M. Stinnett, *A manual on standards affecting school personnel in the United States.* Washington, D.C.: National Education Association, 1974, pp. 46-47.

(continued)

Table **3.6** General Requirements for Teaching Certificates

STATE	U.S. CITIZEN-SHIP	OATH OF ALLE-GIANCE	EVI-DENCE OF EMPLOY-MENT	RECOM-MENDA-TION (COL-LEGE OR EM-PLOYER)	MINI-MUM AGE	FEE	GEN-ERAL HEALTH CERT.	CHEST X-RAY	SPE-CIAL COURSE	NATIONAL TEACHER EXAMI-NATIONS
1	2	3	4	5	6	7	8	9	10	11
Alabama	—	—	—	X	17	$2	—	X	—	—
Alaska[a]	—	—	—	—	18	$10	—	—	X[d]	—
Arizona	—	X	—	X[b]	18	$5-8[c]	—	X	—	—
Arkansas	—	—	—	X	18	None	X	X	—	—
California	—	X[e]	—[f]	X	18	$20	X	—	X[g]	—
Colorado	X	—	—	X	—	$5	—	—	—	—
Connecticut	X	—	—	X	18	None	—	X	—	—
Delaware	—	—[h]	—	—	—	$10[i]	—[h]	X	—	—
Dist. of Col.	X	—	—	X	—	None	X	X	—	—
Florida	X	X	—[j]	—[k]	20	$12	X	—	—	—
Georgia	—	—	—	X[k]	—	None	—	—	—	—
Hawaii	—	—	—	—	—	None	—	—	—	—
Idaho	X[l]	—	—	X	18	$10	—	—	—	—
Illinois	X	X	—	X[m]	19	$13	—	—	X[n]	—
Indiana	—	X	—	X[m]	—	$5	X	—	—	—
Iowa	—	—	—	X	18	$15	—	—	X[o]	—

State				Age	Fee				
Kansas	—	—	X	—	$5	—	—	—	—
Kentucky	—	—	X	18	None	—[p]	—	X[q]	—
Louisiana	—	—	X	—	None	—	—	—	—
Maine	X	—	X	17	None	X	X	—	—
Maryland	X	X	X	18	$10[f]	X	X	—	—
Massachusetts	X[s]	—	—	—	None	—	—	—	—
Michigan	X[t]	X	X	18	None	X	—	—	—
Minnesota	—	—	X	—	$5	—	—	—	—
Mississippi	X	—	X	18	None	X	—	—	X
Missouri	—	—	X	—	None	—	—	—	—
Montana	X[u]	—	X	18	$2[v]	X	X[w]	—	—
Nebraska	X[x]	—	X	—	$8[v]	—	—	—	—
Nevada	X[l]	X	X	18	$3	X	X[w]	X[z]	—
New Hampshire	—	X	X	—	$10	—	—	—	—

[a] Other requirements apply to employment but not to certification.
[b] In-state applicants.
[c] Five dollars for in-state applicants.
[d] Arizona and U.S. Constitutions.
[e] Prior oath was declared unconstitutional and a new oath became effective January 5, 1973.
[f] For some credentials.
[g] U.S. history (or acceptable equivalent).
[h] For state employment, not certification.
[i] For out-of-state applicants.
[j] For part-time or other position where certification cannot be obtained and teacher is needed on emergency basis.
[k] For professional certification.
[l] Or declaration of intent.
[m] In-state graduates.
[n] American history and/or government.
[o] American history or American government.
[p] Medical examination required for student teaching and for employment.
[q] American history, biological and physical science; Louisiana history for elementary teachers only.
[r] Applicants not graduated from Maryland approved programs or not previously employed in Maryland.
[s] A noncitizen may obtain a temporary certificate, valid for six years, to teach his native language provided he meets all other certification requirements and presents a certified copy of his declaration of intention to become a citizen and a school committee requests it.
[t] For permanent or continuing certification only.
[u] Provisional certification may be granted to a noncitizen if requested by the employing district.
[v] A registration fee of $2 is charged for initial certification and $2 for each year of validity.
[w] Or Mantoux test.
[x] Provisional certificates may be issued to exchange students or other qualified aliens if there is a demonstrated need for their services.
[y] Two dollars for nonpublic school certification.
[z] Nevada school law and Constitution and U.S. Constitution (by credit or examination).

(continued)

Table 3.6 (cont.)

STATE	U.S. CITIZEN-SHIP	OATH OF ALLE-GIANCE	EVI-DENCE OF EMPLOY-MENT	RECOM-MENDA-TION (COLLEGE OR EM-PLOYER)	MINI-MUM AGE	FEE	GEN-ERAL HEALTH CERT.	CHEST X-RAY	SPE-CIAL COURSE	NATIONAL TEACHER EXAMI-NATIONS
1	2	3	4	5	6	7	8	9	10	11
New Jersey	X	X	—	X	18	$20[aa]	—	—	—	—
New Mexico	—	—	—	X	18	None	X	X	—	—
New York	X[bb]	—	—	—	18	$5	—	—	—	X
North Carolina	—	X	—	X	18	None	—[h]	—	—	X
North Dakota	X.	—	—	X	18	$5	—	—	—	—
Ohio	—	—	—[cc]	X	—	$2	—	—	—	—
Oklahoma	X	—	—	X	—	$1	X	—	X[dd]	—
Oregon	—	X	—	X	18	$15	—	X	—	—
Pennsylvania	X	X	—	X	18	None	X	X	—	—
Rhode Island	X	—	—	X	19	None	X	X[ee]	—	X
South Carolina	X	—	—	X	18	None	X	—	—	—
South Dakota	X	X	—	X	18	$10	—	—	—	—
Tennessee	—	—	—	X	18	$2	—	—	—	—

State										
Texas	X	—	—	X	18	$2–3[ff]	—	X	X[gg]	—
Utah	—	—	—	X	—	$2	—	—	—	—
Vermont	—	X	X	X	19	$3–10[hh]	—	—	—	—
Virginia	X	—	—	X	18	None	—	—	X[ii]	—
Washington	X	—	—	X	18	$1	—	X	—	—
West Virginia	X	—	—	X	18	None	—	—[ee]	X[kk]	—
Wisconsin	—	—	—	X	—	$5	X[jj]	—	X[mm]	—
Wyoming	X[l]	—	—	—	—	$15[ll]	X	—	—	—

[aa] First instructional authorization, $20; each additional instructional authorization, $10; $20 per authorization for administration, supervision, or special service.

[bb] Or declaration of intent; or valid statutory reason why the applicant cannot become a citizen or declare intent.

[cc] For temporary certificate only.

[dd] Six semester hours in American history and government, and credit in Oklahoma history for social studies majors only.

[ee] Or tuberculin test.

[ff] Two dollars for the provisional certificate; $3 for the professional certificate.

[gg] Texas and federal governments; one year to complete (may be satisfied by examination).

[hh] Three dollars for the probationary certificate; $5 for the standard certificate; $10 for the initial certificate.

[ii] Washington State history and government required for elementary and social studies teachers for standard certification (required within six years of initial, provisional certification).

[jj] Health certificate must be filed with the employing board of education, not with the State Department.

[kk] Cooperatives required of teachers of economics, social studies, and agriculture; conservation required of teachers of sicence and social studies.

[ll] Fifteen dollars for the initial certificate, $10 for the first standard certificate.

[mm] Wyoming and U.S. Constitutions.

SOURCE: T. M. Stinnett, *A manual on standards affecting school personnel in the United States.* Washington, D.C.: National Education Association, 1974, p. 48.

created much interest in inservice, but based simply on the inadequacies of preservice training programs, it is impossible to deny the need.

Because of this need for inservice training, it is important to consider the models through which it is delivered and their effectiveness. Typically, information is presented at meetings. These sessions may be adequate to introduce new teachers to the myriad of forms a particular school district requires, but clearly they are inadequate as a means of training teachers to deal with children. According to Siantz and Moore (1978):

One-shot workshops are not sufficient; training must address, over time and in depth, the knowledge and skills needed to teach children with a specific disability in a specific subject area, in terms of: systematic teaching from an individualized educational plan; decisions about assessment procedures, skills, roles, objectives, and materials; effective communication and cooperative planning with others, including professionals, parents, and students. We are also encouraging consortium arrangements among local education agencies, as well as collaboration between these consortia and institutions of higher education. Moreover, inservice support projects will be needed—projects that provide preparation for those who actually train various target audiences. This kind of training may focus, for example, on special education content, successful and operational service delivery systems, or other skill areas needed for the creation of professional development programs. (pp. 27–28)

The task appears formidable in light of the limited training offered in a four-year undergraduate program.

NATURE OF TEACHING

Is teaching an art or a science? Is it an unrecognizable mixture of both? How necessary is it for the adult in the classroom to be highly trained (that is, educated)? What are the characteristics of school children that encourage successful teaching? How is it that teacher-training programs are allowed not to train teachers? The answers to these questions or, at least, a consideration of the state of the art relating to each, may shed some light on the reasons for the state of personnel preparation.

ACCREDITATION OF COLLEGE TRAINING

Education is a state's right, and its control over education, in part, takes the form of accreditation. Lindsey (1961) found that there were no standards for accreditation of teacher-education programs before 1927. Bush and Enemark (1975), who traced the turbulent history of accreditation, stated:

The accrediting of an institutional program of teacher education, a uniquely American phenomenon, can be either compulsory or voluntary. It is usually compulsory at the state level, where an institution must be approved by the state if its graduates are to be eligible to receive certificates to teach. Accreditation at the national level, through the National Council on Accreditation of Teacher Education (NCATE), is voluntary, although there are *compelling pressures* to "volunteer." (pp. 266–267)

In general, arguments have centered on the composition of NCATE visitation teams (that is, the extent of the teachers', professors', and others' participation), rather than on the more substantive issues of the nature of teaching and standards for training teachers. According to Tom (1980):

There can be little dispute, therefore, that NCATE standards are at the heart of the accreditation process. As a result, one would expect to find a set of clear, valid standards upon opening a copy of the recently revised *Standards for Accreditation of Teacher Education*. No expectation could be more wrong. The reader is greeted with a tangled set of ambiguous prescriptions. The standards have a number of serious shortcomings, including the following: The number and the boundaries of the standards are undeterminate, the standards themselves are vaguely written, and they lack operational definitions. (p. 113)

In his extended discussion of these problems, Tom added:

Since operational definitions are missing, judgment of whether a standard is met is determined basically by the extent to which practices within an institution are consistent with the *implicit* operational definitions possessed by visiting team members and council members. (p. 114)

Given this base, one would expect the NCATE decision making to be unreliable. Tom (1980), reporting on data compiled by an NCATE staff study, noted that "the reversal rate for second evaluations of the same accreditation case was 60 percent; i.e., the review of a case by a second evaluation board resulted in a changed accreditation decision six times out of 10" (p. 114).

Tom went on to describe a "bizarre accreditation case that dramatically illustrates the council's problem with reliably applying the standards" (pp. 114–115). We have tried to paraphrase the incident without losing sight of Tom's message: Dr. Tom was a faculty member at a university that jointly offered a master's program with a nearby liberal arts college. When both schools were visited by NCATE evaluation teams, nearly identical folios were presented by the faculty for each program. Although some aspects of the visiting team decisions were similar, the program was accredited at the university but not at the college. Tom and his colleagues were astonished. The response (Gubser, 1980) of the director of NCATE explained how such an outcome could occur (no graduates in some areas of the college programs, specific area deficits at the college), and he went on to note that the rate of denials of accreditation had risen from 10 percent to 31 percent from the early 1960s to the late 1970s. But his reply does not deal with the issues, raised by Tom, of reliability or rate of reversal. Standards for the establishment and function of teacher-training programs are less than adequate, according to the validity and reliability factors considered important in such decision making.

WHAT ARE THE CHILDREN LIKE?

From the earliest attempts at schooling to the present day, one observation has been consistent: Despite the similarities among children, school classrooms are heterogeneous mixtures of humanity, and a teacher is expected to accommodate these individual differences with a diversified school curriculum. Even when a teacher has an ability-grouped instructional arrangement, he or she is faced with many tasks that require simultaneous actions. Sarason, Davidson, and Blatt (1962) put it this way:

[A] typical classroom day involves the teacher in a number of functions and settings other than those directly concerned with teacher. . . . The teacher, while teaching reading to one group of children, is at the same time an observer, supervisor, and disciplinarian of the other groups in the class. We cannot refrain from noting how surprised many people are when they learn that reading and other skills are rarely taught to an entire class but, rather, are handled separately in groups based on achievement level. This simple fact of classroom life immediately forces the teacher to play, simultaneously, at least two roles: teacher with one group and behavior supervisor with the other. (p. 5)

We would argue that the typical classroom day requires the teacher to carry out, simultaneously, several tasks on several levels at all times: teaching is a complex activity that often bears no relation to what we expect. In a study of first-year teachers' responses to questions about teacher preparation, Ryan, Applegate, Flora, Johnston, Lasley, Mager, and Newman (1979) found two common themes: (1) the limits of teacher-training programs and (2) the value of first-hand experiences. We contend that first-hand experiences enable teachers to see what being in a room with 10, 15, 20, or 30 children is really like, and what they learn from these experiences shows them the inadequacies or limitations of their training.

There is also the issue of whether special education teachers must have different competencies to teach students who are labeled differently. Belch (1979) noted:

Beginning in September, 1977, the state of Pennsylvania discontinued awarding single category teaching certificates in special education and began to award a Comprehensive Certificate which licenses recipients to teach in classes for the mentally retarded, brain injured, emotionally disturbed, physically handicapped, and learning disabled. There will no longer be teacher preparation programs that award certificates in specific areas such as mental retardation, emotional disturbance, or physically handicapped since such programs are to be comprehensive and noncategorical in nature. (p. 129)

Regardless of the labels assigned to the children, the programs are to be noncategorical. As Belch indicated, the idea of undifferentiated certification is not new. Earlier, Laycock (1934) advocated the training of teachers as educational diagnosticians, without regard for special categories. Lord (1956) added that assumed differences among children were of limited utility when considering the delivery of special education services. Hallahan and Kauffman (1977) discussed the significance of the noncategorical movement:

The notion of noncategorical special education has become increasingly popular in the last few years. This movement has occurred for at least two reasons. First, the widespread disenchantment with "labeling" has led many professionals to conclude that placing children in categorically labeled classrooms is ipso facto an unacceptable practice. Second, there is no rational basis, in terms of instructional efficacy, for grouping children in accordance with some of the categorical labels now in use. (p. 139)

To examine the extent of the "national trend toward noncategorical teacher certification (and logically, teacher preparation)" (p. 129), Belch (1979) mailed questionnaires to the teacher education and certification directors for all states and Washington, D. C. Two of the questions pertained to this trend: "1. Does your state offer an equivalent to Pennsylvania's Comprehensive Certificate in special education? 2. Does your state expect to develop something like the Comprehensive Certificate in special education?" (p. 130). (Number 2 was answered when a negative response was received for number 1.) The results of the Belch survey are presented in Table 3.7. Most states do not have a "comprehensive certificate," but

Table **3.7**   Results of Questionnaire Regarding Noncategorical Certification

STATE	QUESTIONS 1	2	STATE	QUESTIONS 1	2	STATE	QUESTIONS 1	2
AL	No	No	KY	Yes		ND	No	No
AK	No	Yes	LA	No	Yes	OH	No	No
AZ	No	No	ME	No	Yes	OK	No	No
AR	No	No	MD	No	No	OR	Yes	
CA	No	No	MA	Yes		PA	—	—
CO	No	No	MI	No	No	RI	No	Yes
CT	Yes		MN	No	No	SC	No	Yes
DE	No	No	MS	No	Yes	SD	No	No
DC	Yes[1]		MO	No	Yes	TN	Yes	
FL	No	No	MT	No	No	TX	Yes[3]	
GA	No	No	NE	No[2]	Yes	UT	No	No
HI	No	No	NV	No	No	VT	Yes	
ID	Yes		NH	Yes		VA	No	No
IL	No	No	NJ	No	No	WA	No	Yes
IN	No	No	NM	No	Yes	WV	No	No
IA	No	No	NY	Yes		WI	No	No
KS	No	No	NC	No	Yes	WY	No	Yes

[1] District of Columbia Public Schools reported two certificates—one for categorical and one for noncategorical programs.
[2] Nebraska has a resource teacher endorsement for the mildly handicapped that includes the educable mentally handicapped, learning disabled, and emotionally disturbed.
[3] Texas has a Generic Special Education Certificate on an experimental basis.

SOURCE: From Toward noncategorical teacher certification in special education—myth or reality? by P. J. Belch, *Exceptional Children*, 1979, *46*, 129–131. Copyright 1979 by The Council for Exceptional Children. Reprinted with permission.

almost half "have already adopted a program of noncategorical, comprehensive certification or appear to be considering a change in that direction" (p. 130).

TEACHERS AS PROFESSIONALS

The question of whether teaching is a profession or a semiprofession periodically resurfaces. The importance of the question is in its implications for training and teacher morale. Typically, a profession is characterized by a common body of knowledge, skills, and behaviors that differentiate it from other professions (Reynolds, 1980). Howsam, Corrigan, Denemark, and Nash (1976) termed this common body a professional culture and lamented its absence among teachers:

The teaching profession is characterized by lack of a common body of knowledge and repertoire of behaviors and skills needed in the practice of the profession. . . . teachers do not possess a common body of professionally validated knowledge and skills which is transmitted in the processes of professional socialization, held in common with other teachers thereafter, and constantly increased through the career span of the teacher. (pp. 10–11)

Attempts to "professionalize" teachers and their training are very competency oriented, and often include statements of what a teacher must do to be competent. For example, in *A Common Body of Practice for Teachers: The Challenge of Public Law 94–142 to Teacher Education* (Reynolds, 1980), 10 "clusters of capabilities" are proposed. The clusters are not offered as competency statements but "simply provide a convenient map of the domains of professional competence that appear to be important to every teacher who participates in the design and implementation of individualized instruction" (p. 8). The 10 capabilities are as follows:

1. Curriculum
2. Teaching basic skills
3. Class management
4. Professional consultation and communication
5. Teacher-parent-student relationship
6. Student-student relationship
7. Exceptional conditions
8. Referral
9. Individualized teaching
10. Professional values

Each capability is presented with a discussion establishing its logic and importance (for example, "It is clear that the presence of exceptional youngsters in regular classes increases the breadth and variety of students' learning needs and skills"; "All teachers should have a general knowledge of the school curriculum that is offered from kindergarten through high school" [pp. 8–9]), a curriculum capability, and a recommendation (see Table 3.8). Similar lists of general teacher competencies can be found in Denmark and Nutter (1980) and in Lindsey (1978).

We would not argue with these capabilities. Our concern is more with the vehicle or training strategies through which teachers are made capable in the proposed areas. For example, to ensure that the "preparation of all teachers. . . include the study of and firsthand experience with preschool through secondary levels," we envision a few curriculum courses being

Table **3.8**   Sample Recommendations for Capabilities in Common Body of Practice for Teachers

CAPABILITY AREA	RECOMMENDATION
Curriculum	The preparation of all teachers should include the study of and firsthand experience with curricular principles, guides, and structures from preschool through secondary school levels. All major subjects that are systematically taught in schools by professionals should be included. The means and procedures by which curriculum is developed, adopted, and changed should be understood and there should be practice in designing and modifying curriculum and materials, especially to suit the individual needs of students.
Teaching basic skills	The preparation of all teachers should include necessary elements to assure competency in teaching the basic skills (defined to include literacy, life maintenance, and personal development skills) and in collaborative practice with specialists in basic skills instruction. Instruction should be provided in teaching the skill areas as such. In addition, supervised practical experience should be provided in teaching of literacy, life maintenance, and personal development skills.
Class management	All teachers should be proficient in class management procedures, including applied behavioral analysis, group alerting, guiding transitions, materials arrangement, crisis intervention techniques, and group approaches to creating a positive affective climate.
Professional consultation and communications	It is essential now that all teachers have opportunities to master the knowledge and practices involved in effective consultation and other forms of professional communication. As part of preservice preparation, every teacher should have instruction and practicum experience leading to assured capability in these areas.
Teacher-parent-student relationships	All teachers should have skills and sensitivity for dealing with parents and siblings of handicapped students; they should have had opportunities to practice skills in this area as part of their practicums in teacher preparation.

SOURCE: M. C. Reynolds, *A common body of practice for teachers: The challenge of Public Law 94–142 to teacher education.* Washington, D.C.: American Association of Colleges of Teacher Education, 1980, pp. 9–13.

added to the already largely irrelevant content of a teacher-training program to guarantee meeting the competencies but actually to do no more than should any other course in improving the quality of the teachers-to-be.

In fact, most of the progress and changes that have occurred in teacher education in the last 50 years have relied largely on reorganizing courses, restructuring programs, and/or redesigning the educational wheel invented by our ancestors. "The adage that 'the more things change, the more they stay the same' can be applied to the pattern and content of pre-service teacher education programs during the past 50 years" (Drummond & Andrews, 1980). To change the nature of teacher preparation, the profession must address questions pertaining to the teaching act. It seems inappropriate to identify the content of courses in teacher training without knowing what teachers do. Similarly, without substantial information about the ways teachers spend their time, it seems useless to address the notion of their competence.

Chapter 4

Issues in Identification

Special and remedial education evolved and exist to serve individuals in need. Such education, however, is virtually worthless if the needy individuals are not identified. Toward this end, a procedure similar to that in medicine has emerged; that is, catalogues of symptoms of various special and remedial conditions are prepared, and diagnostic practices are employed to determine the extent to which an individual has characteristics similar to those of known conditions. The picture of the individual developed from the data collected during a diagnostic evaluation determines that person's classification and, consequently, his or her treatment. In considering this identification process, we must recognize the important issues pertaining to the nature of the classification systems and the effects of the process.

HISTORICAL PERSPECTIVE

We know from anthropology that deviates are found in every society, and that the extent to which the differences they demonstrate violate the dominant social form is the extent to which they are a source for social intervention. For example, around the turn of the century, immigrant children represented about 70 percent of the enrollment in the New York City public schools (Cremin, 1961). The immigrants became a problem because their language interfered with their successful assimilation into contemporary American society. In discussing this problem as it applied to the Cleveland public schools, Miller (1916) noted that "the non-English speaking child cannot keep up with his companions in the regular grades. For this reason he is sent to a special class" (p. 74). For a discussion of the overrepresentation of minority children in special classes during the early 1900s, see Sarason and Doris (1979); and for discussions of the same problem in today's schools, see Dunn (1968); Mercer (1970, 1973); Sarason and Doris (1979); and Tucker (1980). Because the observable difference (that is, language) violated the dominant social form, social intervention (that is, special class placement) was considered appropriate.

Rhodes and Sagor (1976) pointed out that as a consequence of compulsory education laws, more general behavioral differences also became a source of social concern:

Our current national classification systems for children emerged from a nation subjected to constant floods of change: heavy influxes of alien groups; major social philosophies which dominated public thinking in different periods; and strong, charismatic leaders who became spokesmen for such philosophies. (pp. 103–104)

They noted the alarm sounded by Goddard (1921):

There are two million people in the United States who, because of their weak minds or their diseased minds, are making our country a dangerous place to live in. The two million is increasing both by heredity and by training. We are breeding defectives. We are making criminals. (p. iv)

The basis for society's concern about its less fortunate members is the observation that the behavior of a particular individual is different. Vonnegut (1973) pointed out that "bad chemicals" are an insufficient basis for madness; all novice "lunatics" need "some bad ideas, too, so that . . . craziness could have shape and direction" (p. 14). The judgment of when ideas are bad, of course, comes from socially sanctioned decision makers who decide when differences are important.

To deal effectively with the various differences among individuals, society has created a simple system for identifying an individual's problem on the basis of the symptoms the individual manifests. The diagnostic paradigm is essentially straightforward: an observation is made of those characteristics thought to distinguish the afflicted individual, and those data are compared to criteria for known conditions. Data are collected from a number of sources and are used as a basis for decision making. The logic of the process follows this paradigm:

Certain behaviors (B) are characteristic of specific disorders (A).

Certain behaviors (B) are characteristic of certain individuals (C).

Therefore, the disorders (A) are characteristic of the individuals (C).

The individuals (C) have the disorders (A).

Readers who remember elementary logic will recognize that for this form of reasoning to be correct, the characteristic behaviors (B) must be both universal and specific. That is, they must be present in all individuals with the specific disorders (A), and they must occur relatively infrequently in individuals who do not have the disorder.

The extent to which universal and specific characteristics exist among children who fail in school and/or who need special and remedial education, or both, is marginal at best. Werry and Quay (1971) found that the number rather than the kind of behavior symptoms were useful in differentiating psychopathology and that "behavior symptoms are very common in all children" (p. 137). In their study of over 1,700 elementary school children, they found the prevalence of certain symptoms to be very high; for example, 39 percent of the children were restless or self-conscious and easily embarrassed, and 46 percent of the boys were disruptive and tended to annoy others. Phillips, Draguns, and Bartlett (1976) noted that "individuals identically diagnosed in different countries, subcultures, or times have been found to differ perceptibly, and sometimes markedly, in their observable symptomatology" (p. 30); and researchers at the University of Minnesota Institute for Research on Learning Disabilities found that individuals diagnosed differently displayed remarkably similar psychoeducational profiles (Ysseldyke et al., in press). To say that there is overlap among the characteristics of similar children seems to state the obvious. But it is important that those characteristics that are not universal and specific (that is, that overlap) are used to differentiate within and among individuals classified in special and remedial education. As Phillips, Draguns, and Bartlett (1976) indicated, "Many individuals fail to manifest a substantial proportion of the behavioral characteristics that define the category in which they are placed and, in addition, often demonstrate deviant behaviors that help to define other diagnostic headings" (p. 30). We would add that these same individuals also demonstrate many behaviors that do not define any diagnostic headings.

We are not suggesting either that differences among individuals do not exist or that they are not important. We agree with Rhodes's and Sagor's (1976) statement that "it is not argued that differences are not real but that their collective interpretation creates the negative or positive impact of such differences upon the community psyche" (p. 121). Mercer (1976) added, "Because psychologists, educators, and clinicians have neither examined the assumptions underlying traditional practices nor adequately monitored the social implications of institutionalizing procedures based on these assumptions, the standardized testing movement is now being challenged" (p. 131). The so-called scientific process through which the collective interpretation has been formalized is classification. The assumptions that permeate its practice and the social (as well as other) implications of its impact are addressed in the remainder of this chapter.

CLASSIFICATION

Complex systems for classifying differences that society views as critical have evolved over the past century. According to Grossman (1973):

[A] classification system is designed primarily to furnish statistical data about groups of cases. One principal use of such a system will be to furnish classificatory data on incidence, prevalence, characteristics, and concomitant information. Providing a classification system makes possible increased precision in communication, in research work, and in administrative and program planning. The use of a medical classification system which offers descriptive symptoms of clinical conditions is of diagnostic value to physicians and adds new dimensions not found in other classification systems of diseases. (pp. 6–7)

Phillips, Draguns, and Bartlett (1976) also see diagnostic systems "as a basis for compiling census information and statistical data, which, in turn, are utilized in many different kinds of social planning" (p. 31). Clearly, diagnostic classification systems, if not created solely for administrative reasons, largely serve administrative functions (for example, allocation of funds, head counts, program placement decision making). Reynolds (1975b) found that some aspects of the current decision-making paradigm in education "enhance institutional payoff but are incompatible with the enhancement of individual development and welfare" (p. 23).

We contend that classification (as a practice or a system) cannot be evaluated solely on a scientific, technical basis; that is, the extent to which we are classifying sufficient numbers of, or the right, children is an inadequate criterion. We believe that the overall effect of classification also must be evaluated according to the payoff for the individual who is classified. At issue is the fact that the classification systems we have created, although they are largely arbitrary in nature, may have profound effects on our lives. To realize the full impact of our concern, we must analyze classification systems, the importance of measurement precision, and the effects of labeling on the clients of special and remedial education.

MENTAL DISORDERS

One of the earliest known classification systems for mental disorders was made by Hippocrates (460–377 B.C.), who named three syndromes—*mania, melancholia,* and *phrenitis*—to differentiate the clusters of symptoms he observed in different members of Greek society. In 1952, the first volume of the *Diagnostic and Statistical Manual of Mental Disorders* (DSM-I) of the American Psychiatric Association (APA, 1952) listed 8 major categories of "disorders" or "deficiencies," whereas the revised publication (DSM-II; APA, 1968) contained 10 major categories, including one entitled Behavior Disorders of Childhood and Adolescence. The latest version (DSM-III; APA, 1980) contains 17 categories of disorders. The descriptive titles of the disorders classified by the American Psychiatric Association in the DSM series are presented in Table 4.1.

The intent of DSM-III is to provide operational criteria to justify diagnoses. Catalogues such as the *Diagnostic and Statistical Manuals of Mental Disorders* fit nicely into the identification practices followed by psychologists as well as by special and remedial educators; that is, they provide listings of characteristics (B) on which the individual under consideration (C) can be judged. Typically, narrative descriptions accompany the listings of general or specific disorders. For example, in DSM-I, under the general heading "Psychotic Disorders," the following types of disorders are listed:

a. Involutional Psychotic Reaction
b. Affective Reactions
c. Schizophrenic Reactions
d. Paranoid Reactions
e. Psychotic Reactions Without Clearly Defined Structural Change Other Than Above

These "disorders are characterized by a varying degree of personality disintegration and failure to test and evaluate correctly external reality in various spheres. In addition, individuals with such disorders fail in their ability to relate themselves effectively to other people or to their own work" (APA, 1952, p. 24). More specifically, *paranoia* (one of two listed Paranoid Reactions) is described as an "extremely rare" psychotic disorder, characterized by an

intricate, complex, and slowly developing paranoid system, often logically elaborated after a false interpretation of an actual occurrence. Frequently,

Table **4.1** Categories of Psychiatric Disorders by APA Classifications, 1952–1980

DSM–I (1952)

A. Acute Brain Disorders
B. Chronic Brain Disorders
C. Psychotic Disorders
D. Psychophysiologic Autonomic and Visceral Disorders
E. Psychoneurotic Disorders
F. Personality Disorders
G. Transient Situational Personality Disorders
H. Mental Deficiencies

DSM–II (1968)

A. Mental Retardation
B. Organic Brain Syndromes
C. Psychoses Not Attributed to Physical Conditions Listed Previously
D. Neuroses
E. Personality Disorders
F. Psychophysiologic Disorders
G. Special Symptoms
H. Transient Situational Disturbances
I. Behavior Disorders of Childhood and Adolescence
J. Conditions Without Manifest Psychiatric Disorder and Nonspecific Conditions

DSM–III (1980)

A. Disorders Usually First Evident in Infancy, Childhood, or Adolescence
B. Organic Mental Disorders
C. Substance Use Disorders
D. Schizophrenic Disorders
E. Paranoid Disorders
F. Psychotic Disorders Not Elsewhere Classified
G. Affective Disorders
H. Anxiety Disorders
I. Somatoform Disorders
J. Dissociative Disorders
K. Psychosexual Disorders
L. Factitious Disorders
M. Disorders of Impulse Control Not Elsewhere Classified
N. Adjustment Disorders
O. Psychological Factors Affecting Physical Condition
P. Personality Disorders
Q. V Codes for Conditions Not Attributable to a Mental Disorder That Are a Focus of Attention or Treatment

SOURCE: Compiled from the tables of contents of the *Diagnostic and statistical manuals of mental disorders* (DSM-I, 1952; DSM-II, 1968, and DSM-III, 1980) published by the American Psychiatric Association.

the patient considers himself endowed with superior or unique ability. The paranoid system is particularly isolated from much of the normal stream of consciousness, without hallucinations and with relative intactness and perseveration of the remainder of the personality, in spite of a chronic and prolonged course. (APA, 1952, p. 28)

DSM-I is very general and inclusive. The material in DSM-III is similar to that in DSM-I, but the lists of disorders are more specific. For example, in DSM-III the term *psychotic* is not a basis for classification, "in order to avoid classifying the Major Affective Disorders as psychotic, since such disorders usually do not have psychotic features" (APA, 1980, p. 323). Instead, more restrictive terms are used for the major diagnostic categories (for example, Schizophrenic Disorders and Paranoid Disorders). The following diagnostic criteria appear for Paranoid Disorder:

a. persistent persecutory delusions or delusional jealousy.
b. emotion or behavior appropriate to the content of the delusional system.
c. duration of illness of at least one week.
d. none of the symptoms of criterion A of Schizophrenia (p. 188) such as bizarre delusions, incoherence, or marked loosening of associations.
e. no prominent hallucinations.
f. the full depressive or manic syndrome (criteria A and B of major depressive or manic episode, p. 213, p. 208) is either not present, developed after any psychotic symptoms, or was brief in duration relative to the duration of the psychotic symptoms.
g. not due to an Organic Mental Disorder. (APA, 1980, p. 196)

The criteria for Paranoia, a more specific condition, are as follows:

a. meets the criteria for Paranoid Disorder.
b. a chronic and stable persecutory delusional system of at least six months' duration.
c. does not meet the criteria for Shared Paranoid Disorder. (APA, 1980, pp. 196–197)

As diagnostic criteria, these characteristics are presented in DSM-III with more specific description than those presented in other catalogues (see the rest of this subsection). DSM-III provides these listings as "guides for making each diagnosis since such criteria enhance interjudge diagnostic reliability" (APA, 1980, p. 8). The greater specificity of DSM-III, as well as its intended comprehensiveness, makes the publication quite large. In the introduction to DSM-III (APA, 1980), it is said that in

making a DSM-III diagnosis the clinician may find it more convenient to consult the *Quick Reference to the Diagnostic Criteria from DSM-III,* (Mini-D), a pocket-sized booklet sold separately, that contains only the classification, the diagnostic criteria, a listing of the most important conditions to be considered in differential diagnosis of each category, and an index. (p. 11)

With resources such as these, one wonders how soon reference guides and/or computers will make "do-it-yourself" diagnosticians of all of us.

Another classification scheme for mental disorders was developed in 1966 by the Committee on Child Psychiatry of the Group for the Advancement of Psychiatry (GAP). It is a 10-category system intended to rank disorders ranging from less severe to more severe conditions. The diagnostic categories in the GAP classification system are as follows:

 1. Healthy Responses
 2. Reactive Disorders
 3. Developmental Deviations
 4. Psychoneurotic Disorders
 5. Personality Disorders
 6. Psychotic Disorders
 7. Psychophysiologic Disorders
 8. Brain Syndromes
 9. Mental Retardation
10. Other Disorders

The characteristics included in the textual description for Early Infantile Autism, which falls under Psychotic Disorders as one of the Psychoses of Infancy and Early Childhood, illustrates the type of information found in the catalogues:

onset, during the first year of life, failure of infant to develop attachment to mother figure, aloofness, little awareness of human contact, preoccupation with inanimate objects, absent or delayed, non-functional speech, need for maintenance of sameness, resistance to change, sleeping or feeding problems, stereotyped motor patterns, and varied intellectual functioning. (p. 107)

It is interesting to note that the compilers of GAP (1966) discussed the novelty of using Healthy Responses as a category, and they included a qualification stating that "only the passage of time and careful follow-up studies can support the accuracy of this diagnosis when it is made" (GAP, 1966, p. 38). Subsequently, the general nature of Developmental Deviations is qualified by indicating that changes of the "working diagnosis based on follow-up data may be necessary for this, as for any other category, in order to subserve initial classification and more systematic data collection which can further the understanding of the natural history of particular syndromes" (pp. 38–39). There seems to be some confusion regarding the follow-up data: they are necessary to justify healthy responses but serve only to clarify deviations and disorders. Pathology is assumed by classification systems such as these, though diagnostic decisions are often made using the systems as criteria for judgments.

MENTAL RETARDATION

Blanton (1976) noted that the first clear definition of mental retardation was given by J. E. D. Esquirol who stated:

Idiocy is not a disease, but a condition in which the intellectual faculties are never manifested, or have never been developed sufficiently to enable the idiot to acquire such amount of knowledge as persons of his own age and placed in similar circumstances with himself are capable of receiving. (Esquirol, 1845, p. 445)

Based on this definition, identification and classification practices would require information about the relative amount of knowledge the suspected idiot had acquired before a judgment could be made.

In Chapter 2 we presented Seguin's and Howe's descriptions of idiots, simpletons, and fools, and we think they are worth repeating here: To Seguin, an idiot is an individual who *"knows nothing, can do nothing, cannot even desire to do anything"* (Howe, 1848, p. 6). To Howe,

Idiots of the lowest class are mere organisms, masses of flesh and bone in human shape, in which the brain and nervous system have no command over the system of voluntary muscles; and which consequently are without power of locomotion, without speech, without any manifestation of intellectual or affective faculties.

Fools are a higher class of idiots, in whom the brain and nervous system are so far developed as to give partial command of the voluntary muscles; who have consequently considerable power of locomotion and animal action; partial development of the affective and intellectual faculties, but only the faintest glimmer of reason, and very imperfect speech.

Simpletons are the highest class of idiots, in whom the harmony between the nervous and muscular system is nearly perfect; who consequently have normal powers of locomotion and animal action; considerable activity of the perceptive and affective faculties; and reason enough for their simple individual guidance, but not enough for their social relations. (Howe, 1848, pp. 6–7)

Following Seguin, to make a diagnosis, we simply find someone who knows nothing, can do nothing, and so on, and we have found an idiot; according to Howe's more detailed sets of criteria, a diagnosis is not so easy. In fact, Howe indicated that it was difficult to estimate the number

Table **4.2**   Classifications of Retardation Established by American
Association on Mental Deficiency

LEVEL OF RETARDATION	STANDARD DEVIATION RANGE	IQ RANGE BY TEST	
		Binet	Wechsler
Mild	−2.01−−3.00	68–52	69–55
Moderate	−3.01−−4.00	51–36	54–40
Severe	−4.01−−5.00	35–20	39–25
Profound	below −5.01	19 and below	24 and below

SOURCE: J. W. Filler, Jr., C. C. Robinson, R. A. Smith, L. J. Vincent-Smith, D. D.
Bricker, & W. A. Bricker, Mental retardation. In N. Hobbs (Ed.), *Issues in the classification
of children.* San Francisco: Jossey-Bass, 1976, p. 196.

of simpletons using the characteristics he posited, and he pointed out the
arbitrary, nonspecific nature of the simpleton category:

A Russian serf, a Bavarian boor, might enjoy his sinecure office of citizen,
and fill his narrow social circle, with a paucity of intellect such as would inca-
pacitate a man for political rights or social relations in Massachusetts. So,
among the inhabitants of the *least* intelligent and active village population of
Massachusetts, a youth might be thought to be of tolerable capacity, be permitted to go to the polls, and even into society, who would be rated as a simpleton, and treated as such, in the active and hustling crowd of one of our
thriving marts, where the weak sink down and disappear, and the strong
alone live and thrive. And so it may be with regard to time, a century hence,
the standard of intellect and of knowledge may be raised so high as to
exclude from the polls, as simpletons, men equal to some of our generation
who consider themselves qualified, not only to be citizens, but to hold
offices. Who would arrest such progress, provided no qualification but that
of knowledge and virtue could ever be required! (p. 13)

   The current classification system (Grossman, 1973) for mental retardation is based on degrees of intelligence (IQ), as measured by performance
on a standardized test. At first, a diagnosis of mental retardation was
made if a person's IQ score was greater than two standard deviation units
below the mean for the test used (Filler et al., 1976). From this the levels
of retardation can be classified. The current version of the American
Association of Mental Deficiency's *Manual on Terminology and Classification
in Mental Retardation* (Grossman, 1973) lists four levels of retardation based
on IQ scores, which are presented in Table 4.2.

Our presentation of historical and current classification schemes for two mental problems is intended to illustrate the importance of measurement in identification practices. As a professional, the diagnostician always has been concerned with improving the precision of measurement—for the benefit of the client, one hopes. According to Binet and Simon (1916):

To be a member of a special class can never be a mark of distinction, and such as do not merit it, must be spared the record. Some errors are excusable in the beginning, but if they become too frequent, they may ruin the reputation of these new institutions. Furthermore, in principle, we are convinced, and we shall not cease to repeat, that the precision and exactness of science should be introduced into our practice whenever possible, and in the great majority of cases it is possible. (p. 9)

MEASUREMENT PRECISION

The basis for providing services in special and remedial education is categorical identification. The diagnostic decisions are made on the basis of interviews, behavioral information, and standardized tests; and the level of precision for each technique varies considerably.

Interviews

An interview is either a structured or unstructured form of data collection. Structured sessions require the use of a specified series of questions to elicit information on selected topics, for example, the developmental history of an individual or the nature and duration of prevailing symptoms. Similarly, important data may be collected by evaluating qualitative aspects of a client's responses (for example, appearance, attire, eye contact, tone of voice). The characteristics identified during the interview form the basis for diagnostic decisions.

Behavioral Information

Information on behavior is collected in one of two forms: A rating of the extent to which specific symptoms, characteristics, or behaviors are exhibited by a particular individual is made by the individual herself or himself or by someone familiar with the individual; or *direct observation,* is conducted of the extent to which the operationally defined version of the behaviors occurs. There are numerous behavior check lists and rating scales. We shall not discuss them here, but Cone and Hawkins (1977) have reviewed over 150 such devices.

Standardized Tests

All tests are samples of behavior. To facilitate comparisons among the individuals who take the tests, the tests must be administered, scored, and interpreted in a standard way. This practice of standardizing tests has its roots in Binet's early attempts to determine which children were likely to profit from instruction and which were not. Binet and Simon (1916) pointed out that the method for a scientific diagnosis consisted of standardized administration of identical stimuli. The American Psychological Association (1974) published recommended standards for the development and use of standardized tests, and test developers have manuals to accompany their devices to enable standardized administration and scoring. A standardized test without norms for subject comparisons and technical data regarding psychometric characteristics is considered substandard for practice (Salvia & Ysseldyke, 1981). But regardless of the standards we try to impose, there still will be problems at all levels of use of standardized tests (cf. Ysseldyke, 1978).

PSYCHOEDUCATIONAL DECEPTION

Those who assess students simply observe behaviors. On the basis of the behaviors they observe, they may make certain inferences. In fact, most tests, though measures of observed behavior, are designed to help assessors make inferences about global constructs. Tests are called measures of "intelligence," measures of "perception," and measures of "anxiety." Those who assess students observe behaviors and infer the extent to which specific constructs are evidenced. According to the relative presence or absence of the inferred construct, assessors assign diagnostic (categorical) labels to describe students. For example, students may be said to be mentally retarded because they display relatively little of the inferred construct intelligence. For the most part, the titles assigned to tests tell us very little about the specific behaviors sampled by those tests.

The name Illinois Test of Psycholinguistic Abilities (ITPA) suggests a device to measure psycholinguistic abilities, but a clear definition of those skills is not readily available in the test manual or professional literature and must be inferred from the test content. The ITPA comprises 12 subtests, each with a different name. One is called Auditory Reception. It seems that an important psycholinguistic ability should be auditory reception or the ability to comprehend the spoken word. Who would argue with the importance of knowing whether an individual possesses it? One would expect, then, that the Auditory Reception subtest of the ITPA measures the ability to comprehend the spoken word. As a test, it must sample behavior: to identify the behavior by one definition and description, but to measure it by another criterion would be deceptive.

In fact, the ITPA Auditory Reception subtest requires a child to answer a series of general information questions with "yes" or "no"; the ability to comprehend the spoken word may be measured by it. For example, if a child answers all the questions, or answers none of them, this ability (or the lack of it) should be obvious. What if, as is more likely the case, a child answers some questions but not others? Has he or she demonstrated the ability to comprehend the spoken word? The test developers (and most devout users) base their decisions about the youngster on the number of items he or she answers correctly. That score is evaluated and serves as a critical indicator of the ability or dysfunction. For example, a significantly different, low score in auditory reception reflects a critical or significant problem in auditory reception for the participant taking the test (Bush & Waugh, 1976). The fact that the participant has performed the behavior (that is, has given a "yes" or "no" answer to a general information question) on specific items is ignored. The fact that low performance may be due to item content is ignored. But the deception that the child has an auditory reception dysfunction is exercised. An analysis of all the ITPA subtests and those of most other psychoeducational devices reveals a similar possibility for deception. It is the content of the items that is the basis for the raw score, not the presumed ability or actual behavior sampled.

Many tactics have evolved that make test-naming deceptions less obvious. A set of pseudostandards has become the hallmark of "good" tests, and educational psychologists, statisticians, and other professionals have led the test-consuming, or test-requiring, public to believe that necessary and sufficient conditions can be met in developing a good test. They have ignored the underlying assumption that what is being tested must be somehow observable, and they have dismissed the accepted practice of testing constructs which are named to the advantage of the test developer.

A test's validity is considered an important measurement of its adequacy. Content validity is relatively easy to establish; a test should contain items indicating the content being measured. A mathematics test should contain mathematical items. But what should an intelligence test contain? A psycholinguistic test? A perceptual test?

There are more difficulties with construct validity or predictive validity, especially since most of our tests purport to measure nonobservable behaviors (for example, intelligence, auditory reception). The common practice is to correlate a test of unknown validity with one of accepted validity. If the correlations are high, then the second test is said to be credible, even though there may be major construct validity problems with the first measure. Multiple tests that measure the same unknown to the same level serve no purpose. When the validity of tests is in question, to strive for or to achieve reliability is absurd. Just as a research project not worth doing is not worth doing well, a test that does not measure what it is supposed to measure is not improved by measuring it well (that is, consistently).

In fact, the most important information on a child's test performance can be found by analyzing the right and wrong responses to items. The deception that occurs when these raw scores are transformed to other forms is perhaps the most sophisticated and dangerous one. For example, people often misinterpret age or grade equivalents to mean that a child performed as a child of the obtained age or grade would. This is not true. The scores simply mean the child got the same number of items correct that an average child of that age or grade did. Since it is possible to obtain any different combinations of right and wrong items, the important information (what was right and wrong) is lost when the score becomes "3.2" or "8–10." Because the raw score alone tells very little, test developers transform it to something that is seemingly more meaningful (yet has less utility), rather than analyzing it as it is and saying what it really means. The score is thus transformed, disguised, and stripped of any chance for constructive analysis. Similar unnecessary sophistication is apparent in the derivation of cluster scores and/or scores based on groups of subtests. If the original subtest loses its value when the raw score is transformed, it seems obvious that the scores consisting of groups of already limited scores are valueless.

Identification (that is, testing and classifying children) will likely continue in American education: in fact, in 1979, more than 250 million standardized tests were administered to America's 44 million school children. Obviously, the practice is considered important by many people. Of interest from our perspective is how the effects of the process are determined as positive or negative for the individuals tested.

LABELING

Classifying and labeling youngsters is an ubiquitous activity. Szasz (1970) argued that "today, particularly in the affluent West, all of the difficulties and problems of living are considered psychiatric diseases, and everyone (but the diagnosticians) is considered mentally ill" (p. 4). The labeling issue in special and remedial education is straightforward: the extent to which the negative effects outweigh the positive effects of being classified (that is, labeled). Algozzine and Mercer (1980) indicate that these effects may be studied from two perspectives: "1. the impact of the label on the perceptions and behavior of the child himself, and 2. the impact of the

Figure **4.1**   Critical Aspects of the Labeling Issue

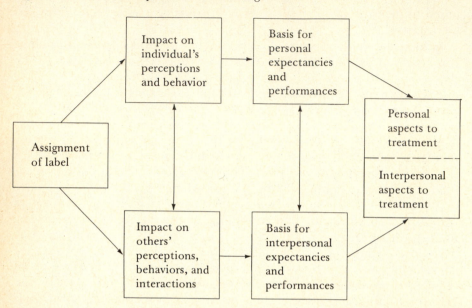

label on the perceptions and behavior of others who interact with the child'' (p. 288). The important aspects of the labeling issue are summarized in Figure 4.1, and the advantages and disadvantages of labeling are discussed in the following subsections.

PRESUMED ADVANTAGES

The major advantage of a label is the admission to some form of special service. According to a group of parents, Gorham, Des Jardins, Page, Pettis, and Scherber (1976), ''Practically speaking, 'good' labels are those that a parent can use to open doors for his child and maximize chances of marshalling resources on his behalf'' (p. 155). Labels that serve as ''passports'' to improve educational services are the ideal. Gallagher (1976) pointed out that labels serve other purposes as well; in his discussion, he suggested describing the ''sacred'' uses of labeling as follows:

1. A means for beginning a classification, diagnosis, and treatment sequence peculiarly designed to counteract certain identifiable negative conditions.
2. The basis for further research which will give more insight into etiology, prevention, and possible treatment applications of such conditions in the future.

3. A means for calling attention to a specific problem in order to obtain additional resources through special legislation and funding (p. 3).

Algozzine and Mercer (1980) also found advantages in labeling:

The primary objective that ultimately permeates the rationale for labeling exceptional children is that the label will directly or indirectly facilitate treatment. Labeling and consequent treatment are more conspicuous in some instances than in others. For example, the label "hearing impaired" more often implies specific treatments than the label "learning disabled." The use of labeling to improve communications among researchers, establish prevalence estimates, determine etiologies, design prevention programs, place in special education, and obtain funds are examples of indirect and direct uses of labeling to provide or improve treatment efforts. (p. 289)

PRESUMED DISADVANTAGES

The difficulties associated with labeling elicited the following observation from Algozzine and Mercer (1980):

The problems of labeling may be viewed along two major fronts. First, to the extent that a label fails directly or indirectly to lead to differentiated treatment for an individual child, it fails to serve a useful function. Second, labeling may actually be harmful to the child. When a child's perceptions and behaviors, as well as those of others, are altered by labeling in a manner which results in restricting the social, emotional and/or academic growth of the child, labels are harmful. (p. 289)

Hallahan and Kauffman (1977) noted widespread disenchantment with labeling and the fact that "there is no rational basis, in terms of instructional efficacy, for grouping children in accordance with some of the categorical labels now in use" (p. 139). This disenchantment is the basis for a move toward noncategorical special education. There is little evidence that individual programming decisions based on categorical labels or diagnostic classifications are different from those based on a child's behavioral needs, regardless of the diagnostic label. Labels seem, at best, to serve as passports which in no way guarantee differential treatment.

There is evidence that labeling may be harmful. According to Gorham, Des Jardins, Page, Pettis, and Scherber (1976):

Labels have damaged many children, particularly minority-group children whose cultures and lifestyles differ sufficiently from the "norm" to make any measurement of their abilities and aptitudes by norm-biased scales a certain disaster for them. Placing minority children in classes for the retarded on the basis of IQ tests has been one of the more flagrant abuses of the labeling process. (p. 155)

Gallagher (1976) listed the "profane" use of labeling as follows:

1. A means for tranquilizing professionals by applying labels (i.e., autism or minimal brain dysfunction) to children without following with subsequent differentiated programs of treatment, merely filling a need for closure on a difficult diagnostic issue.
2. As a means to preserve a social hierarchy by using labels to keep minority group children from opportunities and to force them to remain at the bottom of the social ladder.
3. To delay needed social reform by focusing the problem on the individual, rather than on complex social and ecological conditions needing specific change and repair. (p. 3)

The data on the effects of labeling are probably not complete. To analyze those data that are available, it is necessary to develop a sense of how the system works or how the effects of labeling occur.

THE PROCESS

In his book *The Slaying of the Dragons Within,* Joel Macht (1980) described a child (David) whose handwriting was different from that of two peers. This difference set in motion the process we call identification which resulted in the opinion that David had a processing or perceptual problem. Macht questioned the value of the search for an underlying cause, even though it is often justified by professionals as a necessary step to effective treatment. He added that the pressures of treatment can greatly alter the child's life circumstances:

It was suggested that David receive some treatment for his supposed processing problem. His parents, however, questioned the existence of the organic difficulty. Instead, they helped the child learn how to hold a pencil, learn how to keep a piece of paper from slipping off a desk, and learn how to write. That was the parents' choice. Another parent, however, whose child was also having difficulty producing his name to the satisfaction of an authority, might have believed the assertion of a processing problem and might have accepted the suggestion that special help was needed—not to solve the handwriting difficulty, but to resolve the organic dysfunction. The parents might have accepted the assertion that if something wasn't done immediately, the child would suffer further serious learning problems.

Under that pressure the parents might start searching out other *differences* manifested by the child. The parent might change the way he or she normally responds to the child for fear of doing more harm. Sensing the change, the child might begin to pick up on his apparent differences as well as the differences now being manifested by his parent. Fairly soon, both parent and child might begin to believe that something, indeed, is wrong. (Macht, 1980, p. 70)

It is difficult to argue that the labeling process does not cause changes in the relationships between labeled and nonlabeled individuals. The manner in which this process affects individuals has been discussed by many professionals (cf. Algozzine & Mercer, 1980; Berger et al., 1966; Brophy & Good, 1974; Cooper, 1979; Entwistle & Webster, 1972; Finn, 1972; Foster, 1976; Jones, 1977; McGuire, 1966; Schain, 1972; Sutherland, 1976). In general, explanatory models suggest that labels must be attended to, understood, and retained by an individual who responds to their effects. A model demonstrating labeling effects is presented in Figure 4.2. Within this context, labels may be thought of as cues that help to organize people's knowledge, personal perceptions, and behavior. They serve as distinguishing features to which individuals assign various other characteristics, qualities, and/or behavioral attributes in the attempt to establish, alter, or verify a personal belief system.

When labels are presented to target individuals who may react to them, the proposed model is set into operation. If teachers, parents, and/or other caretakers have attended to, comprehended, and retained the label, it may help to establish, alter, or verify a belief or preconceived bias they hold. This first level of transmission is clearly essential for any additional effects to be observed.

After the initial phase, the next possible level is transmission to the subject on whom the now-existent bias will have its effect. Of course, this child or subject must attend to, comprehend, and retain the transmitted bias for it to establish, alter, or verify any differential performances. It must be stressed that the effects at this level are dependent on the establishments, alterations, and verifications at previous levels. To observe only outcomes (that is, effects) may lead to spurious conclusions unless each previous stage of the model has been shown to be operational with regard to the stimuli being investigated.

THE EFFECTS OF LABELING

Jones (1977) presented a perspective from which the effects of the labeling process can be evaluated. He stated that there are two key points in labeling deviance:

1. The idea that particular types or categories of people are *expected by others* to display certain additional characteristics and/or be consistently deviant.

Figure **4.2**   Possible Model for Explaining Interpersonal Expectancies

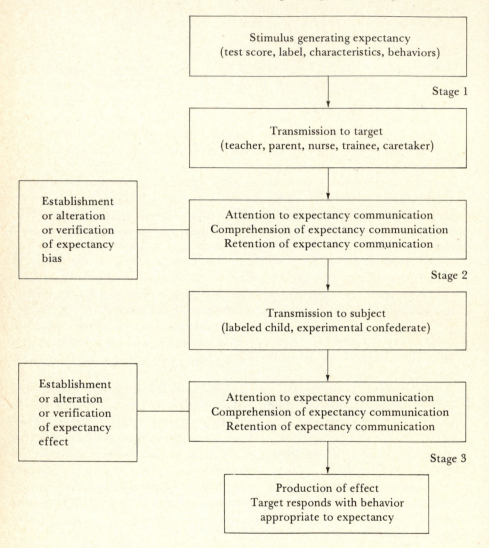

2. Once we have discovered that another is a certain type, we react to them
   in ways that push them into secondary and/or career deviance, thereby
   confirming our initial expectations. (p. 90)

Algozzine and Mercer (1980) considered that:

Labels serve as convenient reference points upon which to make predictions
as to the future behaviors of labeled individuals, as well as representing key

words to which a variety of other characteristics may be associated. It is when these implied stereotypical characteristics and/or expectations are negative that labels become a problem. Few people would mind being called a "genius" unless that meant they would always be expected to say and do brilliant things and to only associate with other people thought to be in their same category. Similarly, it is not the special education label *per se* that is problematic but the fact that that label serves as an expectancy-generating stimulus which has less than favorable associated qualities. (pp. 295–296)

There has been much research on the effects of various special and remedial education labels. In a major analysis, MacMillan, Jones, and Aloia (1974) reviewed studies in which the "mentally retarded" label had been evaluated. They concluded that "regardless of the dependent measure employed [self-concept, acceptance, lowered achievement, post-school adjustment], the evidence does not support the conclusion that there is a detrimental labeling effect" (p. 252). Guskin, Bartel, and MacMillan (1976) concluded their discussion of the effects of labeling from the "perspective of the labeled child" by stating that "there is no simple predictable consequence of labeling for the individual" (p. 209). Algozzine and Mercer (1980) reviewed studies "reported concurrently with or subsequent to the MacMillan, Jones, and Aloia (1974) review" and concluded that "differential effects have been demonstrated in studies which have manipulated various special education labels" (p. 296). They pointed out that their analysis considered the sequential aspects of effect transmission, whereas that of MacMillan, Jones, and Aloia did not.

We have analyzed studies in which the effects of the mentally retarded label were reported concurrently with or subsequent to the MacMillan, Jones, and Aloia review, and some of the studies we analyzed are summarized in Table 4.3. We grouped them according to their relevant stage(s) of transmission (see Figure 4.2).

From the results presented in Table 4.3, it seems safe to conclude that labels are expectancy-generating stimuli (see the interpersonal expectancy model presented in Figure 4.2). Within the context of the biasing factors that result in differential expectancy effects (cf. Brophy & Good, 1974), labels seem to represent powerfully biasing stimuli. It is important to note, however, that other factors may be more powerful biasers; for example, competence at a task may override the label of mental retardation. (For a label to influence outcomes, it must be believable; mental retardation and competence seem to be inconsistent.)

Approximately half the studies reported and analyzed in Table 4.3 demonstrated negative effects for the mentally retarded label, either in comparison with other labels or within the category of mental retardation (for example, severe vs. mild). Those studies in which no labeling effects were indicated tended to include other biasing factors that may have

Table 4.3 Selected Investigations of Effects of Mentally Retarded (MR) Label

INVESTIGATOR	LABEL(S) BEING STUDIED	METHOD OF INVESTIGATION	TARGET INDIVIDUAL(S)	RESULTS
		Studies of Stage 1 Transmission		
Gottlieb, 1974	Mentally retarded vs. normal; competent vs. incompetent	Videotaped presentation—Experimental comparison	Transmission to classmates	Fourth-grade children were more influenced by degree of competence than by labels
Aloia, 1975	Mentally retarded vs. normal vs. no label; attractive vs. unattractive	Experimental comparison	Transmission to teacher credential students	Physical stigmata (i.e., photographs of Down's syndrome children) influenced ratings; no labeling effects
Gottlieb, 1975	Mentally retarded vs. normal; aggressive vs. passive behavior	Videotaped presentation—Experimental comparison	Transmission to third-grade pupils	Attitudes more favorable for normal fifth grader and for passive child
Yoshida & Meyers, 1975	Mentally retarded vs. normal	Videotaped presentation—Experimental comparison	Transmission to regular and special teachers	No labeling effect
Gottlieb & Gottlieb, 1977	Mentally retarded vs. crippled children	Case study paragraphs—Experimental comparison	Transmission to jr. high school students	More favorable attitudes toward crippled children

Author, Year	Comparison	Description/Method	Transmission	Findings
Kurtz & Gottlieb, 1977	Mentally retarded vs. non-mentally retarded	Case report—Experimental comparison	Transmission to undergraduate education majors	Greater immediacy reflected in body leans toward MR child
Seitz & Geske, 1977	Mentally retarded vs. non-mentally retarded	Videotaped presentations of mother-child interactions were presented in labeled and nonlabeled conditions	Transmission to mothers of normal children and graduate students	Mothers rated retarded children differently whether or not the label was present; graduate students did not respond similarly; some altruistic response tendencies were noted relative to "retarded" child
Foster & Keech, 1977	Mentally retarded vs. normal	Hypothetical and videotaped presentations—Experimental comparisons	Transmission to undergraduate students	Mentally retarded child rated more negatively in both presentations
Siperstein & Gottlieb, 1977	Down's syndrome vs. children with normal appearance in competent or less competent portrayal	Audiotaped presentations of spelling performance depicted for retarded or nonretarded child	Transmission to fourth and fifth graders	Competent, nonstigmatized children were rated higher than noncompetent, stigmatized children; some respondent sex and popularity differences were indicated
Severance & Gasstrom, 1977	Mentally retarded vs. non-mentally retarded	Description of ten-year-old boy or girl was manipulated to portray success or failure at a puzzle; "mentally retarded" label was sometimes present	Transmission to undergraduate students	Ability, effort, and task difficulty were perceived differently for labeled as compared to unlabeled target children

(continued)

Table 4.3 (cont.)

INVESTIGATOR	LABEL(S) BEING STUDIED	METHOD OF INVESTIGATION	TARGET INDIVIDUAL(S)	RESULTS
		Studies of Stage 1 Transmission		
Kennon & Sandoval, 1978	Mentally retarded	Questionnaire regarding attitudes toward mentally retarded	Transmission to regular and special teachers	Both groups of teachers rated mentally retarded similarly; some ethnic differences were indicated
Siperstein & Gottlieb, 1978	Severely vs. mildly retarded	Completion of questionnaires regarding school and community integration	Transmission to parents, teachers, and others likely to be interested in mainstreaming	Attitudes expressed toward community and school integration were more positive for mildly retarded individuals
Palmer, 1980	Educable mentally retarded	Experimental analysis of effects of several types of case studies	Transmission to elementary school teachers	No label effects relative to attributions; knowledge of achievement level did influence instructional programming and placement decisions
		Studies of Stage 2 Transmission		
Farna, Thaw, Felner, & Hust, 1976	Normal vs. mentally retarded vs. mentally ill	Labeled confederates —Experimental comparison	Transmission to undergraduate students; transmission to labeled subject	Shocks to subject thought to organically retarded were shorter and of less intensity than those to normal or mentally ill (nonorganic) subjects; no measure of performance by "labeled" individual

Study	Subjects	Method	Source	Findings
Bryan & Wheeler, 1976	Severely retarded, trainable mentally retarded, learning disabled, normal	Naturalistic observation of classroom interactions for two school days	Teachers	Differences in classroom interactions received by children of different classifications
Grant & Moores, 1977	Levels of mentally retarded	Naturalistic observation in two hospitals for the retarded	Hospital staff	Differential interactions with patients as function of levels of independence, adaptive behavior, and behavioral maladaption; no comparison of similar factors in interactions with nonretarded individuals
Dembo, Yoshida, Reilly, & Reilly, 1978	Educable mentally retarded *vs.* educationally handicapped	Naturalistic study in which teacher-pupil classroom interactions were analyzed for educable mentally retarded and educationally handicapped	Transmission to handicapped child by teachers	No differential interaction patterns were evident within different types of special classrooms

Studies of Stage 3 Transmission

Study	Subjects	Method	Source	Findings
Buium, Ryders, & Turnure, 1974	Down's syndrome and normal children	Analysis of audiovisual tape recordings of mother-child interactions	Parents	Different "linguistic input" for Down's syndrome children

(continued)

Table **4.3** (cont.)

INVESTIGATOR	LABEL(S) BEING STUDIED	METHOD OF INVESTIGATION	TARGET INDIVIDUAL(S)	RESULTS
		Studies of Stage 3 Transmission		
Buckhart, Rutherford, & Goldberg, 1978	Down's syndrome and nonretarded infants	Observational analysis of verbal and nonverbal interaction	Parents	Differences in rate of speech but not complexity as a function of child's condition
Richardson, 1978	Mentally retarded	Follow-up study at age 22 for selected variables	Retarded young adults and comparison peers	Four times as many retarded as nonretarded young adults were unemployed; some differences in job-related and interpersonal factors
Margalet & Schuchman, 1978	Educable mentally retarded	Follow-up study of parents, students, and employers	Retarded young adults	Differences in vocational adjustment as a function of training; no comparison with nonretarded subjects
		Study of Complete Model		
Badad, 1977	Educable mentally retarded with high or low learning potentials	Experimental study in one school year	Transmission to teachers; transmission to students	Unexpected inferiority of the "high" expectancy group on several measures; no measure of what teachers actually did with students

counteracted the effects observed when the labels were studied in isolation. For example, Gottlieb (1974) found that children responded more to competence than to labels, and Aloia (1975) reported that physical stigmata were more influential than labels. Other investigators suggested that labels were not detrimental, but they failed to realize or indicate the confounded nature of their research.

Yoshida and Meyers (1975) presented teachers with a videotape in which a child's performance improved over four sets of trials. The teachers were told that "they were participating in a teacher judgment experiment" and were asked to rate the "probable future performance of the child" (p. 524). An analysis of the results indicated that the teachers perceived an improvement in performance and that no labeling effects were present: in light of the improved performance, the label of mental retardation may have been less believable.

Reschly and Lambrecht (1979) conducted a similarly confounded study. They presented a videotape of children labeled gifted, educable mentally retarded, or normal, who performed 6 of 10 items correctly on the tape during 4 different trials. The initial estimates of bias favored the gifted and disfavored the retarded children, but after four measurements, all the children were rated similarly. Reschly and Lambrecht (1979) interpreted this outcome to mean that labels have no effect over time but are confounded by the child's "average" performance (that is, 6 of 10). In fact, the gifted child and the retarded child would be expected to perform 60 percent better or worse, respectively, and, therefore, the labels again would become unbelievable in light of more salient information (that is, actual performance).

Other reports of unexpected outcomes favoring the MR label or not showing any negative effects can be analyzed similarly. For example, Kurtz, Harrison, Neisworth, and Jones (1977) reported a favorable response to the MR label when teachers favored labeled over nonlabeled children. The investigators based their interpretation on Mehrabian's (1972) theory relative to the meaning of immediacy. The results also could be interpreted as a sign of the MR children's anticipated helplessness and/or their expected need for closer guidance. The label had an effect; it is the interpretation that is in question. Foley (1978) also reported favorable responses to the MR label. He introduced a possible source of confounding: a teacher was present in the videotaped scene, and she responded either positively or negatively to the child. The subjects may have responded to the teacher's behavior which would have influenced their responses to the labels. In analyzing the effects of labeling, it is important to consider other situational aspects which also are salient and may lead to unexpected outcomes.

No child can benefit from the intended advantages of special and remedial education without being identified as eligible. The negative effects, as well, will not accrue without identification. The current system on which decisions to classify children as needing special and remedial education is founded on a logically weak base. Therefore, many children are identified, and in fact, the estimates of those in need are as high as 50 percent to 60 percent of all of school children (Rubin & Balow, 1971). And although waiting lists of children referred but not placed in some school districts number over a thousand students, a common solution is to hire more school psychologists or to improve identification by developing or searching for better tests. Questions such as "What can we do to improve the current system?" or "How can the 'right' children be found?" are old questions, and new answers to them will be limited by the appropriateness of the initial question. Answers to new questions that address the rationale for referring significant numbers of students and/or the usefulness of identification information that does not provide knowledge regarding instruction will serve as the foundation for future decisions in special and remedial education.

Chapter 5

Issues in Assessment

It is estimated that over 250 million standardized tests are administered each year to the 44 million students who attend American elementary and secondary schools. In addition, teachers and educational support personnel regularly collect data on students through classroom tests, informal and formal observation, and interviews with students' biological or surrogate family members or care takers. Clearly, assessment, and specifically that part of assessment that includes testing, is a major activity in America's schools.

ISSUES OF DEFINITION

TESTING CONTROVERSY

Tests and testing have been the subjects of considerable controversy in both the popular press and the professional literature. Both the instruments and their uses have been criticized. This opposition is understandable, given the significance of tests in decisions affecting students' future social and economic status. Indeed, in a number of the court cases brought against school systems and educators by students and parents (see Chapter 8), the substantive issue has been abuse in intellectual and psychological assessment.

In some of the litigation, school personnel were charged with excluding students from educational programs because of their performance on standardized tests (Mills v. Board of Education, 1972). The courts have ruled that ability grouping, or the assignment of students to different educational tracks on the basis of their performance on standardized tests, is unconstitutional (*Hobson* v. *Hansen,* 1969). Although educators and educational researchers have observed that black students and students from low socioeconomic environments usually obtain scores about one standard deviation lower on measures of intelligence than the scores of white middle-class students, the extent to which the tests are biased against minority students has recently become a judicial issue. In a significant decision (Larry P. v. Riles, 1978), the judge restrained educators and psychologists in California from using intelligence tests to place black students in classes for the educable mentally retarded. However, in an Illinois case(PASE v. Hannon, 1980), the judge refused to order educators and psychologists to discontinue the use of tests to make placement decisions for black students. The judge, after personally reviewing the commonly used individual intelligence and achievement tests, reported that he was able to identify only a very small number of items that he considered biased against black students and he ruled that pupil performance on those few items would not result in the inappropriate placement of normal students.

Public and professional controversy also have focused on what has been called "truth in testing." At issue are the tests used to make college admissions decisions. It is argued that the students, after taking the tests, should be given a set of all test questions and possible correct responses (Nairn & Associates, 1980). This procedure would give the students the opportunity to challenge the appropriateness of both the questions and the answers scored as correct. The New York State legislature recently passed a "truth in testing" bill requiring test publishers to provide copies of test questions and their answers to students who have taken tests. Test publishers argue that this practice will invalidate each edition of a test and will require the expenditure of millions of dollars for the construction of new editions.

Cronbach (1975), in his review of 50 years of controversy over mental testing, argued that the popular criticism of testing often has lacked scientific merit: "Public controversy deals in stereotypes, never in subtleties" (p. 1). He also argued that public controversy confuses the goodness of tests with the use to which the tests are put: "Sound policy is not for tests or against tests, what matters is how tests are used. But all the public hears is endless angry clamor from extremists who see no good in any test, or no evil" (p. 1).

CONCEPTS AND DEFINITIONS

Much of the controversy over tests and test use is actually conceptual and definitional in nature. School personnel believe that intelligence or learning aptitude is related to how much students profit from schooling; that is, they believe that students who have more of the attribute called intelligence will profit more from instruction than will students who have less intelligence. Hence they administer intelligence tests to measure how much intelligence a student has. Many educational personnel also believe that students have perceptual or perceptual-motor abilities (that is, those abilities assessed by measures of figure ground, visual closure, eye-hand coordination, visual association, or body image), and they administer tests to try to identify students with such difficulties (that is, do not have perceptual or perceptual-motor abilities). Many school personnel believe that some students have severe social and emotional difficulties or personality disturbances that interfere with and sometimes are the cause of academic difficulties. Thus they administer personality tests or measures of socia-emotional functioning to try to discover the specific difficulties. Consequently, some students are said to be depressed, anxious, neurotic, or even psychotic, according to how their test performances are interpreted.

No one has ever seen whatever it is that is called intelligence. No one has ever seen figure-ground pathology, a visual closure problem, depression, or anxiety, either. We only observe behaviors, and it is from these behaviors that we infer the existence of underlying traits or abilities. Intelligence, perceptual-motor ability, depression, and anxiety are inferred constructs whose labels or names describe constellations of behaviors. When tests are used to assess these nebulous qualities to which we have assigned tremendous importance, it is little wonder that there is so much controversy over the assessments themselves.

Tests are also used to classify students. Students are said to be mentally retarded, learning disabled, or emotionally disturbed, depending on their performances on tests. The current definitions of mental retardation and specific learning disabilities are given in Chapter 2, and the numerous conceptual and definitional issues are readily apparent. Students labeled mentally retarded are said to have subaverage intellectual functioning, but what is subaverage intellectual functioning? Students labeled mentally retarded are also said to demonstrate deficits in adaptive behavior, but when is behavior adaptive (or maladaptive), and how does a student show a deficit in adaptive behavior? There are many measures of adaptive behavior (see Salvia & Ysseldyke, 1981, for descriptions), but measurement experts continue to struggle to develop technically adequate measures of adaptive behavior and to define the term specifically. In the midst of this confusion, educators classify students as mentally retarded on the basis of performance on measures of intelligence and adaptive behavior, as learning disabled on the basis of performance on process measures, and as emotionally disturbed on the basis of performance on personality tests.

Public Law 94–142 includes a definition of specific learning disabilities. However, the definitions of learning disabilities regulating classification in the individual states differ considerably (Mercer et al., 1976). The reason for these discrepancies is the considerable conceptual confusion regarding the meaning of the classification. The definition states that students with specific learning disabilities have a "disorder in one or more of the basic psychological processes. . . . " But we do not know what the basic psychological processes are. If we do not know what they are, how can we expect to develop tests to measure them? Mann (1971) aptly noted that most of the process and ability deficits that are said to cause academic difficulties are "test-identified." For example, when we ask teachers and school psychologists to define visual sequential memory deficit and figure-ground disorders, they typically tell us only that students with visual sequential memory deficits earn low scores on the Visual Sequential Memory subtest of the Illinois Test of Psycholinguistic Abilities and that students with figure-ground disorders perform poorly on the Figure-Ground subtest of the Developmental Test of Visual Perception. We often are left wondering whether the disorders would exist if we did not have tests to measure them. We believe that they would not.

Whenever there is conceptual confusion regarding terminology, there is conceptual confusion in measurement. Diagnostic personnel have incredible difficulty demonstrating that a test is valid—that it measures what it says it measures—when they cannot define or describe what it is they are trying to measure. Hence, courts and legislatures have challenged diagnostic practices, and controversy and confusion reign supreme.

THE PRACTICE OF ASSESSMENT: MAGNITUDE AND ORIENTATION

At the beginning of this chapter we noted that about 250 million standardized tests are administered annually to students in school settings. Routine achievement tests account for a substantial number of the measures administered but many—perhaps too many—of the assessments take place under the umbrella of "special education planning." In trying to describe the magnitude of assessment activities, Thurlow and Ysseldyke (1979) surveyed 44 federally funded model programs for learning-disabled students. They found that the model programs used different tests to decide whether students were eligible for special education services and individually appropriate instructional interventions. Often, tests that were developed and intended for one purpose were diverted to different purposes. Similar findings were reported by Ysseldyke, Algozzine, and Thurlow (1980) in their study of decision making by placement teams and by Ysseldyke, Algozzine, Regan, Potter, Richey, and Thurlow (1980) in their computer simulation study of the decision-making process. Ysseldyke and Thurlow (1980), in their report of a longitudinal study of the assessment and decision-making process in eight individual cases, found that although the actual number of tests used in making the decisions varied considerably, much time was spent assessing students and deciding what to do for or about them.

In some cases, assessment and decision making may require as much as 13 to 15 hours of professional time. If we estimate an average charge of $15 per hour by each professional, then the costs of assessment are obviously very high. Mirkin (1980) estimated that it costs as much as $1,800 to assess and make decisions for one student. And the practical knowledge gained from such activities is marginal at best.

When we look at the magnitude of the assessment process, at the large numbers of tests administered to students, we repeatedly ask why. Why is it that school personnel administer so many tests in order to make decisions about students? Is it because they learn so much about the students and how to teach them? Apparently, educational personnel believe so. We think, however, that there is much evidence to indicate that assessors learn very little about students from the students' performances on standardized tests. Ysseldyke, Algozzine, Richey, and Graden (in press) investigated the correspondence between decisions made by placement teams and the extent to which the data supported the decisions, and they reported very little correlation (range: -.13 to +.29) between the team decision and the empirical support for the decision. Why, then, do decision makers expend so much energy on assessing students? Sarason and Doris (1979) addressed this same question in relation to the assessment of mentally retarded students. To them, "diagnosis is a pathology-oriented process activated by someone who thinks something is wrong with somebody else" (p. 39), and they described the assessment process as follows:

The diagnostic process is always a consequence of somebody saying that someone has something wrong with him. We put it this way because frequently it is not the individual who decides to initiate the process. This is the case with children, but there are also times when adults are forced by pressure from others or by legal action to participate in the process. In all of those instances people individually or society in general communicate four ideas: something may be wrong with someone; our lives are being affected; we should find out the source of the trouble; and we should come up with solutions to alter the individual's status and allow us to experience our lives in the way we wish. (Sarason & Doris, p. 16)

Although the assessment process is problematic, teachers refer very large numbers of students for evaluation. In New York City alone, during 1978, the backlog of students awaiting psychoeducational assessment exceeded 16,000. Teachers refer students because they think that "something is wrong," either academically or socially, and that the students are not performing as they are expected to. The professionals who assess students presume that something is wrong with them, and tests are administered until the professionals are able to identify some pathology, which they nearly always can. In New York City, during 1978, 95 percent of those students who were referred for evaluation were declared eligible for special education services.

BIAS IN ASSESSMENT

The concern with bias in assessment is legitimate and has arisen for three reasons:

1. The concern with bias arises directly out of the ways in which American society evaluates the worth of individuals. With some exceptions, of course, people are evaluated on the basis of their presumed intelligence. The IQ has become a very potent yardstick, and educators become concerned when a student's achievement is not commensurate. Even mothers repeat their children's IQ scores as if they were indices of worth. Kamin (1974) illustrated how society has used intelligence to evaluate a person's worth: Arguments of limited intellectual potential have been advanced to limit immigration; advocate sterilization; and explain criminal tendencies, mental and physical defects, and degeneracy. Kamin stated, "Since its introduction to America, the intelligence test has been used more or less consciously as an instrument of oppression against the underprivileged—the poor, the foreign born, and racial minorities" (p. 1). Kamin illustrated this use of tests to oppress people by repeating quotations from early psychologists and congressional witnesses in support of limiting immigration.

2. Different racial groups, as groups, achieve different average scores on intelligence tests. This finding has been fashioned into an instrument of oppression, according to Kamin (1974), but it also has kindled consid-

erable professional controversy over the reason for the observed differences.

3. There is a disproportionate representation of minority students in special education classes, which is a concern apparent in both litigation and legislation (see Chapter 8). Nonetheless, disproportionate representation has not changed. Tucker (1980) reported the results of an eight-year study in the Southwest, which demonstrated that the number of students in the total special education population had increased by 10 percent and, further, that the trend toward placing minority students in special education classes in disproportionate numbers has continued, despite national preventive efforts. Tucker observed that the present trend is to label minority students, especially Blacks, as learning disabled.

Given the legitimate and necessary concern of professionals with bias in assessment, let us look at how educators and psychologists have addressed the problem.

A PROFESSION ADDRESSES A PROBLEM

Early observations that minority students earned lower scores, on the average, than did nonminority students, led to long and heated debates on the relative contributions to intelligence of genetic and environmental variables (Bayley, 1965; Bereiter, 1969; Bijou, 1971; Bloom, 1964; Cronbach, 1969; Elkind, 1969; Gordon, 1971; Hirsch, 1971; Jensen, 1967, 1968a, 1968b, 1969a, 1969b). The debate still goes on. Kamin (1974) noted the general assumption that 80 percent of variation in IQ scores is genetically determined. Bijou (1971) responded to that statement by arguing that we are not doing a very good job with the other 20 percent. Then Kamin (1974), on the basis of his analysis of the data, observed, "There exist no data which should lead a prudent man to accept the hypothesis that I.Q. test scores are in any degree heritable" (p. 1). And so the debate continues; the observed differences continue to exist; and children continue to fail in school.

Observed differences between groups also have led to investigations of the fairness of tests. We have seen large-scale comparative studies of the performances of groups on specific tests (Goldman & Hewitt, 1976; Hennessey & Merrifield, 1976; Jensen, 1976, 1979; Matusek & Oakland, 1972; Mercer, 1973). Studies of group differences in performances on psychometric devices have persuaded other investigators to examine the fairness of specific items used with members of minority groups (Angoff & Ford, 1971; Fishbein, 1975; Newland, 1973; Scheyneman, 1976). How biased specific tests and test items are has been examined for both linguistic bias (Berry & Lopez, 1977; Matluck & Mace, 1973; Matluck & Mace-Matluck, 1975; Vasquez, 1972) and sex bias (Dwyer, 1976; Harmon, 1973; Lockheed-Katz, 1974; Tittle 1973; Tolor & Brannigan, 1975).

Research revealing the differences between groups in performances on tests or test items, along with assertions that bias existed in the selection and employment of people, has led several psychologists to develop models to evaluate test fairness and to try to define the concept of culture fairness. Both Cole (1973) and Petersen and Novick (1976) devised a useful conceptualization of six different models of fairness. Without going into detail, they are the Quota Model, Regression Model (Cleary, 1968), the Subjective Regression Model, the Equal Risk Model (Guion, 1966), the Constant Ratio Model (Thorndike, 1971), and the Conditional Probability Model (Cole, 1973).

Some investigators have reviewed the several models of test fairness (Hunter & Schmidt, 1976; Linn & Werts, 1971; McNemar, 1975; Petersen & Novick, 1976) and concluded that there is little agreement among them. It is readily apparent that major measurement experts have been unable to agree on a definition of a fair test, let alone a test that is fair for members of different groups. There also is little agreement on the concept of nondiscriminatory assessment. Petersen and Novick (1976) noted:

The Regression, the Constant Ratio, the Conditional Probability, the Equal Probability, the Equal Risk and the Culture-Modified Criterion Models are each explications of general concepts of what constitutes the fair use of tests in a selection situation. There seems to be nothing in the literature that clearly indicates when, if ever, one of the models is preferable to the other five models. Thus, the practitioner has no clear guidance in the choice of a culture-fair selection model. Further, we have suggested that the Constant Ratio, the Conditional Probability, the Equal Probability Models and their converses are *internally contradictory*. (pp. 23–24)

This nation and its researchers have invested considerable effort, time, and financial resources in attempts to develop or identify assessment devices that are not biased against members of racial or cultural groups. Given the history of psychologists' efforts to address the concept of fairness and their generalized lack of success, it troubles us to see educators these days trying to find *the* fair test to use with specific groups, arguing about the fairness of specific test items, and generating state-approved lists of fair tests. What would it mean if, somehow, we found *the* fair test? An end to abuse in assessment? Would bias in assessment and decision making cease to exist? We think not. Even given a fair test or a set of tests, there is considerable evidence that the bias in decision making would not be ameliorated. The review of testimony before the congressional committee on the Protection in Evaluation Procedures Provisions of Public Law 94–142 reveals an obviously much broader concern than simply that of the fairness of tests and test items that are administered to members of minority groups. This broader concern is with the subject of abuse in the entire process of using assessment data to make decisions regarding pupils. Abuse is evident in many areas related to the assessment of children and includes (1) inappropriate and indiscriminate use of tests; (2) bias in the assessment of handicapped children and in the identification as handicapped of children who are not; (3) bias throughout the decision-making process; and (4) bias following assessment.

The following two excerpts from U. S. Senate Report No. 94–168 illustrate the statement that the real concern is with abuse in assessment and decision making:

The Committee is deeply concerned about practices and procedures which result in classifying children as having handicapped conditions when, in fact, they do not have such conditions. At least three major issues are of concern with respect to problems of identification and classification: (1) the misuse of appropriate identification and classification data within the educational process itself; (2) discriminatory treatment as the result of the identification of a handicapping condition; and (3) misuse of identification procedures or methods which results in erroneous classification of a child as having a handicapping condition. . . .

The Committee is alarmed about the abuses which occur in the testing and evaluaton of children; and is concerned that expertise in the proper use of testing and evaluation procedures falls far short of the prolific use and development of testing and evaluation tools. The usefulness and mechanistic ease of testing should not become so paramount in the educational process that the negative effects of such testing are overlooked. (U. S. Senate, Report No. 94–168, Education for All Handicapped Children Act, June 2, 1975, pp. 26–29)

Educators can and probably will argue for a long time over which of these interactions is fair. There would be more progress made by addressing something that could be affected: bias in the entire process of decision making.

THE BIASING EFFECT OF NATURALLY OCCURRING PUPIL CHARACTERISTICS

Recent research has demonstrated the extent to which naturally occurring characteristics influence the kinds of decisions made on pupils. Ross and Salvia (1975) examined how much students' physical attractiveness affects teachers' decisions. The investigators grouped school pictures of third-grade children into 10 piles by means of a Q-sort technique, and then they asked the raters to rank the pictures from least to most physically attractive. The pictures of four third-grade children—a boy and girl who had been ranked the most attractive physically and a boy and girl who had been ranked the least attractive physically—were affixed to identical psychological reports. All four reports included the same objective, borderline data on pupil intellect and prior achievement; that is, they could be used to support a diagnosis of either mentally retarded or normal.

The four reports and pictures were given to four groups of classroom teachers. They were asked to diagnose the pictured children on the basis of the objective data. Although the teachers had received identical information about all four children, their diagnoses differed according to the children's appearance. Thus, the personal attractiveness of students was demonstrated to be a biasing factor in the diagnostic decisions made by educators.

Algozzine (1975) extended this research by looking at how much the pupils' physical attractiveness affected teacher-pupil interactions. He found that teachers interacted significantly less often and more negatively with unattractive pupils than with attractive pupils. Salvia, Algozzine, and Sheare (1976) investigated the effect of physical attractiveness on the grades given out by elementary teachers. They examined the cumulative records of those children who had been identified as attractive or unattractive in the previous study by Ross and Salvia (1975). Although there were no differences among the groups of students on intelligence tests and measures of academic achievement, the teachers rated attractive students one grade point higher. In other words, teachers assigned higher grades to physically attractive students.

Further research on the extent to which naturally occurring characteristics affect decision making was completed by Salvia and Podol (1975). They obtained a photograph of a child with a visible repaired cleft palate and had a copy made in which the repaired cleft was made invisible. Two groups of speech therapists were given copies of the same speech sample and told that they were to evaluate the speech of a child with a repaired cleft palate. One group was shown the picture of the child in which the repaired cleft was visible, and the other group was shown the retouched photo. There were significant differences in the therapists' ratings of the same speech sample.

The studies reported here, and others, plainly showed bias in decision making. In each case, decision makers who were given objective data reached different conclusions on the basis of diagnostically irrelevant pupil characteristics.

School personnel regularly must decide which students experiencing academic and/or behavioral difficulties or both should be declared eligible for and receive special education services. They spend considerable time and effort collecting data and making the decisions. Professionals charged with the task of making psychoeducational determinations routinely administer standardized tests to referred students or use the results of pupil performance on these tests to make decisions. Such test data and relevant pupil information are collected to facilitate decisions on screening, eligibility-classification-identification-placement, intervention, and evaluation (Salvia & Ysseldyke, 1981). But how many and which of these data are actually used in making the decisions?

A recent investigation at the University of Minnesota Institute for Research on Learning Disabilities was designed to ascertain how much the assessment process relies on the differences in referral information—that is, to what extent diagnostic personnel actually use the different kinds of assessment information—and to ascertain how much the different, naturally occurring characteristics influence their decisions on pupils.

The investigation was a computer-simulated decision-making program. Data were collected on both test use and the extent to which the decision-making process and its outcomes were biased by referral information. At the same time, information was gathered on the decision makers' knowledge of assessment and on how they used technically adequate tests, obtained information from test manuals, and went beyond scores to evaluate how youngsters earned those scores.

The participants in the investigation were 159 Minnesota educators and school psychologists who had taken part in at least two placement team meetings. As administrators, school psychologists, special education teachers, regular education teachers, and support personnel (such as counselors, nurses, and social workers), they represented a spectrum of specialities and experience in providing both direct and indirect services in educational settings.

Each participant was asked to read a case-folder description of a child and then to participate in a simulation of diagnostic activities. The program gave the participants access to informaton from an archive containing the results of various assessment measures. The specific test scores available were for intelligence, achievement, perceptual-motor ability, personality, and language; performance scores on adaptive behavior scales and the results of several forms of behavioral observation or behavior check lists also were included. The program was set up to provide the participants with consistent data indicating that each pupil's test performance was within the average range. Each participant was allowed to select specific tests, such as the Wechsler Intelligence Scale for Children—Revised and the Illinois Test of Psycholinguistic Abilities, from the seven domains until he or she was ready to make the diagnostic decision. The program then presented a series of decision questions.

The data collected in assessments should be functionally useful in educational decision making. In this investigation, the decision makers were presented with referral information that varied only in the child's sex, socioeconomic status, physical appearance, and type of referral problem. They were given the opportunity to select specific kinds of assessment data (all of which indicated pupil performance and behavior within the average range), to make diagnostic and prognostic decisions, and to report the extent to which specific kinds of test data and naturally occurring pupil information influenced their decisions.

In the analysis of the participants' decision-making behavior, it was found that across conditions, achievement tests were used most often. Referral information affected the decisions, but only for one of the four independent variables. The referred students' sex, socioeconomic status, and physical appearance had no effect on the diagnostic and prognostic decisions. The reason for referral had a significant effect on the decisions. Although all the assessment data indicated average or normal performances for all students, those referred for behavior problems were significantly more often diagnosed as, and labeled, emotionally disturbed than were students who were referred for academic problems. In short, the statement of referral problem biased the outcome decisions.

Decision makers perceived different kinds of assessment data as affecting their outcome decisions. Overall, the scores on achievement and intelligence tests, and the disparity between the two, were perceived to be the most useful and influential. The scores on personality tests and the records of observed or perceived behaviors, however, were seen as having a greater influence on outcome decisions when the referred students demonstrated behavioral rather than academic problems.

Further, the participants viewed naturally occurring pupil characteristics as influencing their decisions as follows: (1) Socioeconomic status influenced decisions more when the students were from high rather than low socioeconomic backgrounds. (2) Sex, socioeconomic status, and reason for referral had a greater influence on outcome decisions than did physical appearance, but only when the reason for referral was academic in nature. (3) The reason for referral had a pronounced effect on outcome decisions, and this effect was significantly greater than that of sex, appearance, or socioeconomic status.

Obviously, referral information biases such decisions. Although there was no difference in the kinds of test information supplied to the participants, different referral conditions produced different outcome decisions. At the same time, the participants perceived their decisions as having been influenced by different kinds of data and pupil characteristics, and these differences were a function of the referral information. In sum, whatever concern educational and psychological decision makers may have about achieving nondiscriminatory assessment, the more immediate problems are bias in the decision-making process and abuse in the use of assessment data on which important decisions regarding students are made.

CONTEMPORARY ASSESSMENT AND DECISION-MAKING PRACTICES

Although tests are administered to students for one or more purposes, testing is only one part of the broader conception of assessment. Testing refers to the sampling of behaviors in students to obtain quantitative indices (that is, scores) of relative standings. Assessment can be described as a process of collecting data to make decisions about students (Salvia & Ysseldyke, 1981). Assessment data are obtained, in part, from norm-referenced and criterion-referenced tests, observation, interviews, searches of school records, medical evaluations, and social histories.

Salvia and Ysseldyke (1981) identified five kinds of decisions regarding students (evaluation of the individual, program evaluation, screening, placement, and intervention-planning decisions) made by using assessment data. These data are supposed to facilitate correct decision making, although the misuse of assessment data can lead to inappropriate decision making and adverse effects on students' life opportunities. In the next section we examine current practices (and abuses) in the use of assessment data.

EVALUATION

Schools regularly gather data to evaluate the extent to which individual students or groups of students are progressing in the instructional programs to which they are assigned. These data also give schools information on their effectiveness. If students progress, schools are judged to be effective. Parents, teachers, and students themselves have both a right and a need to know whether and how much progress is being made. Parents, at the time of annual or semiannual parent-teacher conferences, often are given test scores as indices of their children's progress. School personnel regularly administer group achievement tests to obtain comparative data (Have the students under one teacher progressed as much as the students under a different teacher have? Have the students in one school or school district progressed as much as students in comparable administrative units have?) and to measure the progress of individuals, thereby detecting students who, for any number of reasons, may not be profiting from instruction.

Schools use tests to evaluate the effectiveness of instructional programs. The practice of administering group achievement tests serves two purposes: to let parents and school personnel know how much the students are profiting from instruction and to evaluate the general effectiveness of the instructional program.

When school personnel observe that students in their school profit more from instruction in one year than do students in other schools, they tend to be proud of their instructional programs. On the other hand, when they observe that pupils in their school profit less, on the average, than do students in other schools, they search for reasons why. School officials may become concerned about the quality of instruction in their schools, or they may attribute the observed differences to the inferior quality of their students.

At a curricular level, tests often are used to evaluate the effectiveness of specific instructional interventions. In the simplest form, school personnel give tests before and after instituting new teaching methods or materials, and they compare the gain in achievement with the gain that followed some other intervention. Using data obtained from such tests, administrators try to sort "good" from "bad" programs.

SCREENING AND/OR SELECTION

Tests are administered regularly to students to facilitate admission decisions. College admissions officers use test data (from the Scholastic Aptitude Test or the American College Testing Program) to assist them in deciding which applicants should and should not be accepted, and graduate school personnel also use test scores (from the Graduate Record Examination or the Miller Analogies Test) as one criterion.

Assessment data are used in elementary and secondary schools to identify students who are not profiting from educational programs. School personnel regularly review pupil performance on routinely administered group tests to identify students who may need remediation or who should be referred for additional assessment because they may be eligible for special education intervention. Much as routine vision and hearing screening are used to discover students with possible vision or hearing difficulties, the results of screening tests that assess learning aptitude, academic achievement, or perceptual-motor functioning are used to discover students with potential difficulties in these areas.

School personnel also screen students at the preschool level in order to identify those with potential problems. Under Public Law 94–142, schools are required to do this, to identify handicapped students.

ELIGIBILITY, PLACEMENT, AND/OR CLASSIFICATION DECISIONS

The kinds of decision making that can have, perhaps, the most profound effects, are whether students are eligible for special or remedial education services, can be classified as handicapped, and should be placed in special education programs. It may be advantageous to distinguish among these three decisions, although in practice it is nearly impossible to do so. Ysseldyke, Algozzine, and Thurlow (1980) reported that most teams make eligibility, classification, and placement decisions concurrently.

On paper, at least, eligibility, classification, and placement decisions are made on the basis of assessment data. All states have special education rules and regulations that specify eligibility criteria for special education services. The criteria differ considerably among states (Mercer, Forgnone, & Wolking, 1976), and within states, typically, there is considerable variation in the extent to which local education agencies use the state criteria. Ysseldyke, Algozzine, and Mitchell (in press) tried to identify the kind(s) of decisions made at special education team meetings by videotaping 32 meetings and carefully analyzing the contents. They reported that it was impossible to specify the decisions made by the teams. In addition, at the conclusion of meetings the teams did not regularly state or formally write down the decisions they had reached.

CONFUSING PURPOSES

Let us take another look at assessment as a process of collecting data to make decisions regarding students. The process can lead to five kinds of decisions: pupil evaluation, program evaluation, screening, placement-classification, and intervention. Tests also are administered to students for purposes other than those for which they were designed (Ysseldyke, 1979).

When they are confronted with a referred student, diagnosticians typically ask, "What test(s) should I administer?" We believe that several questions need to precede this one and that asking them highlights a major issue in assessment. The very first question that one should ask is, "What decision am I being asked to make?" The assessment process and the kinds of tests used should depend on the decisions to be made and, thus, should differ accordingly. To make a placement decision, one must collect data different from those needed to plan an instructional intervention.

Diagnosticians regularly administer and use the results of tests for purposes other than those for which they were designed. At its very simplest level is the use of the results of a pupil's performance on a screening measure to make a classification or placement decision. More often, tests are used for more than one purpose, and in the process, they are used for purposes for which they were not designed. (In an earlier publication, Ysseldyke (1979) demonstrated how the profile analysis on the Wechsler Intelligence Scale for Children—Revised (WISC-R), is used in a way that differs from the test's purposes.)

Diagnostic personnel regularly analyze profiles of pupils' performances on standardized tests in order to spot individual strengths and weaknesses and to design individual instructional interventions on the basis of the profile analyses. There is no empirical support for this practice, and it repeatedly has been shown to be unproductive (Arter & Jenkins, 1979; Ysseldyke, 1973; Ysseldyke & Mirkin, in press; Ysseldyke & Shinn, 1981; Ysseldyke & Stevens, in press).

THE USE OF TECHNICALLY INADEQUATE TESTS

Professionals who assess students to make decisions about them use technically inadequate data-collection procedures. We stress this fact because the decisions can have very significant effects on the students' lives. Educators are purported to have the best interests of the students at heart when they make decisions, though they often base the decisions on data from technically inadequate tests.

Three characteristics determine the technical adequacy of tests: norms, reliability, and validity. Norms are simply standards of comparison. A norm-referenced test is developed by standardizing it on a sample of students that actually represents the population on whom the test will be used. The performance of an individual on the test can then be compared with, or evaluated according to, the performance of other members of the population. The nature of the norm group, the group with whom one is being compared, is important, because it is the performance of the norm group that is used to judge the quality of the individual's performance.

Suppose you were the personnel manager for a large industrial firm and that part of your job included hiring typists. You regularly require applicants for positions as typists to take a typing test which you score for both speed (number of words per minute) and accuracy. You usually try to hire those applicants who are the fastest and most accurate. How do you know that you are hiring the best possible typists? You actually do not, unless you have a standard according to which the applicants can be evaluated. Hence, you decide to develop a typing test that requires applicants to type from both handwritten copy and dictation. Even if you gave every applicant the same test, you still would have to have some way of evaluating the performance. So you decide to standardize your test, that is, to develop a set of norms according to which applicant performance can be evaluated.

The way in which our hypothetical typing test is standardized will have a significant effect on the evaluation of each applicant's performance. There are several groups on whom your typing test could be standardized:

1. All high school seniors in your local school district.
2. All high school seniors in your local school district who have been enrolled in a business curriculum and who have taken at least one full year of typing classes.
3. A representative national sample of high school seniors who have been enrolled in a business curriculum and who have taken at least one full year of typing courses.
4. All those persons who, over a three-year period, have applied for employment with your company.
5. All those persons who, over a three-year period, have applied for employment as typists with your company.
6. Persons currently employed as typists in your company who have better than "satisfactory" performance evaluations from their immediate supervisors.

The nature of the norm group you select will influence your judgment of an applicant's typing skills. An applicant could look very good compared with high school seniors but very poor compared with currently employed, successful typists. Besides the test score and a set of norms for evaluating that score, you still will need to know the nature of the group on whom the test was standardized, that is, the nature of the norm group. Because the decision to hire or not to hire a person is influenced by his or her performance relative to the norm group, your decision might well be in error if you do not know the nature of the group on whom the test was standardized.

An underlying assumption in psychological and educational assessment is that the acculturation of the person being assessed is comparable to, although not necessarily identical with, that of the people on whom the test was standardized (Newland, 1980; Salvia & Ysseldyke, 1981). Acculturation refers simply to one's set of background experiences and opportunities. This assumption is typically addressed by test developers when they select a sample representative of the population of concern. Representativeness in the testing industry is usually achieved by stratifying a norm sample on a number of characteristics specified in the *Standards for Educational and Psychological Tests* developed by a joint committee of the American Psychological Association and the American Educational

Table **5.1**   Tests with Norms That Are Inadequately Constructed or Described

Arthur Adaptation of the Leiter International Performance Scale
Auditory Discrimination Test
Bender Visual Motor Gestalt Test
Culture Fair Intelligence Tests
Cognitive Abilities Test
Developmental Test of Visual-Motor Integration*
Developmental Test of Visual Perception
Diagnostic Reading Scales*
Durrell Analysis of Reading Difficulty*
Full-Range Picture Vocabulary Test*
Gates-McKillop Reading Diagnostic Tests*
Gilmore Oral Reading Test
Goodenough-Harris Drawing Test
Gray Oral Reading Test
Henmon-Nelson Tests of Mental Ability
Illinois Test of Psycholinguistic Abilities
Memory for Designs Test
Primary Mental Abilities Test
Purdue Perceptual-Motor Survey
Quick Test
Silent Reading Diagnostic Tests
Slosson Intelligence Test
Stanford-Binet Intelligence Scale
Wide Range Achievement Test

*These tests include norms in their manuals but include *no* data about the group on whom the test was standardized.

SOURCE: Reprinted with permission from J. Salvia & J. E. Ysseldyke, *Assessment in special and remedial education* (2nd ed.). Boston: Houghton Mifflin, 1981, p. 536.

Research Association (APA, 1974; see also Salvia & Ysseldyke, 1981). The characteristics of that normative sample that must be considered in developing a test and that must be reported by a test's developer(s) include age, grade, sex, acculturation of parents (as usually indicated by some combination of socioeconomic status, income, occupation, or education), geographic region, and race. For achievement tests it is important to consider the cognitive functioning (intellectual level) of the norm group.

In addition, one must be certain that the representative sample is made up of correct proportions of the kinds of people in the total population, that is, "the various kinds of people should be included in the *same proportion* in the sample as in the population" (Salvia & Ysseldyke, 1981, p. 115). The test's norms also must be current. The joint APA-AERA committee recommended that tests be revised at regular intervals, usually at least once every 15 years.

All this discussion leads up to what we view as a major issue in educational assessment: the use of tests with inadequately constructed or described norms. Educators make judgments about the quality of a pupil's test behavior by evaluating it in reference to the performance of an unknown norm group. Some of the most widely used measures of intelligence, achievement, personality, and perceptual-motor functioning were standardized on inadequately constructed and/or described norms. Salvia and Ysseldyke (1981) evaluated the composition of the normative group for over 100 norm-referenced tests. Table 5.1 lists the tests whose norms are inadequately constructed and/or described.

The second important technical characteristic is reliability, which refers simply to consistency in measurement. Assessment instruments are said to be reliable when students make approximately the same scores whenever they take the test. In the evaluation of pupil performance, we want to be certain that we are obtaining a reliable index of performance. It is necessary for test developers, as part of the developmental process, to provide evidence that their tests are reliable. Salvia and Ysseldyke (1981) evaluated the evidence for reliability in each test they reviewed, and they concluded that for very many of the tests there was insufficient evidence of reliability. Table 5.2, from Salvia and Ysseldyke (1981), lists the tests with inadequate reliability.

There are standards for reliability, which change according to the decision to be made. Salvia and Ysseldyke (1981) indicated that tests should have reliability coefficients in excess of .60 (1) when the scores are to be used for administrative purposes and (2) when test data are to be reported for groups of individuals. However, when tests are to be used to make decisions regarding individuals, they must have reliability coefficients over .90. Table 5.3 lists commonly used tests and their reliabilities, as reported in the tests' technical manuals.

The third important technical characteristic is validity, which refers to how much a test measures what it purports to measure. Evidence for validity is not only considered essential by the APA Standards for Educational and Psychological Tests but also is required by law. The regulations for Public Law 94–142 state, "Tests must have demonstrated validity for the purpose(s) for which they are used." Test developers must provide consumers with evidence of test validity. Tests are invalid when they provide inappropriate information for decision-making purposes.

Table **5.2**   Tests with Inadequate Reliability Data

Arthur Adaptation of the Leiter International Performance Scale
Developmental Test of Visual Perception
Durrell Analysis of Reading Difficulty
Full-Range Picture Vocabulary Test
Gates-McKillop Reading Diagnostic Tests
Gilmore Oral Reading Test
Gray Oral Reading Test
Illinois Test of Psycholinguistic Abilities
Primary Mental Abilities Test
Quick Test
Stanford-Binet Intelligence Scale
System of Multicultural Pluralistic Assessment
Test of Auditory Comprehension of Language

SOURCE: Reprinted with permission from J. Salvia & J. E. Ysseldyke, *Assessment in special and remedial education* (2nd ed.). Boston: Houghton Mifflin, 1981, p. 537.

Table 5.4, from Salvia and Ysseldyke (1981), lists the tests with inadequate or no evidence of validity.

The technical adequacy of tests currently used to make decisions on students has been evaluated in several recent investigations. Thurlow and Ysseldyke (1979) evaluated the technical adequacy of tests used in 44 model programs for learning-disabled students, the Child Service Demonstration Centers. They found that of 30 tests used by 3 or more centers, only 5 (16.7 percent) tests had technically adequate norms. Only 10 (33.3 percent) of the 30 tests had reliability adequate for decision making, and only 9 (30 percent) had technically adequate validity. The model programs—among the very best special education programs in the nation—made decisions regarding students by using tests that, for the most part, were technically inadequate.

Many kinds of abuse can occur in the use of assessment data to make decisions regarding students: (1) from the use of tests for purposes other than those for which they were designed, (2) from comparisons of students who differ systematically in several characteristics, and (3) from the use of technically inadequate tests to collect data on students. Abuse also occurs when investigators go beyond their data to infer underlying pathology and then to predict later academic difficulty. Throughout the assessment process, evaluators create bias on the basis of pupils' naturally occurring characteristics.

Table **5.3**   Reliabilities of Frequently Used Tests

TEST	RELIABILITY
AAMD Adaptive Behavior Scales	.37–.92[e]
Arthur Adaptation of the Leiter International Performance Scale	None
Auditory Discrimination Test (Wepman)	.91–.95[b]
Bender Visual Motor Gestalt Test	.50–.90[b]
Blind Learning Aptitude Test	.92–.95[c]
Boehm Test of Basic Concepts	.12–.94[c]
Cain-Levine Social Competency Scale	.75–.91[a]
California Achievement Tests	.59–.95[a]
Cognitive Abilities Test	.91–.99[a]
Denver Developmental Screening Test	.80–.95[c]
Developmental Test of Visual-Motor Integration	.83–.87[b]
Developmental Test of Visual Perception (subtests)	.29–.70[b]
Diagnostic Reading Scales	.30–.96[b]
Durrell Analysis of Reading Difficulty	None
Full-Range Picture Vocabulary Test	None
Gates-MacGinitie Reading Tests	.77–.89[b]
Gates-McKillop Reading Diagnostic Tests	None
Gilmore Oral Reading Test	.53–.94[d]
Goldman-Fristoe-Woodcock Test of Articulation	.95–.96[b]
Goodenough-Harris Drawing Test	.60–.70[b]
Gray Oral Reading Test	.96–.98[d]
Henmon-Nelson Tests of Mental Ability	.84–.97[a]
Illinois Test of Psycholinguistic Abilities (subtests)	.12–.90[b]
Iowa Tests of Basic Skills	.89–.97[a]
Keymath Diagnostic Arithmetic Scales	.39–.90[a]
Lee-Clark Reading Readiness Test	.56–.88[b]
McCarthy Scales of Children's Abilities	
Verbal	.86–.92[c]
Perceptual-Performance	.75–.90[c]
General Cognitive	.90–.94[c]
Quantitative	.77–.86[c]
Memory	.72–.83[c]
Motor	.60–.84[c]
Nebraska Test of Learning Aptitude	.92–.95[c]
Northwestern Syntax Screening Test	None
Otis-Lennon School Ability Tests	.84–.92[b]
Peabody Individual Achievement Test	.42–.94[b]
Peabody Picture Vocabulary Test–Revised	.73–.91[b]

(continued)

Table **5.3** (*cont.*)

Pictorial Test of Intelligence	.87–.93[a]
Preschool Inventory–Revised	.84–.93[c]
Purdue Perceptual-Motor Survey	None
Quick Test	.60–.96[d]
Short Form Test of Academic Aptitude	.82–.94[b]
Silent Reading Diagnostic Tests	.85–.97[c]
Slosson Intelligence Test	.97[b]
SRA Achievement Series	.54–.94[a]
Stanford Achievement Test	.65–.97[a]
Stanford Binet Intelligence Scale	None
Stanford Diagnostic Mathematics Test	.84–.97[a]
Stanford Diagnostic Reading Test	.75–.94[c]
Test of Auditory Comprehension of Language	None
Tests of Basic Experiences	.64–.78[b]
Tests of Written Language	.62–.96[b]
Tests of Written Spelling	.78–.96[a]
Vineland Social Maturity Scale	.57–.98[b]
Wechsler Intelligence Scale for Children–Revised	
Verbal	.91–.96[c]
Performance	.89–.91[c]
Full Scale	.95–.96[c]
Subtests	.62–.92[c]
Wechsler Adult Intelligence Scale	
Verbal	.96[c]
Performance	.93–.94[c]
Full Scale	.97[c]
Subtests	.60–.96[c]
Wechsler Preschool and Primary	
Verbal	.93–.95[c]
Performance	.91–.95[c]
Full Scale	.96–.97[c]
Subtests	.62–.91[c]
Woodcock-Johnson Psycho-Educational Battery	
Subtests	.46–.97[c]
Clusters	.67–.98[c]
Woodcock Reading Mastery Test	.02–.99[c]

[a]Internal consistency   [d]Alternate form
[b]Test-retest   [c]Interrater
[c]Split-half

Table **5.4**   Tests Having Questionable Validity

Bender Visual Motor Gestalt Test
Developmental Test of Visual-Motor Integration*
Developmental Test of Visual Perception
Durrell Analysis of Reading Difficulty*
Full-Range Picture Vocabulary Test*
Gates-McKillop Reading Diagnostic Tests*
Gilmore Oral Reading Test*
Gray Oral Reading Test*
Henmon-Nelson Tests of Mental Ability
Illinois Test of Psycholinguistic Abilities
Northwestern Syntax Screening Test
Purdue Perceptual-Motor Survey
Stanford-Binet Intelligence Scale*
System of Multicultural Pluralistic Assessment
Wide Range Achievement Test

*No validity data are included in the manuals for these tests.

SOURCE: Reprinted with permission from J. Salvia & J. E. Ysseldyke, *Assessment in special and remedial education* (2nd ed.). Boston: Houghton Mifflin, 1981, p. 538.

TEAM DECISION MAKING

Assessment and decision making in school settings are supposed to be done by multidisciplinary teams, a requirement specified in Public Law 94–142. This requirement was written into the law in order to limit unilateral decision making and the making of important decisions by individuals. Team decision making, however, does raise questions: Just what is it that the teams are supposed to accomplish? Who, among the many possible professionals in school buildings, should be included in the team and participate in the team decision making? Given that certain individuals must participate in team meetings, what does participation mean? Is mere presence at a meeting evidence of participation? What kinds of data are typically presented at team meetings? Who, specifically, makes the decisions? These issues have been the subjects of recent research, and this research has raised many new questions at the same time that it has analyzed the team decision-making process.

With our colleagues at the University of Minnesota's Institute for Research on Learning Disabilities, we have been using several different methods to investigate issues in the placement team's decision-making

Table **5.5**   Composition of Multidisciplinary Teams Responsible for Making
Screening, Placement, and Instructional Planning Decisions: Percentages of
Directors of Special Education Listing Each Team Member ($n = 97$)

	TYPE OF DECISION		
TEAM MEMBER*	Screening	Placement	Instructional Planning
Parent	61%	91%	84%
School Administrator	72%	89%	55%
Special Education Teacher	48%	85%	89%
School Psychologist	64%	81%	48%
Regular Classroom Teacher	82%	78%	72%
Speech-Language-Audiology Specialist	69%	68%	51%
LD Specialist	47%	62%	68%
Educational Diagnostician	47%	62%	47%
Director of Special Education	38%	60%	38%
School Counselor	56%	58%	28%
Child	41%	39%	42%
Nurse	47%	38%	12%
Social Worker	29%	33%	14%
Physician	15%	20%	6%
Psychiatrist	8%	13%	6%
Paraprofessional Aide	9%	4%	16%
Physical Therapist	3%	3%	3%
Occupational Therapist	2%	2%	2%

*Only those members mentioned by more than 1 director are included here, and an additional 16 team members were identified only by 1 director.

process: we have sent questionnaires to a representative sample of directors of special education throughout the nation, videotaped more than 30 actual team meetings, and interviewed school building professionals after they participated in team meetings (Poland et al., in press). One hundred directors of special education were asked to describe the team decision-making process as it was carried out in their schools. Specifically, they were asked to identify the people who typically participate in team meetings, the major steps in the assessment and decision-making process, the factors thought to influence the process and its outcomes, and the problems experienced in the process.

Although team make-up was relatively consistent across school districts, there was much variation in the actual assessment and decision-making sequence. Professionals identified as participating in the process

Table **5.6**   Percentages of Directors of Special Education
Mentioning 13 Steps of the Assessment–Decision-Making
Process

STEP	PERCENTAGE
Child found or referred	96.9
Review of referral	31.7
Appoint assessment team	11.3
Obtain parental permission to assess	46.4
Assessment	97.9
Review of assessment results	20.6
Eligibility determination	18.6
Contact parent after assessment	12.4
Develop IEP	77.3
Placement decision	35.1
Parental permission for placement	27.8
Develop strategies to implement IEP	4.1
Implement program	62.9

differed according to the decision that the team had to make. Table 5.5
lists the professionals who were said to participate in the various kinds of
team meetings.

Screening decisions were made most often by teams composed of regular classroom teachers, school administrators, speech-language-audiology
specialists, school psychologists, and parents. Placement decisions, on the
other hand, most often were made by teams composed of parents, school
administrators, special education teachers, school psychologists, and regular education teachers. Special education teachers, parents, and regular
education teachers most often sat on the teams that made instructional
planning decisions.

There was much variation in the steps identified by the directors of special education as characteristic of the decision-making process in their
schools. Table 5.6 is a list of these steps and the percentage of directors
who identified each. Of special interest is the fact that parental permission
was obtained to assess students in only 46 percent of the decisions.

The videotape studies of each placement team's decision-making process provided especially enlightening information. It was very difficult to
find meetings that could be called placement decision-making sessions.
Many team meetings were held, but most can be described as meetings to
get ready for the meetings to get ready for the meeting. Often, placement

decisions were made at the same meetings at which many other kinds of decisions were made. We repeatedly had difficulty attempting to specify decisions that were actually made at meetings because in most instances it was apparent that the decisions were made before the actual meetings took place. We also had difficulty getting individuals to assume responsibility for the decisions that were made. When we asked people after the meetings, "Who actually made the decision," nearly all claimed that someone else had been responsible for it and that they, personally, had had little power in the process. We learned to refer to this finding as the "Little Red Hen" phenomenon. (When we asked who made decisions, we consistently were told, "Not I!")

Ysseldyke, Algozzine, and Allen (in press) evaluated the participation of regular education teachers in placement team meetings. They found that although teachers were present at the meetings, they participated (presented data, asked and answered questions) very little. Regular education teachers reported general dissatisfaction with the process and stated that their views of individual children were not changed by the meetings. Ysseldyke, Algozzine, Richey, and Graden (in press), investigating the relationship between the data presented at the team meetings and the decisions reached by the teams, found very little congruence. Hence they questioned the extent to which the collected assessment data were actually used in the decisions that were made.

After Ysseldyke, Algozzine, and Mitchell (in press) evaluated the videotapes of 32 placement team meetings and determined how many characteristics of effective meetings were in evidence, they reported that the team meetings tended to be unstructured, nongoal oriented, and limited in the extent to which all individuals actually participated in the decision making. Ysseldyke, Algozzine, Rostollan, and Shinn (in press) evaluated the same 32 placement team tapes for the specific discussions of the meetings. They found (1) that about twice as much time was spent discussing academic data, as opposed to behavioral data; and (2) that when assessment data were discussed, the discussions focused on classroom data and on performance on intelligence and achievement tests.

The issue can be simply stated: Do team meetings make a difference? Are decisions regarding students better when they are made by teams of educators, rather than by individuals? We think that the research evidence to date indicates serious problems in the team decision-making process.

DIAGNOSING INSTRUCTION

The dominant theme in assessment today, as we have noted throughout this chapter, is to assess what is wrong with students. Reynolds (1975b) addressed this issue as follows:

The dominance of the prediction orientation in measurement can no longer be supported because while decisions based on it may be beneficial for institutions, too frequently they are painful for those individuals who are rejected and misleading for other individuals. In a school system that purports to serve all children, such efforts are intolerable. . . . We are in a zero demission era; consequently, schools require a decision orientation other than simple prediction; they need one that is oriented to individual rather than institutional payoff. In today's context, the measurement technologies ought to become integral parts of instruction, designed to make a *difference in* the lives of children and not just a *prediction about* their lives. (p. 15)

The issue is also addressed by Hunt (1975) who states that:

Psychological assessment should guide teaching. It should tell a teacher what kinds of assignments and curricular materials a given child can utilize profitably to foster his psychological development and pick up the knowledge and skills which he must acquire in order to adapt to his culture. The form of psychological assessment now most prevalent in education fails utterly to do this. (p. 545)

Engleman, Granzin, and Severson (1979) described an approach to assessment that focuses on the diagnosis of instruction: "Traditional diagnostic approaches usually occur outside the instructional context and focus on the learner. Accurate conclusions about the learner, however, can only be reached after an adequate diagnosis of instruction" (p. 355). In instructional diagnosis the focus is on both determining the extent to which the learner's failure is caused by inadequate or inappropriate instruction and on devising strategies or techniques that teachers can use to remedy academic and social problems. Assessment assumes different forms when it is addressed from this perspective. Instructional diagnosis has been described elsewhere as task analysis (Ysseldyke & Salvia, 1974), precision teaching (Kunzelmann et al., 1970), and direct instruction (see Chapter 6).

ASSESSMENT GUIDELINES

Obviously, many of the critical issues in special and remedial education are related to assessment. The reason is the challenges to how screening, placement, evaluation, and instructional intervention decisions regarding students are made. The data used to make these decisions are derived from assessment, and the substantive issue in many court cases relevant to special education has been abuse in assessment (see Chapter 8). Repeated judicial decisions have led legislators to pass major special education legislation that has included numerous mandates which, in many instances, are simply impossible to comply with.

Assessment is also controversial because the change in its practice is occurring so rapidly. Given current legislation, educators must lay bare, as never before, their assessment and decision-making practices and must put themselves up for public scrutiny for both what they do and do not do. Yet, appropriate assessment is not a "pie-in-the-sky" ideal but is possible. We offer some guidelines for improving assessment practice and addressing the issues raised in this chapter:

The first action to take when a student is referred for psychoeducational evaluation is twofold: (1) Clarify the nature of the problem for which the student has been referred, and (2) articulate the decision that must be made. Problem clarification sometimes may be difficult, but without it appropriate assessment is not possible. Not infrequently, one observes situations in which students are referred for problems, for example, in "attending" behavior. The assessor gathers data on attending behavior and institutes an intervention that results in increased attention; only then does the referring agent tell the assessor that the real problem was the student's frequent spelling errors. If the nature of the problem for which the student is being referred is not clearly established, new problems can keep coming up. It is necessary to establish specifically, on referral, the decision that must be made because assessment strategies, including the tests selected for use, should differ according to the decision to be made.

When one clearly understands the specific reason for referral and the decision to be made, the next question is still not "What test should I use?" but "What behaviors do I want to sample?" Any test is a sample of behavior, and tests or subtests should be selected to sample behavior.

In selecting a test or subtest to administer, an assessor must ask repeatedly whether the behavior assessed by the test is relevant to the presenting problem and the decision to be made. Too many assessors engage in "knee-jerk" assessment; they administer the same tests or subtests without carefully considering either the decision that must be made or the kind(s) of behavior(s) that the tests sample. In addition, the assessor must evaluate the assessment devices for their technical adequacy. We emphasized (see section, "The Use of Technically Inadequate Tests"), that much contemporary assessment practice consists of administering technically inadequate tests to students and then making decisions regarding those students on the basis of their test performances. There are technically adequate tests that can be used to gather data for decision-making purposes, and there are tests that are based on appropriate norms and that have the necessary reliability and validity (see Salvia & Ysseldyke, 1981): these tests should be used to gather information for decision-making purposes. It is incumbent on the personnel who assess students to use the technically adequate tests and to refuse to use technically inadequate devices.

Improved assessment practices should lead to better decision making for handicapped or potentially handicapped students. Better decision making should result in a better press for assessment practices and in fewer challenges by parents. Only by improving assessment practice can we take assessment out of the judicial system and keep it in the educational process where it belongs and where it may be used to improve what happens to students.

Chapter 6

Issues in Intervention

Despite considerable disagreement over what it is that should be taught in schools, there is a national consensus that the primary function of schools is to teach students. Thus, educators develop curricula with the general goal of educating all students to their maximum potential, and the curricula, typically, are designed to meet the assumed capabilities of the majority of students. Because schools are organized according to the students' age-grade, a general core curriculum is made up for each grade. It is the responsibility of the school personnel to adapt these core curricula according to the appropriate emphases for all or select groups of students. If these students fail to profit from the core curricula developed for their ages and grades, they are given special or remedial programs or interventions. The critical issues in special and remedial interventions are reviewed in this chapter.

Most special and remedial interventions are developed to accommodate learners' individual differences, that is, the differences in the extent to which they profit from instruction. Educators usually have assumed that individual differences in rates of learning or in the extent to which students profit from instruction are due to individual differences in learning ability. Ysseldyke and Salvia (1980) noted:

Observed differences in achievement are characteristically attributed to differences in learning ability. The notion of learning ability, as conceptualized within the framework of modern learning theory, is abstracted or inferred from observations of performance in learning situations. (p. 3)

They also quoted Estes (1970), who attributed differences in learning rate to differences in learning ability:

Substantial individual differences with respect to any measure of speed of learning are universally observed when a group of individuals, however similar on any selection criteria the experimenter may use, are run through an identical experimental routine. And this is true whether the situation be as simple as classical conditioning or as complex as classroom learning. If the individuals are well matched with regard to whatever previous experience is relevant to the particular task, then these differences in observed rates of learning are attributed to differences in learning ability. (p. 4)

In early American educational history (see Chapter 2), a dual-track system compensated for individual differences in learning ability: a student either received and profited from instruction in lock-step graded classes or was educated in a special school or class. To tailor instruction to the learner's needs, educators placed them in homogeneous groups, assuming that those with similar characteristics should be taught using the same instructional methods or techniques. Special education classrooms were self-contained. Classes of deaf, blind, and mentally retarded students (defined on the basis of performance on standardized tests) were established according to the considerable research on the learning characteristics of these children. More recently, students have been grouped categorically, both in response to pressure from parents and advocacy groups and because we do not have a knowledge base derived from research on the students' characteristics and how to teach them (Hallahan & Cruickshank, 1973).

In the late 1950s and early 1960s there were many serious challenges to educators on the efficacy of self-contained special classrooms for handicapped students. It was demonstrated over and over that students who received special education services did not improve academically and socially over those handicapped peers who were kept in regular classrooms and not offered special educational interventions. Although early efficacy studies were plagued with methodological problems (for example, failing to demonstrate that the groups were comparable), they did cause educators to question the efficacy of self-contained programs for handicapped students.

At the same time that educators were questioning the benefits of special education and, especially, of self-contained classrooms, they recognized that there were as many variations within categories of students as among them. This recognition returned the focus of education to individual differences rather than to categories, and instruction was tailored to the learner's own needs.

Special and remedial education have evolved to the point that today educators speak of "continua of placements" and of a "variety of alternative placements and services" in a continuum from regular class placement with tutorial or resource teacher assistance to isolation from the regular classroom program. Deno (1970) pictured the continuum of placements as in Figure 6.1. Reynolds (1978) elaborated and refined the cascade model, developing a triangular conception with regular class placement as the base (see Figure 6.2). Reynolds considered abnormal anything other than regular class placement. In Deno's conception, students with special needs are sifted out of the regular classroom to settle downward in a variety of increasingly restrictive environments. In Reynolds's triangular conception, students are seen as moving individually and deliberately up from regular classroom placement, with the goal of returning as soon as possible to regular classroom placement. Reynolds's triangular conception goes beyond the "places" where instruction occurs to consider how instructional services are delivered.

Public Law 94–142, the Education for All Handicapped Children Act of 1975, specifies that all handicapped students have the right to a free, appropriate public education to meet their particular needs. Simply placing students in classes or programs for the handicapped is not enough; schools must ensure that the instruction delivered is appropriate to the

Figure **6.1**   Cascade Model of Special Education Service

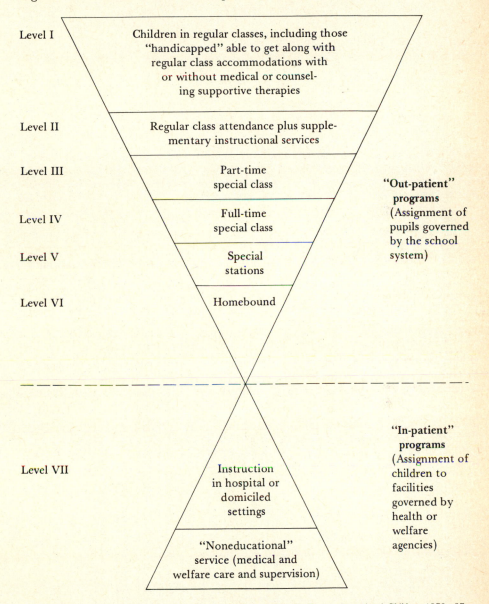

Level I — Children in regular classes, including those "handicapped" able to get along with regular class accommodations with or without medical or counseling supportive therapies

Level II — Regular class attendance plus supplementary instructional services

Level III — Part-time special class

Level IV — Full-time special class

Level V — Special stations

Level VI — Homebound

"Out-patient" programs (Assignment of pupils governed by the school system)

Level VII — Instruction in hospital or domiciled settings

"Noneducational" service (medical and welfare care and supervision)

"In-patient" programs (Assignment of children to facilities governed by health or welfare agencies)

SOURCE: From Special education as developmental capital by E. Deno, *Exceptional Children,* 1970, *37,* 229–237. Copyright 1970 by The Council for Exceptional Children. Reprinted with permission.

Figure **6.2** Reynolds's Triangular Conceptualization of Instructional Alternatives

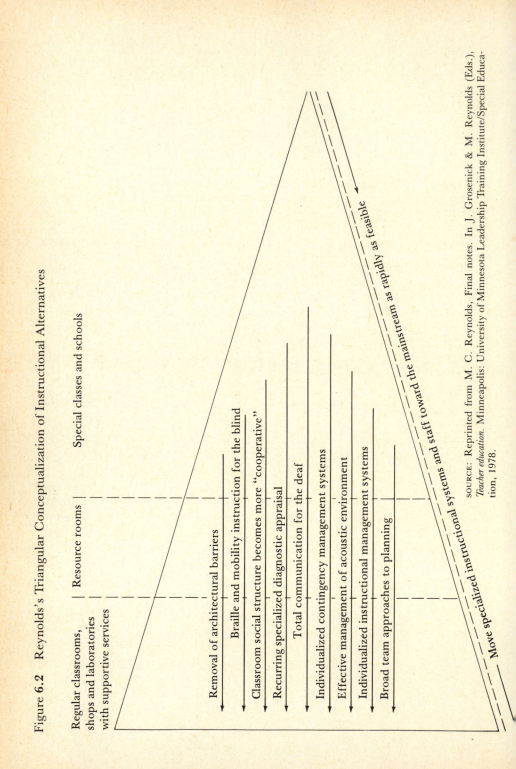

SOURCE: Reprinted from M. C. Reynolds, Final notes. In J. Grosenick & M. Reynolds (Eds.), *Teacher education*. Minneapolis: University of Minnesota Leadership Training Institute/Special Education, 1978.

needs of each learner. Thus, in examining the issues in intervention, it is necessary to look beyond placements and to scrutinize the instructional treatments that are or can be delivered. In order to match instruction to the learners' needs, schools have adopted a variety of assessment-intervention approaches.

DERIVATION OF INTERVENTIONS

Any discussion of the critical issues in intervention should start by analyzing the assumptions underlying intervention and the many different ways in which educators conceptualize the purposes of intervention. Cromwell, Blashfield, and Strauss (1975) described assessment and intervention as parts of an ongoing process. They identified four categories of diagnostic and intervention data and labeled them A, B, C, and D. Category A consists of historical and/or etiological information, the precursors of currently observed behavior or characteristics (for example, phenylketonuria as a precursor of mental retardation). Category B is made up of data on currently assessable pupil characteristics (for example, "intelligence" or skill in adding single-digit numbers). Category C refers to specific treatments or interventions (or levels of treatment or interventions), and category D refers to the particular outcomes that result from particular interventions. By using the categories A, B, C, and D, the interrelations of historical-etiological information, currently assessable pupil characteristics, specific kinds of interventions, and the outcomes of those interventions can be examined. The several kinds of assessement-intervention paradigms propsed by Cromwell, Blashfield, and Strauss (1975) are sketched in Table 6.1

This conceptualization of assessment-intervention programs is useful for two reasons: (1) it helps us to describe the current interventions used in special and remedial intervention, and (2) it helps us to differentiate between valid and invalid assessment-intervention approaches. According to Cromwell and his colleagues (1975), assessment-intervention approaches that include both C and D data (ACD, BCD, CD, and ABCD) are valid because they include treatments on the basis of known outcomes. Three approaches do not pertain to interventions (AD, BD, and ABD) and are not useful in helping us to establish a science of instruction. Four approaches (AB, AC, BC, and ABC) have little value for the educator because they describe relationships among historical-etiological data, pupil characteristics, and treatments, but pay no attention to the outcomes of differential treatment. Many instructional interventions — AC, BC, and ABC — now used in schools are invalid, assigning students to interventions or treatments with no evidence of their effectiveness or outcomes.

Table **6.1**   ABCD Assessment-Intervention Paradigms

LABEL	NATURE OF PARADIGM
AB	Describes relation between historical events or etiologies and current pupil characteristics or behaviors without considering treatment or its outcomes.
AC	Describes relation between historical events or etiologies and particular treatments or interventions without considering pupil characteristics or treatment outcomes.
AD	Links generalized outcomes to etiology without considering differences among pupils or treatments.
ABC	Plans interventions for students according to their history-etiology and current characteristics without evidence of the effectiveness of the outcomes.
ABCD	The complete assessment-intervention paradigm: treatments with known outcomes or effects are prescribed according to etiology and current pupil characteristics.
BC	Assigns pupils to treatments according to their current characteristics without evidence regarding known outcomes of the treatment.
BCD	Assigns pupils to interventions with known outcomes on the basis of their current characteristics without considering the etiology or historical development of their conditions.
CD	Describes relationships between treatments and outcomes without considering etiology or current characteristics.
BD	Investigates relationships between student characteristics and instructional outcomes without considering the etiology of the characteristics or the differences in treatment programs.

SOURCE: Adapted from R. L. Cromwell, R. K. Blashfield, & J. S. Strauss, Criteria for classification systems. In N. Hobbs (Ed.), *Issues in the classification of children.* San Francisco: Jossey-Bass, 1975.

Mercer and Ysseldyke (1977) described five models used by educators in developing interventions: medical, social system (deviance), psychoeducational process, task analysis, and pluralistic. These models are helpful in considering the kinds of instructional interventions employed in schools, and they are outlined in Table 6.2.

Each of the five models has a different definition of abnormality, or perception of deviance, from "normal" behavior. In the medical and psychoeducational process models, disorders are traced to pupil disease or dysfunction. Normality is defined as the absence of disease or dysfunc-

Table 6.2   Outline of Different Assessment Models

ELEMENTS OF THE MODELS	MEDICAL MODEL	SOCIAL SYSTEM (DEVIANCE) MODEL	PSYCHOEDUCATIONAL PROCESS MODEL	TASK ANALYSIS MODEL	PLURALISTIC MODEL
Definition of abnormal	Presence of biological symptoms of pathology.	Behavior that violates social expectations for specific role.	Psychoeducational process and/or ability deficits.	No formal definition of normal or abnormal. Each child is treated relative to himself and not in reference to a norm.	Poor performance when sociocultural bias controlled.
Assumptions	Symptoms caused by biological condition. Sociocultural background not relevant to diagnosis and treatment.	Multiple definitions of normal are role and system specific. Biological causation not assumed.	Academic difficulties are caused by underlying process and/or ability deficits. Children demonstrate ability strengths and weaknesses. Processes or abilities can be reliably and validly assessed. There are links between children's performance on tests and the relative effectiveness of different instructional programs.	Academic performance is a function of an interaction between enabling behaviors and the characteristics of the task. Children demonstrate skill development strengths and weaknesses. There is no need to deal with presumed causes of academic difficulties. There are skill hierarchies; development of complex skills is dependent upon adequate development of lower-level enabling behaviors.	Learning potential similar in all racial-cultural groups. Tests measure learning and are culturally biased.
Nature of treatments or interventions	Treat biological organism. ABCD-type constructs.	Teach child socially expected behaviors. BCD- and BD-type constructs.	Compensatory or remedial ability training. BD-type constructs.	Test-teach-test. Teach enabling behaviors. BC(D)-type constructs.	Nonspecific estimate of performance level. ABD- and BD-type constructs.

SOURCE: Reprinted with permission from J. Mercer & J. E. Ysseldyke, Designing diagnostic-intervention programs. In T. Oakland (Ed.), *Psychological and educational assessment of minority children.* New York: Brunner/Mazel, 1977.

tion, and abnormality is defined as the presence of pathology or process-ability deficits. In the other three models, abnormality is traced to environmental (including school) influences on the student. In the social system model, abnormal behavior is perceived as behavior that deviates from society's expectations. In the task analysis model, normal or abnormal behavior is not defined but is viewed as normal or abnormal only in accordance with the context in which it occurs. In the task analysis model, "abnormality is the sort of deviance that calls for and sanctions the professional attention of psychiatrists, clinical psychologists, and other 'mental health' professionals" (Ullmann & Krasner, 1969, p. 1).

The models for or perspectives on intervention programs differ in their assumptions of what causes difficulty and, thus, lead to the design of different kinds of interventions. The medical model views symptoms, difficulties, or problems as originating in the individual's biological condition. In the psychoeducational process model, difficulties are seen as the direct result of underlying process dysfunctions. In the social system model, it is assumed that normality and abnormality are role and system specific, and in the task-analysis model academic performance is viewed as the function of an interaction between the particular set of background experiences an individual brings to the learning setting and the demands of the tasks he or she is asked to perform.

These models lead to different interventions. Proponents of the medical model design interventions to treat the biological organism. When disorders cannot be treated by medical (pharmacological or surgical) intervention, educational programs are designed to compensate for or to bypass them. Those who support the social system model and who believe that specific behaviors are abnormal only in that they deviate from role or system expectations, design treatments to teach students socially expected behaviors. Advocates of the psychoeducational process model design interventions to remediate or compensate for underlying causes (process dysfunctions) of behavior. Treatment consists of ability training. The task-analysis model emphasizes teaching enabling skills, subskills necessary to perform more complex behavior.

Quay's formulations (1973) (see Chapter 2) also are useful in conceptualizing interventions. He believes that the particular interventions one chooses to apply usually accord with one's view of the causes of exceptionality, and he identified four views: process dysfunction, experiential defect, experiential deficit, and interactive.

The perspectives or models of the assessment-intervention process formulated by Cromwell and his colleagues, Mercer and Ysseldyke, and Quay have much in common, and all can be used to analyze the assessment-intervention process and to understand better the kinds of interventions used in schools.

FACTORS THAT INFLUENCE
INTERVENTION DECISIONS

In this section we describe how decisions to use specific interventions with students are made. Educators decide to use certain interventions because they believe that they will improve the students' academic and/or social functioning. No food and drug administration controls the use of interventions: any intervention can be used by anyone, and interventions are selected and used because of a "bandwagon effect," blind faith, or research findings.

BANDWAGON EFFECT

The bandwagon effect is probably more often the source of most special and remedial interventions than any other base.

The bandwagon effect, wherein an idea or a cause suddenly becomes popular and gains momentum rapidly, may not have been invented in this country, but we have surely perfected it. Our propensity for faddism extends from diets, fashions, and games to major political, educational, or sociological movements. We also tend frequently to be more concerned with the appearance of things than with the substance of things. This is the issue of form versus content. Thus, I wrote elsewhere, "we live in a society which tends to evaluate its devoutness by counting the number of people who go to church rather than the number of people who believe in God. We promote university professors on the basis of the number of publications they have authored, with little consideration for the quality of the contents. We evaluate the progressivism of a public school system by the number of new things it is doing, rather than concerning ourselves with whether it is doing any of them well" (Trachtman, Note 26). The form versus content issue interacts with the bandwagon effect to produce hastily conceived, poorly implemented innovations or programs, the failure to achieve anticipated goals, and consequent disillusionment with the original idea, or backlash. In turn, backlash may lead to equally precipitous abandonment of meritorious programs and ideas which have not been adequately conducted or sufficiently tried. This situation establishes a state of readiness for the next bandwagon and places us constantly at the mercy of what Hyman (1979, p. 1024) called the panacea mongers. (Trachtman, 1981, pp. 140–141)

Parents have been instrumental in encouraging, indeed, sometimes nearly forcing, educators to get on a variety of bandwagons. To strengthen the bandwagon, the parents form clubs or organizations to popularize, promote, and push specific treatments or interventions, and in the process of doing so they push educators to adopt the interventions. Educational fads come and go and usually are adopted with no regard for the empirical evidence of their effectiveness. Then each, in turn, is replaced by a new fad, equally untested.

TRADITION AND PRECEDENT

It is a cliché that the more things change, the more they stay the same. In special and remedial education, many practitioners choose to use specific interventions either because of tradition ("We've always done it this way") or because of history ("The treatment worked before"). Some educators employ the same intervention with all students who have academic and social problems simply because they have always used it, and others prescribe a program just because it once worked for another student.

CASH VALIDITY

Many educational interventions are adopted because they have "cash validity," that is, they sell well. Just as school systems use specific group tests because other school districts use them, interventions are selected because they sell well. This phenomenon is one way that bandwagons begin rolling.

Unfortunately, when there is little information on how to treat specific kinds of educational difficulties, and parents and teachers are looking for simple solutions to complex problems, the environment is ripe for someone to come up with a panacea. Thus, because their developers are looking for profits, many instructional interventions are developed and marketed with no evidence of their effectiveness. Lynn (1979) illustrated "cash validity" by using a statement attributed to one Mel Levine:

I would like to call Doubleday and have them come over here, tell them I'm a Harvard professor and that I've found out, from seeing lots and lots of patients, that air pollution causes learning disabilities and that I'd like to write a book about it. I could have that book done in a few months' time, full of anecdotal evidence about how it hits the kid nearest the city, or tell stories about a kid who lived near a factory and when he moved there his schoolwork got worse, and when he moved away it got better and how that got me thinking. . . .

This book would sell a million copies.

I would then go to Arthur D. Little, which is a consulting firm, to see what they could do about designing me a mask for kids to wear that will filter the air they breathe. Let them design that mask for me, put activated charcoal in the mask so they'll breathe pure air, and then sell these for $15.95 each—you can send away for them—to parents of LD children.

I'll say have them wear the mask at least eight hours a day; kids will go to school with their masks on. I'll have a following around the country—the

"Levine Dyslexia Society." It will be extraordinary, with parents who can provide abundant testimony as to how their child's whole life was changed when they started using the Levine method. I'll be famous; I'll get on the "Today" show with my mask; and I'll continue to make money because we'll patent it and sell replacement cartridges that you have to get for $6.95 every six months.

No problem. It will be antitechnological, which is in the spirit of the times; antiauthoritarian (it's those big boards of directors that are poisoning our kids' brains). . . . I'll guarantee you that my air pollution idea will come up within the next three or four years. (Lynn, 1979, pp. 116–117)

Interestingly, Levine may have shown considerable foresight, as we note that today residents of the Three Mile Island region in Pennsylvania are claiming that the recent leakage of the Three Mile Island nuclear power plant may be affecting the learning and behavior of youngsters in that region.

"DOCTOR TESTED"

A well-known remedy for hemorrhoids has been advertised as "doctor tested, found effective in many cases." Other medical products use slogans like "Four out of five doctors surveyed recommend. . . . " Such statements, of course, do not provide evidence of the effectiveness of a product but merely try to convince consumers that if a product is doctor tested and used or recommended by a physician, then it is something the consumer should buy. Educators have used many interventions simply because they were "doctor tested"; that is, their use was urged and no evidence for their effectiveness was provided.

JOINT DISSEMINATION REVIEW PANEL RECOMMENDATION

In all our years of reading the final reports of projects funded by the old U. S. Office of Education, we (the authors) never came across a project intervention that did not work. Investigators whose intervention studies are funded by the government somehow manage to present evidence that, they say, supports the effectiveness of their particular interventions. People just do not tell their sponsoring agencies that their funded programs were ineffective. How then does the consumer select, from all these "effective" interventions, those that actually have merit and ought to be adopted?

In the mid-1970s the U. S. Office of Education established a mechanism for reviewing educational interventions and identifying those that were worthy of dissemination. In the belief that the government should encourage schools to adopt only "validated" educational interventions, the Joint Dissemination Review Panel (JDRP) was formed. Educators who use specific interventions evaluate their effectiveness and submit their findings to the JDRP for review and endorsement. Only after JDRP endorsement are projects, programs, or interventions disseminated for adoption in new settings. The idea is a good one, but unfortunately, many inadequate and technically and methodologically unsound interventions have been validated and recommended for dissemination.

RESEARCH

We believe that the decisions to use particular interventions on students should be based on evidence that the intervention is effective. Unfortunately, there are few research findings to support specific interventions. Joyce and Weil (1972) stated:

There have been several hundred studies comparing one general teaching method to another, and the overwhelming portion of these studies, whether curriculums are compared, specific methods for teaching specific subjects are contrasted, or different approaches to counseling are analyzed, show few if any differences between approaches. Although the results are very difficult to interpret, the evidence to date gives no encouragement to those who would hope that we have identified a single, reliable, multipurpose strategy that we can use with confidence that it is the best approach. (p. 4)

Although we do not have evidence that specific curricula are universally effective, many data support the contention that interventions must be designed for the individual and monitored frequently to ensure their effectiveness. Intervention is equivalent to research and is a process of hypothesis testing:

At the present time we are unable to prescribe specific and effective changes in instruction for individual pupils with certainty. Therefore, changes in instructional programs which are arranged for an individual child can be treated only as hypotheses which must be empirically tested before a decision can be made on whether they are effective for that child. (Deno & Mirkin, 1977, p. 11)

FACTORS THAT INFLUENCE INTERVENTION EFFECTIVENESS

Educators spend considerable time trying to evaluate the effectiveness of alternative instructional interventions. The effectiveness of an intervention is typically evaluated according to two criteria: the payoff for the individual (the student is smarter, reads better, or is better behaved) and the payoff for the institution (things go more smoothly in classrooms; the school is able to account for the programs it uses with students).

At its simplest level, intervention effectiveness is evaluated by administering tests to students and seeing how much they gain from the interventions (see Chapter 5). Gain is usually expressed as progress (or loss) in achievement.

Samuels (1981) grouped a number of factors that influence learning under the headings of school, task, and student. Variables that the school controls are (1) underlying assumptions, (2) personnel, (3) training and supervision of personnel, (4) curriculum, (5) time, (6) structure, and (7) evaluation. Task variables are (1) content (decisions on what to teach), (2) sequence (decisions on when to teach), and (3) method (decisions on how to teach). Student variables are (1) prior knowledge, (2) special aptitudes, and (3) motivation (including alertness, attention, and persistence). From this perspective, intervention effectiveness is based on the interaction among the variables controlled by the schools, tasks, and students.

We believe that it is very difficult to know what instruction works, and we believe that, to date, educators' views of intervention effectiveness have been too simplistic. We see educators repeatedly trying to figure out what kinds of programs work with particular kinds of students. To try to do so, in our view, is too simplistic. We (Ysseldyke & Algozzine, 1979) believe that the effectiveness of an intervention is determined by at least five factors in complex interaction, which are: pupil characteristics, nature of treatment, teacher characteristics, setting variables, and the behavior one tries to change.

PUPIL CHARACTERISTICS

Like Samuels (1981), and nearly all educators, we believe that pupil characteristics influence the effectiveness of particular instructional interventions. A student's level of skill development affects both the access to and the outcomes of intervention. These characteristics determine whether the students are referred for psychoeducational interventions, and they usually must be referred before they can be given special placements and/ or treatments. Schools assume that students who are referred and subsequently placed in special settings do need help, and many research findings support the contention that the referral and the decision-making process are biased (Algozzine & Stoller, 1980; Algozzine et al., 1980; Richey et al., 1980; Ysseldyke, Algozzine, & Thurlow, 1980; Ysseldyke & Thurlow, 1980).

Students' characteristics also influence how much they profit from interventions. A student's sensory equipment (vision and hearing) affects the extent to which he or she profits from instruction. Similarly, the student's level of skill development (for example, few would expect a student who cannot add and subtract to profit from instruction in multiplication) and motivational characteristics (students must attend to instruction to profit from it; we do not believe in education by osmosis) also determine intervention effectiveness.

NATURE OF TREATMENT

What schools do with students affects what they learn, although perhaps to a lesser extent than we might imagine. Berman and McLaughlin (1978) found that the variance in instructional methods made less difference in their outcomes than might be expected. Instead, what seems to matter is how committed the teachers and administrators are to a program and how confident they are that it will work.

TEACHER CHARACTERISTICS

Teacher characteristics (training, teaching style, and personality) interact with both student characteristics and the nature of the treatment to influence intervention effectiveness. There are numerous examples in which treatment A worked with student Q when it was taught by teacher W but not by teacher M. Similarly, teacher tolerance of student differences affects the teacher's acceptance of a student with special needs.

SETTING VARIABLES

Setting variables, including general school climate and specific instructional arrangements, determine how well instructional programs work. Specific interventions may work in one school but not in another, in a resource room but not in a regular classroom, and so on. One factor contributing to this selective response is the adaptation of instructional programs. Berman and McLaughlin (1978) showed that when specific projects (for example, Title III interventions) are disseminated from one school district to another, the adopting school almost always modifies, adjusts, or changes the intervention to fit its own needs. Interventions are adapted to different settings, and thus their effectiveness is determined by the characteristics of the setting in which they are used.

THE BEHAVIOR ONE TRIES TO CHANGE

Learning is behavior change; and educators try either to increase or decrease certain behaviors. Some interventions work with specific students in specific settings with teacher X to bring about particular kinds of behavior changes; other kinds of behavior change require other variables.

Obviously, intervention is complex and is influenced by the complex interaction of many different variables. We think that one reason for our dismal track record in creating interventions that work in special and remedial education is that our efforts have been too simplistic in identifying effective programs. Given the interaction of all these complex factors at once, it is no wonder that educators are devoting so many resources to the problem.

TYPICAL SPECIAL AND REMEDIAL INTERVENTIONS

Despite these failures, schools have developed many different kinds of interventions to compensate for, or remediate, student-learning difficulties. Global interventions that range from exclusion and tracking to bilingual education were described in Chapter 2. In this section we describe in more detail the kinds of interventions that have been used with students.

NONSYSTEMATIC INTERVENTION

In many instances intervention is nonsystematic; that is, either all pupils get the same instruction, or the intervention is haphazard. Morse, Cutler, and Fink (1964) conducted an extensive survey of the teaching methods used with emotionally disturbed students. On the basis of their observations they labeled one approach "haphazard-chaotic"—all students were working on different tasks—but they could identify no basis for the assignment of the students to the tasks. The method had no underlying logic.

DIAGNOSTIC-PRESCRIPTIVE TEACHING

The dominant methodology in special and remedial intervention is diagnostic-prescriptive teaching, also called ability training (Ysseldyke & Salvia, 1974). This approach tries to identify strengths and weaknesses in the pupil and to design instructional programs based on the diagnosis. The model is rooted in the philosophy that academic and behavioral difficulties result from deficits, dysfunctions, or disabilities in the pupil and that it is necessary to remediate, or compensate for, these disorders before the pupils can be expected to profit from instruction. Educators long have recognized that different students learn differently, but it was not until the

1960s that major programs were initiated to teach handicapped students by means of specific methods and techniques based on their particular strengths and weaknesses. This movement characterized all of the special and remedial education in the 1960s and early 1970s, and it continues to affect intervention efforts today. The many examples of this method are described under the headings Optometric Vision Training, Visual-Perceptual Training, Auditory-Perceptual Training, Perceptual-Motor Training, and Neurological Organization.

Optometric Vision Training

There have been numerous proposals for and descriptions of optometric vision training in the professional literature on special and remedial education for almost two decades (Coleman & Dawson, 1969; Dilbard et al., 1972; Forrest, 1968; Getman, 1962, 1966a, 1966b, 1972; Getz, 1973; Gould, 1962; Greenspan, 1973; Halliwell & Solan, 1972; Kane, 1972; Kirshner, 1967; Mullins, 1969; Rosner, 1963; Sloat, 1971; Swanson, 1972; Swartwout, 1972; Tramonti, 1963). Keogh (1974) identified at least three groups of optometrists who were participating in optometric programs for learning-disabled students: (1) those concerned with acuity and conventional eye care, (2) those in orthoptic training (use of eye exercises to enhance vision or to remedy visual problems), and (3) those promoting programs of developmental vision training:

> Optometric vision training programs are based on assumptions that vision is learned; that vision has motoric and sensory motor bases; that problems in learning are due to disturbances of underlying functions in terms of visual efficiency and sensory motor organization; that vision and visual organization can be trained; and, importantly that visual training will affect educational performance. Developmental vision advocates rely directly upon the work of Gesell, Kephart, Barsch, Strauss, Doman, Delacato, and Renshaw. Leadership in the organized program of developmental vision training has come primarily from Getman, Skeffington, and Harmon. (Keogh, 1974, p. 220)

Keogh reviewed the research on the effectiveness of optometric training programs and reported that the research results were mixed. She observed that there is a problem in being unable to determine why optometric training succeeds or fails and in being unable to link student and program characteristics in producing or contributing to intervention outcomes.

Visual Perceptual Training

Especially during the 1960s, many schools instituted visual-perceptual training programs. Many students, particularly children of prekindergarten, kindergarten, and first-grade ages, were enrolled in programs designed to provide visual-perceptual training. The fundamental assumption underlying such treatments has been that visual-perceptual problems cause academic problems and that unless these visual-perceptual problems are remediated, the student will continue to have academic difficulties. The major proponents of this approach have been Arena (1969); Barsch (1965, 1967, 1968), Frostig and Horne (1964); and Johnson and Myklebust (1967).

Visual-perceptual training programs were developed after educators observed a connection between students' performances on measures of academic achievement and measures of visual perception. Larsen and Hammill (1975) reviewed more than 60 studies reporting over 600 correlations between performance on perceptual measures and achievement tests; but they reported no correlations above .35 and concluded that "the combined results of the correlational research treated in this paper suggest that measured visual-perceptual skills are not sufficiently related to academic achievement to be particularly useful" (pp. 287–288).

Educators have based many visual-perceptual training programs on the presumption that poor readers have more visual-perceptual problems than good readers do. Hammill, Larsen, Parker, Bagley, and Sanford (1974) examined this contention and reported that visual-perceptual measures did not discriminate between groups of readers.

During the early 1960s, educators enrolled large numbers of students in visual-perceptual training programs, some students on the basis of presumed deficits and others on the basis of demonstrated deficits (Ysseldyke, 1973). For example, many school systems simply assumed that disadvantaged students had visual-perceptual deficits (after all, they performed poorly in reading), and so they developed extensive programs to provide visual-perceptual training to all disadvantaged students (Alley et al., 1968). Other school systems set up massive screening programs designed not only to find those students who had visual-perceptual difficulties but also to specify the nature of those difficulties. Such efforts led directly to intensive remedial, or compensatory, programs intended to alleviate or ameliorate the underlying visual-perceptual disorder. One of the most common training programs was the Frostig-Horne Program for specific training in eye-hand coordination, spatial localization, position-in-space, figure-ground, and form constancy. Hammill and Wiederholt (1973) reviewed the research on the effectiveness of the Frostig-Horne Program and concluded that "the research indicates that the Frostig training program in perception has no effect on reading and has a questionable effect on school readiness and perception itself" (p. 44).

Mann (1970, 1971), Mann and Phillips (1967), and Ysseldyke (1973) criticized the logic of, and the theoretical assumptions underlying, training students in visual perception. They argued that the very basis for providing training in visual perception was questionable. To date, there has been no support for specific visual-perceptual training, although Arter and Jenkins (1977) reported that it is still popular in special and remedial education programs.

Auditory Perceptual Training

Special educators have regularly assigned students to special and remedial programs designed to provide auditory-perceptual training, assuming that many academic problems result from auditory-perceptual deficits, disorders, or disabilities. Sabatino (1973) stated, "Although very little is known about the diagnosis and remediation of auditory-perception problems, and no agreement exists as to what constitutes auditory perception, diagnostic instruments and ability-training programs are being developed" (p. 49). Auditory-perceptual training programs were developed after educators found high correlations between pupils' performances on reading achievement tests and measures of auditory perception (auditory discrimination, auditory sequential memory, and the like). Sabatino (1973), indicating the extensive product marketing that grew from this observation, identified 17 tests that specifically assessed auditory perceptual skills and 16 instructional programs that trained learners deficient in auditory-perceptual processing.

The research on how much the auditory-perceptual training helps students to profit from academic instruction has been generally depressing. Hammill and Larsen (1974) reviewed 33 studies in which performance on auditory-perceptual measures was correlated with performance on reading-ability measures. They reported that auditory-perceptual skills are not sufficiently related to reading to be particularly useful for school practice.

Perceptual-Motor Training

Based largely on the theoretical and practical formulations of Newell Kephart, educators have developed, and continue to use, interventions intended to remediate students' perceptual-motor disabilities. According to Kephart, it is logical to assume that all behavior is basically motor and that muscular and motor responses are the prerequisite for any more complex behavior. Based on his notion of the perceptual-motor match, Kephart (1971) devised an extensive perceptual-motor assessment and training program which emphasizes training in posture, balance, directionality, and body image. He designed a test, the Purdue Perceptual-Motor Survey, to assess balance and posture, body image and differentiation, perceptual-motor match, ocular control, and form perception.

Goodman and Hammill (1973) reviewed 42 interventions using the Kephart techniques. They concluded that 26 of the studies were not adequate to evaluate the effectiveness of the techniques. After reviewing the

16 remaining studies, the investigators concluded that the results of the training were, for the most part, insignificant.

Neurological Organization

Interventions based on the concept of remediating deficient or defective neurological organization were the direct result of the early work of Doman and Delacato. They believed that adequate neuropsychological development must precede the development of higher-order processes like language and reading and that the individual's development (ontogeny) goes through the same stages as the evolution of the species (phylogeny) does. Their belief was often paraphrased as "Ontogeny recapitulates phylogeny." When individuals have academic or behavior problems, it is recommended that their level of neurological organization be assessed. Handedness (hand dominance) and eyedness (eye dominance) are assessed to evaluate cerebral dominance. Those shown to be deficient are assigned to developmental interventions and are required to go through "patterning," an intervention in which their parents put them through a series of neuromuscular developmental activities, such as teaching them to crawl in specified ways. The assumption is that the brain, rather than the symptoms, is being treated.

The Doman-Delacato treatment programs became popular despite the absence of supportive empirical evidence, and thus in 1968, several professional associations banded together to take an official position on the approach. The American Academy for Cerebral Palsy, American Academy of Physical Medicine and Rehabilitation, American Congress of Rehabilitation Medicine, Canadian Association for Children with Learning Disabilities, Canadian Association for Retarded Children, Canadian Rehabilitation Council for the Disabled, and National Association for Retarded Children adopted an official statement criticizing the Doman-Delacato approach on the following grounds:

1. Promotional methods put parents in a position where they could not refuse treatment without calling into question their adequacy and motivation as parents.
2. The treatment regimens prescribed were so demanding and inflexible that they led to neglect of other family members' needs.
3. The approach asserted that anything less than 100 percent effort on the part of parents in carrying out the program would result in damage to the child's potential.
4. Though unwarranted by supportive data, restrictions were often placed on age-appropriate activities, such as walking or listening to music, of which the child was capable.
5. Claims made for "rapid and conclusive diagnosis" according to a "developmental profile" were of no known validity.

6. The program's undocumented claims for cures in a substantial number of cases, making normal children superior, easing world tensions, and hastening the evolutionary process.
7. Without supporting data Doman and Delacato indicated that many typical child-rearing practices limited a child's potential, thereby increasing the anxiety of already burdened and confused parents.
8. The theory supporting the program is based on questionable and oversimplified concepts of hemispheric dominance and relation of individual sequential development to phylogenesis.
9. Results of therapeutic interventions published by the Institutes for Achievement of Human Potential were inconclusive. There were no data available to contradict the likelihood that any improvement observed with this method of treatment could be accounted for on the basis of growth and development, intensive practice of isolated skills, or the non-specific effects of intensive stimulation. (Hallahan & Cruickshank, 1973)

After carefully evaluating the theory of neurological organization and the accompanying treatment program, Robbins and Glass (1969) concluded:

There is no empirical evidence to substantiate the value of either the theory or practice of neurological organization. . . . If the theory is to be taken seriously . . . its advocates are under an obligation to provide reasonable support for the tenets of the theory and a series of experimental investigations, consistent with scientific standards, which test the efficacy of the rationale. (p. 96)

Psycholinguistic Training

Special educators have developed elaborate diagnostic-prescriptive systems to diagnose and remediate psycholinguistic disorders in children. The approaches are based on the assumption that many academic problems are linked to psycholinguistic disorders.

In the early 1960s, Samuel Kirk and his colleagues at the University of Illinois developed the Illinois Test of Psycholinguistic Abilities, an instrument designed to diagnose students' psycholinguistic strengths and weaknesses. Subsequent to the development of the test, educators devised instructional interventions that could be used to train psycholinguistic abilities (for example, visual association, auditory sequential memory, grammatic closure, and manual expression). The test and the subsequent training program immediately gained widespread popularity in special education, and educators today continue to debate the efficacy of remedial psycholinguistic training.

Newcomer and Hammill (1975) reviewed 28 studies in which performance on the Illinois Test of Psycholinguistic Abilities (ITPA) was related to performance on measures of reading, spelling, and arithmetic achievement. They reported that 9 of the 12 ITPA subtests lacked validity for any aspect of achievement. They also reviewed 22 studies of the diagnostic validity of the ITPA, focusing on studies in which researchers, using the ITPA, attempted to differentiate among divergent groups of readers. Newcomer and Hammill reported that none of the ITPA subtests differentiated among groups of readers.

Hammill and Larsen (1974) reviewed 38 studies using psycholinguistic training based on the model of the ITPA and concluded that the effectiveness of psycholinguistic training had not been demonstrated. Minskoff (1975) and Lund, Foster, and McCall-Perez (1978) challenged the Larsen and Hammill analyses, arguing that most of the research on psycholinguistic training had been ineffectively designed to serve as an actual test of the model. The debate goes on: one group of educators argues that psycholinguistic training does no good, and another argues that the training is necessary and works and that studies to demonstrate its effectiveness are plagued by inadequate research design.

Summary

There have been many efforts to intervene in students' educational programs and to provide training programs to alleviate the underlying process or ability deficits supposedly causing the students' academic difficulties. To date, there is little empirical support for the contentions that (1) specific processes and/or abilities exist, (2) specific processes and/or ability deficits can be reliably and validly assessed, (3) specific processes and/or abilities can be trained, and (4) specific processes and/or abilities are relevant to instructional success (Ysseldyke, 1978). Yet as Arter and Jenkins (1979) reported, educators still are trained extensively in diagnostic-prescriptive teaching from an ability-training viewpoint; they are still taught that the majority of academic problems are caused by process-ability deficits; they still try to diagnose ability strengths and weaknesses; and they still believe in the efficacy of ability identification and ability training.

DIRECT INSTRUCTION

Direct instruction, an alternative to diagnostic-prescriptive teaching, differs markedly from the methods just discussed in its views of the causes of students' academic difficulties and its assumptions regarding the best ways to proceed in ameliorating or alleviating observed difficulties. This approach is based on the belief that exceptionality results from either experience deficits or an interaction between experience deficits and process dysfunctions. Although in interventions, it is recognized that some students may have biological or sensory dysfunctions, the emphasis is on addressing those aspects of instruction that a teacher can control. The focus of assessment is the student's skills rather than the causes of his or her academic difficulties. Assumptions regarding causality are viewed as irrelevant (Stephens et al., 1978). Thus, the academic and social environment in which the student is learning and his or her behavior are the most effective points of educational intervention: it is not necessary to look for internal conditions to treat (Tharp & Wetzel, 1969). Gardner (1977) labeled this the "behavioral" approach.

The behavioral approach does not attempt to "cure" the child since no assumption is made that there are some "central" or "core" etiologic factors which, if changed or eliminated, would reciprocally alleviate a range of symptomatic learning and behavior difficulties. Rather, a direct attempt is made to change those learning, behavioral, and environmental features involved in, and which comprise, the child's difficulties. The behavioral position, as noted, assumes that all consistent learning and behavior characteristics of children, appropriate and inappropriate, are the end results (symptoms, if you wish) of a history of experiences and of a contemporary set of conditions as these have and do interact with specific physical and psychological characteristics. (p. 186)

Direct approaches to intervention are characterized by a focus on the "development of appropriate behaviors and not on behavioral deficits, inadequacies, disabilities, shortcomings, or difficulties" (Gardner, 1977, p. 193).

Rosenshine (1976) identified several variables associated with student achievement and labeled a set of these as direct instruction. He reported that the approach was marked by (1) spending time on reading and math, instead of on other activities or the students' concerns; (2) spending time in supervised groups, as opposed to students working alone; (3) drill, consisting of frequent, low-level questions followed by teacher feedback; and (4) instruction composed of small steps appropriate to the students' performance levels. Carnine (1979) gave the following description of a direct instruction approach:

The University of Oregon's Direct Instruction Program assumes that a major determinant in a child's cognitive and affective development is the quality of the interaction between the learner and the environment. The programme carefully structures this interaction to maximize learner growth. The programme is characterized by increased teaching time (through the addition of paraprofessionals, small-group instruction, and scheduling more time for instruction), carefully designing curricula, various direct instruction teaching techniques (pacing, corrections, cues for participation, and reinforcement), quality control procedures (periodic criterion-referenced testing, monitoring of child progress, and preservice and inservice teacher-training and supervision), and active parent involvement. (pp. 29–30)

When the effectiveness of preschool programs was evaluated by Abt Associates, they reported that of all the various models followed in the programs, Direct Instruction resulted in superior gains for students in basic skills, cognitive skills, and affective development:

The data from the Abt study on the *Direct Instruction Model* suggest that significant improvement is possible in the education of children who are likely to fail in school. The design procedures indicate that an explicit technology is available for designing instructional programmes that contribute to child performance. These design procedures reflect an instructional and an activist orientation: instructional in that they have immediate implications for classroom behaviour in contrast to explanations that require interventions outside the classroom, such as eradicating poverty, providing counselling to the parents, repairing neuronal damage, etc. Although these factors undoubtedly influence child performance, they are not under the teacher's control; the selection of examples, teaching procedures, and the like are under the teacher's control.

The orientation is activist in that it suggests specific interventions to bring about change. Rather than waiting for a child who is not "ready" to learn to read, a *Direct Instruction* teacher would construct a reading operation, identify and sequence the modules and clusters, pretest the child on these, and begin instruction at the child's skill level. Similarly, a *Direct Instruction* teacher would not delay instruction in the use of rules because a child's performance was not at the appropriate Piagetian developmental level. An assessment would be made and appropriate instruction would be provided. (Carnine, 1979, p. 44)

Ysseldyke and Mirkin (1981) and Ysseldyke and Shinn (1981) reviewed the published research on both the diagnostic-prescriptive and the direct instruction approaches and concluded that there is little support for the diagnostic-prescriptive approaches but that instruction based on direct instruction, for the most part, is successful.

CHARACTERISTICS OF EFFECTIVE INTERVENTIONS

It has been very difficult to identify known practices that we can say with assurance will work with students. One reason is the obvious fact that intervention effectiveness depends on the complex interaction of numerous variables, only a few of which are under the control of the teacher. For this reason, education is necessarily experimental: educators must form hypotheses for what will work with students, must teach in accordance with those hypotheses, and then must continually evaluate the effectiveness of their interventions.

Research data on the characteristics of effective reading programs help us to identify and understand those factors that interact to determine the effectiveness of any instructional intervention. Samuels (1981) conducted an extensive review of the characteristics of successful reading programs. After examining six major studies of exemplary reading programs, he described the characteristics of successful and unsuccessful programs. Contrary to what one might expect, the difference was greater in administrative arrangements than in curricular methodology. The following discussion draws heavily on Samuels's findings:

Successful and unsuccessful reading programs differ in their underlying assumptions. Successful programs, according to Samuels (1981), are based on two important assumptions: (1) that "the school *can* have a significant impact on the academic achievement of its students" and (2) that "most children are capable of mastering the basic skills" (p. 2). In both assumptions the school is seen as responsible; it is not absolved of the responsibility for failing to educate students. This is not the prevailing mood of the day. In Chapter 2 we described a 1979 survey by the National Education Association, in which 92 percent of the classroom teachers attributed student academic problems to home and family problems or to deficits within the students.

A second set of characteristics shared by successful reading programs is what Samuels labeled personnel characteristics. Successful programs had strong administrative leaders who provided "time for planning and carrying out decisions, securing financial support, and running interference against counterforces" (p. 4). They also employed teacher aides in direct instruction and reading specialists who worked with teachers and aides to assist them in planning instruction. According to Samuels, the teacher's attitude was critical to success. He found that successful programs were consistently staffed by teachers who, because they were committed, dedicated, and supportive of project goals, devoted considerable time and energy to achieving project goals. They were teachers who believed that student success and failure depended on what happened in the classroom.

Further, according to Samuels, successful reading programs were characterized by practical training and supervision in which regular staff meetings focused on actual problems. In successful programs teachers were given the opportunity to observe and model other successful teachers and programs, and furthermore, they participated in decision making.

Samuels reported that successful reading programs have clearly stated and specific goals and objectives and that the most successful programs use a task-analysis (direct instruction) approach as well as creating a warm, friendly classroom atmosphere. These programs emphasized teaching skills, gave students opportunities to practice those skills, and used instruction and instructional materials relevant to the attainment of the objectives.

Successful programs were those that provided ample time for instruction and in which time was used efficiently. Instruction was kept at a low level of complexity. Classes were fairly structured. Teachers frequently and directly measured their pupils' progress (Samuels, 1981).

Unsuccessful instructional programs were, according to Samuels, programs based on what Trachtman (1981) labeled the bandwagon syndrome. The programs were developed more in response to the availability of federal funding or to parental pressure than to demonstrated need. They lacked systemwide commitment, either because they were based on "bottom-up" motivation (the teachers were committed to the program, but the administrators were not) or "top-down" motivation (the administrators required programs to which the teachers were not committed).

Samuels felt that unsuccessful programs consistently failed to allow enough start-up and development time, had narrow, piecemeal approaches, and used time inefficiently (Samuels, 1981).

Educators have spent an incredible amount of time and effort in (1) creating models of intervention or of the assessment-intervention process, (2) trying to relate assessment results to intervention effectiveness, and (3) presuming that academic difficulties are caused by process dysfunctions that must be remediated or compensated for. They have spent comparatively little time actually teaching and making formative and summative evaluations to identify the parameters of effective intervention.

Chapter 7

Issues in Research

NOTES FROM AN EARLY DUTCH RESEARCHER

The following notes were found in the archives of an early Dutch investigator:

Experiment 1812
Purpose. Determine the effects of appendage removal on jumping ability of a frog.

178

Apparatus. A two-foot by eight-inch board was used, and a three-foot yard-stick was placed perpendicular to the board.

Method. 1. The frog was removed from the cage and placed on the board immediately in front of the yardstick.
   2. Experimenter shouted, "Jump," and released frog.
   3. Distance of frog's horizontal movement (i.e., "jump") was measured.

Phase 1. Baseline data were collected until stability of response was observed. For seven baseline *jumping trials,* each preceded by the loud shout, "Jump," three-to four-inch horizontal movements (i.e., "jumps") were recorded.

Conclusion. This frog can "jump" three to four inches on command.

Phase 2. The right foreleg of the frog was surgically removed. Experimental *jumping trials* were followed by two- to three-inch "jumps."

Conclusion. Removing one foreleg of a frog does not significantly affect jumping ability.

Phase 3. The left foreleg of the frog was surgically removed. Experimental jumping trials were followed by three- to four-inch "jumps."

Conclusion. Removing the two front legs of a frog does not significantly affect jumping ability.

Phase 4. The right backleg of the frog was surgically removed. Experimental jumping trials were followed by two- to three-inch "jumps."

Conclusion. Removing three legs of a frog does not significantly affect jumping ability.

Phase 5. The left back leg of the frog was surgically removed. Experimental jumping trials were *not* followed by "jumps."

Conclusion. Removing the four legs of a frog causes it to go deaf.

This early researcher may have jumped to the wrong conclusion in the analysis of his data. Unfortunately, the history of research in special and remedial education is characterized by too many similar leaps. We agree with an analysis of the research on teacher preparation offered by Sarason, Davidson, and Blatt (1962): they observed that "there have been too many studies in which the initial hypotheses and the final conclusions bear little or no relationship to the data collected" (pp. 15–16). Yet, the issues raised by research in special and remedial education go far beyond the relatively simple problem of drawing inappropriate conclusions from one's data. In this chapter we examine these issues and give special attention to the kinds of research attempted, how the research is conducted, and what to look for in deciding whether the research is "decent" (that is, whether the problem studied is significant, the methodology is adequate to answer the questions asked, sufficient data are collected, data are appropriately analyzed and interpreted, conclusions are appropriately drawn from the data, and so on). Research contributes to our knowledge base of a discipline in all its ramifications. Indeed, many of the issues (for example, assessment, personnel preparation, and intervention) discussed throughout this book often are the subjects of research.

BACKGROUND AND PERSPECTIVE

The process of research in education, as in any field, can be defined as asking questions, collecting answers, and drawing conclusions from the answers that represent new knowledge. Prehm (1976) took a relatively narrow view of research when he suggested:

[Research is] an intellectual enterprise, a process whereby objective answers are obtained to specific questions. The overall objective of research is the identification of unequivocal relationships between variables, and through repeated demonstrations of these unequivocal relationships, a research finding achieves the status of a fact. Through the application of the research process, the researcher attempts to understand and explain relationships between variables. The emphasis on answering questions and on understanding relationships makes research intellectual in character. (p. 11)

What Prehm described is a laboratory model of research in which it is possible to manipulate variables endlessly to create relationships. But researchers do more than identify unequivocal relationships; they point out, compare, and/or experimentally predict the way things are, or may become, in the environment being studied.

TYPES OF RESEARCH

Research is founded on the desire to answer questions by means of information about some aspect of the world that is of interest to the researcher. Turney and Robb (1971) see research as an extension of one's system of thought, and they identified three kinds of research:

Historical research allows us to determine what has led to existing circumstances and prepares the way for *descriptive research,* which makes it possible to determine what actually exists now. This knowledge prepares us for *experimental research,* based on past and present conditions, which enables us at least partially to predict and control our future existence. (p. 59)

Other theorists have offered similar descriptions (cf. Fox, 1969). We believe that all research is descriptive by nature and that the focus of the description distinguishes the type of research. Sometimes researchers wish to describe the "state of the art", the differences or similarities among groups or individuals, or the relations that will enable them to make predictions. Thus, the conclusions drawn from research are illustrative, comparative, and/or predictive, and the research is labeled as such.

ILLUSTRATIVE RESEARCH

When questions about the state of the art are addressed, the research is illustrative. The investigator tries to represent the subject under study as accurately as possible. The subject(s) for illustrative research may be the literature on a topic of interest, one person or a group, a school, a program, or a theory. The certification requirements in various states, characteristics of specific kinds of students (for example, mentally retarded), or the publishing policies of special education journals are examples of factual information isolated by illustrative research.

COMPARATIVE RESEARCH

Besides finding out (that is, illustrating or representing) the status quo in an area of interest, researchers are often interested in systematically describing differences between or among persons (or groups of persons), places, or things: such descriptions are comparative. In comparative descriptive research, information about selected aspects of a topic is collected, recorded, analyzed, and evaluated, and conclusions of a comparative nature are drawn. Investigations of the relative achievement of boys and girls in resource rooms, of differences in reading performance among children of various intellectual levels, and of successful and unsuccessful teachers' scores on a teaching exam are examples of comparative descriptive research.

PREDICTIVE RESEARCH

In explaining the ways of the world, researchers often are interested in predicting the nature of relations among topics, subjects, and/or areas of interest. There are two kinds of predictions, relational and experimental. Studies of relational predictions identify the simultaneous occurrences of selected variables. Research on the relations between intelligence test scores and achievement test scores or relations among various measures of psycholinguistic abilities are examples of relational predictive research.

We also are interested in experimental predictions; that is, how well we can selectively predict the change in a variable (for example, an improvement in performance) by systematically controlling the presence or absence of certain conditions. Studies of how various types of reading programs affect differences in reading achievement or how differing amounts of study time influence test performance are examples of experimental predictive research. Examples of illustrative, comparative, and predictive research are listed in Table 7.1.

The body of knowledge in any field of study is related to the amount and kind of research conducted. Our current compilation of educational

Table **7.1**   Sample Topics for Different Types of Research

TYPE OF RESEARCH	POSSIBLE TOPICS
1. Illustrative	1. Nature of teachers' activities during the school day. 2. Publishing practices of a special education journal. 3. Topics of illustrative research. 4. Number of children enrolled in special education in each state.
2. Comparative	1. Differences in rates of rejection for APA and AERA journals. 2. Differences in performance scores of boys and girls. 3. Differences in behavioral characteristics of ED, LD, and EMR children. 4. Differences in reading rates for children in three reading groups.
3. Predictive a. Relational	1. Extent that IQ and achievement are related. 2. Predictors of school failure. 3. Relationship between teaching behaviors and student success. 4. Predictors of success in graduate school.
b. Experimental	1. Effects of two reading programs. 2. Effects of study time on test performance. 3. Extent that different teaching styles can influence student behavior. 4. Extent that faculty productivity can be altered by reward system.

facts today was drawn from systematic illustrative, comparative, and predictive research. At the same time, however, our lack of factual information on certain educational problems reveals the absence of some types of research relating to important questions. For example, we do not have a detailed knowledge of what teachers do because we have not done illustrative research in that area; we do not know the differences in productivity of "good" and "poor" researchers because we have not done the necessary comparative research; and we do not know whether learning to read by means of formal instruction is quantitatively and qualitatively different from learning to read without such instruction because we have avoided, or found it difficult, to do the relevant experimental, predictive research.

When students, professors, and other professionals decide to carry out research, a common question is, "What is good research?" Clearly, the answer is not related to the kind of research being considered, as any and all research of the different types described will answer questions. And although the issue of the "goodness" of research is important, we believe that the "what" and "how" of research contain more provocative issues. The researcher, young or old, novice or experienced, is constantly faced with problems of what to study and how to study it.

FACTORS INFLUENCING DECISIONS TO CONDUCT RESEARCH ON SPECIFIC TOPICS

The purpose of research is to advance knowledge, and thus, it suggests the continuous breaking of new ground. Unfortunately, not all research is so directed: some areas are ploughed over and over, and others are ignored completely. The reason, often, is that many decisions on what to study and how to study it are made in regard to who is paying for the research and what conditions must be met in order to qualify for the support.

BASIC VERSUS APPLIED RESEARCH

A distinction is often made between basic and applied research. Travers (1964) suggested the following difference:

Basic research is designed to add an organized body of scientific knowledge and does not necessarily produce results of immediate practical usage. Applied research is undertaken to solve an immediate practical problem and the goal of adding to scientific knowledge is secondary. (p. 4)

Kerlinger (1977), on the other hand, pointed out that the purpose of any research is to explain theory which may or may not be relevant to practice. In other words, research may be basic (that is, simply hypothesizing relations or events) or applied (that is, simply solving practical problems or events). The concern of basic researchers with theory is evidenced in such statements as the following:

The basic purpose of scientific research is theory. . . . Theory is held in high esteem by behavioral scientists—and rightly so. The high esteem springs from science's basic purpose, and theory is the vehicle for expressing the basic purpose. Science, then, really has no other purpose than theory, or understanding and explanation. (Kerlinger, 1977, p. 5)

If basic research is considered to be science, then its domain of study and modus operandi is theory.

The concern of applied researchers for theory is clear in the articles published in the various journals of applied studies that one can find in university libraries. Sometimes it is stated explicitly in the instructions to authors. For example, the editor of the *Journal of Applied Physics* (1977, No. 11) notes that manuscripts are welcome that describe "significant new experimental or theoretical results in applied physics . . . ;" and the goals of the *Journal of Applied Behavior Science* (1977, No. 4) include: "To develop or test theoretical and conceptual approaches to planned change that have both predictive and explanatory power and clear implications for further actions." (Shaver, 1979, p. 4)

Successful research only confirms or rejects a hypothesis (theory), and its implications for application may or may not be indicated. Research findings may or may not translate to real-life solutions to problems. According to Kerlinger (1977):

Most people assume that educational research can solve educational problems and improve educational practices. The assumption is false. And it creates expectations that cannot be fulfilled. Educational research does not lead directly to improvement of educational practice. The solution of a research problem is on a different level of discourse than the solution of an action problem. (p. 6)

Kerlinger, of course, is biased toward experimental predictive research. We agree with his position, but we would argue that it is limited: the solution of illustrative and comparative research problems, which are basic or applied by nature, also may not lead to changes in educational practice. For example, determining the factor structure of a mentally retarded individual's intelligence test performance or how various instructional arrangements are used to educate special children may or may not improve practice. Yet if such problems are studied in an appropriate, scientific manner, theory may be advanced.

POTENTIAL PRACTICAL PAYOFF

Educational personnel (for example, teachers and principals) often are convinced that research outcomes are of little value: for example, "It's too theoretical, too general!'' or ''What does it say that helps my situation?'' (Schubert, 1980). Jackson and Kieslar (1977) pointed out:

There is no army of educational practitioners expectantly waiting to hear what the fundamental researchers have to say, nor is there a corresponding group of researchers. The truth is that most practitioners do not turn directly to researchers for advice, nor do most researchers offer it. The two groups talk more among themselves than they do to each other—and so they should if they are to do justice to their respective tasks. (p. 13)

An example of the extent of the gap between the products of research and the needs and beliefs of practitioners was given by Arter and Jenkins (1977). They reviewed the research on the effectiveness of teaching using students' demonstrated modality preferences (for example, teaching auditory learners auditorily and visual learners visually) and concluded that there was no empirical support for differentiating instruction on the basis of modality preferences. But, when Arter and Jenkins surveyed teachers, they found that most teachers believed it was important to differentiate instruction according to modality preferences and that they felt there was much research supporting their belief. Arter and Jenkins offered several reasons for this outcome. Regardless of the explanations, the fact that teachers report beliefs and practices counter to those supported by much of the literature is provocative.

Traditionally, the solution to the research-practice gap has been to recommend more applied research. When this strategy fails to yield significant improvements and the pendulum swings too far toward applied research, the researchers go back to emphasizing basic research in the belief that successful practice is grounded in theory. Sax (1968) explained this perspective:

Basic research has too often been neglected and overlooked by those intent upon improving educational practice. . . . Unless there is a background of theory and empirical research to back up some proposed educational innovation, it may be necessary to evaluate every whim and fad in the public schools to see if they will work.
    Unfortunately this is exactly what has happened in education. (p. 33)

We believe that the basic-versus-applied research argument is fruitless in regard to educational practice. Like questions about how effective psycholinguistic training is or the effects of violations of homogeneous variance assumptions on statistical tests, addressing the question of whether research should be basic or applied has little chance of improving educational practice. In fact, there may be a need to reconceptualize research or to develop practical research.

To be useful, research must address real problems. But under the present system, the research that is conducted depends largely on the organizations that fund it and the panels that review research proposals. If either fails to recognize the importance of practical (n.b., not applied) problems, then practical research is neither conducted nor encouraged.

When engaging in practical, action research, special and remedial educators take their leads from educational practitioners and work in situation-specific settings. Traditional concerns with generalizability may be unnecessary, but the principles of scientific rigor in inquiry (for example, design, methodology, analysis) still must be followed. In considering this redirection, the question of who takes the lead in research becomes important because the extent of the redirection may be based on the answer to this question.

THE PEOPLE WHO DO THE RESEARCH

In 1976, the National Institute of Education (NIE) funded the American Registry of Research and Research-related Organizations in Education (ARROE). The participants in this massive illustrative research project "sought to determine how many organizations were doing educational research and related work, the nature of the institutions in which these organizations were located, the staffs they employed, the money they spent, and the topics they dealt with" (Sharp & Frankel, 1979, p. 6). To be included in this study, the activities of research (R), development (D), and evaluation (E) organizations had to be "systematic and designed to establish new facts or principles (research); to invent new or improve existing solutions to educational problems (development); to assess the effects of existing programs or determine the feasibility of new ones (evaluation); or to disseminate R & D results" (Sharp & Frankel, 1979, p. 7). Over 6,000 organizations were identified as eligible for inclusion, and based on these general criteria, data were collected from 2,434.

The distribution of research organizations according to the sectors in which their work is done is presented in Table 7.2; relative percentages of the total active organizations ($n = 2,434$) in the ARROE project (Sharp & Frankel, 1979) are also indicated. Of more interest is the distribution of money and personnel among these organizations:

—51% of the funds and 58% of the staff are located in the academic sector;
—33% of the funds and 27% of the staff are in the private sector; and
—16% of the funds and 15% of the staff are in the public education sector. . . .
80% of all funds were spent by 20% of all organizations. However, there are very few giants in this universe: only two public agencies, 13 universities, and 10 private sector organizations reported 1977 expenditures in excess of $5 mil-

Table **7.2**   Active Educational Research Organization Data 1976–1977

SECTOR	NUMBER OF ORGANIZATIONS
Public education (state and intermediate education agencies and local education agencies whose enrollment is 10,000 or greater)	688 (28%)
Academic (subdivisions of public and private two-year and four-year colleges and universities)	1268 (52%)
Private (all other organizations, especially profit and nonprofit research and development organizations, but also hospitals, publishers, foundations, associations, and so forth)	478 (20%)

SOURCE: Data and definitions are adapted from L. M. Sharp & J. Frankel, Organizations that perform educational R & D: A first look at the universe. *Educational Researcher,* 1979, *8,* 6–11.

lion. Defining "major performers" more modestly as those with expenditures in excess of $1 million during fiscal year 1977, we found a total of 172 such organizations; most of these "major performers" are in the academic (53%) or private (34%) sectors. These major performers accounted for nearly 70% of all reported expenditures. (pp. 8–9)

In regard to the focus of activities in these research organizations, Sharp and Frankel reported that "practically all organizations spend at least some of their funds for research, but research is emphasized most heavily in the academic and private sectors, while development and evaluation studies dominate in public education agencies" (p. 9). Thus, although it can be argued that locally based practical research is a possible attractive alternative to traditional basic and applied theoretical research, the likelihood of its taking the lead in educational research activities without support from the academic and private sectors is small. Pancrazio (1978) discussed five ways in which research-oriented interactions between state and university researchers could be organized to facilitate cooperation; but Sharp and Frankel concluded, "It is clear from our findings that, in the aggregate, state, intermediate, and local education agencies have made meager allocations for research and research-related activities, and that relatively little truly locally anchored work is being carried out" (p. 10).

THE AGENCIES AND PEOPLE WHO FUND RESEARCH

Prior to the 1950s most of the money spent in educational research was related to test development and construction. The educational research and development community was very small, and a $50 grant to do research under the auspices of a university research and development council was a "big event" (Shutz, 1979). Big-time, organized educational research originated in 1957 with passage of the Cooperative Research Act, the first law to authorize federal funds for research related to the education of handicapped children (Prehm, 1976). Shutz (1979) explained, "The public force for this initiative was neither the general education community nor researchers. It was the special education interest group operating in conjunction with a handful of deans of Colleges of Education" (p. 7).

The first congressional appropriation of approximately $667,000 in 1957 (that is, half the total) was designated for research with mentally retarded children. But according to Mueller (1976), "There was a steady decline in the proportion of education research funds focused on needs of handicapped children" (p. 151). "The second major federal breakthrough came in 1963 with Public Law 88–164. This law authorized funds for research and demonstration projects related to the education of all categories of handicapped children" (Prehm, 1976, p. 14). The mid-1960s marked the beginning of a major era in general education research as well (Shutz, 1979). Appropriations for research programs in special education increased steadily from 1964 to 1971 and leveled off somewhat at that point. Data on funding compiled by Mueller (1981) are presented in Table 7.3.

The budget for fiscal year 1981 for the Department of Education was $15.5 billion, of which over $200 million was requested for "research, development, dissemination, evaluation, policy study and statistics, of which $163 million is targeted for R & D activities" (Florio, 1980). It is apparent that research and development activities are accepted by the federal government as critical to the improvement of public school education. The primary federal agency supporting research in special education was the Bureau of Education for the Handicapped (BEH), established in November 1966 with the enactment of Public Law 89–750 (Burke, 1976; Mueller, 1976; Prehm, 1976) and absorbed into the Office of Special Education and Rehabilitative Services (OSERS) in 1980 when the Department of Education was organized.

In fiscal year 1975, BEH awarded approximately $11 million for educational research relating to handicapped children. Glickman (1975) showed a breakdown of these funds based on types of handicaps and BEH priorities, which is presented in Table 7.4. Citing Glickman's research, Prehm (1976) noted that:

Table **7.3**   Appropriations and Actual Obligations for Handicapped Research Funding

FISCAL YEAR	APPROPRIATIONS	NEW PROJECTS	OBLIGATIONS
1964	$ 1,000,000	34	999,739
1965	2,000,000	21	2,000,000
1966	6,000,000	92	5,994,231
1967	8,100,000	58	8,049,041
1968	11,100,000	65	10,794,113
1969	13,100,000	67	13,168,750
1970	13,785,000	27	13,881,536
1971	15,300,000	29	16,970,459
1972	11,105,000	23	8,380,595
1973	9,916,000	32	11,577,494
1974	9,916,000	50	10,878,210
1975	9,916,000	56	10,790,698
1976	16,535,897	95	16,368,642
1977	11,000,000	66	11,000,000
1978	11,345,000	55	11,288,720
1979	11,668,151	67	11,668,151
1980	11,767,912	67	11,767,912
1981[a]	10,000,000	55	10,000,000

[a] Data for 1981 are estimated.

SOURCE: M. Mueller, personal communication to J. Ysseldyke, June 22, 1981.

Approximately 47% was allocated to research in noncategorical areas of exceptionality, 25% in mental retardation, 8% in the visually handicapped, and another 8% in the hearing handicapped. The remaining 12% was distributed in the areas of the crippled and health imparied, learning disabled, emotionally disturbed, and the speech handicapped. Viewed topically by BEH priority areas, the distribution of funds was as follows: full school services (49%); child advocacy, career education, and personnel development (13% each); severely handicapped (7%); early childhood education (5%); and combined priority areas (1%). (p. 14)

The federal government does not simply give away money (see Chapter 1); yet "the funding of educational research has become almost entirely a federal responsibility" (Krathwohl, 1977, p. 11). The question of how an individual or organization can draw on federal dollars is obviously important to consider and may help to clarify the issue of what is studied in educational research.

Table 7.4 Distribution of 1975 Federal Handicapped Research Funding According to Handicaps and BEH Priorities

BEH PRIORITIES	TYPES OF HANDICAPS							TOTAL
	Crippled & Otherwise Health Impaired	Emotionally Disturbed	Hearing Handicapped	Mentally Retarded	Speech Handicapped	Visually Handicapped	Non-Categorical	
Combined objectives	0	0	0	0	0	0	(1)* 152,871	(1) 152,871
Early childhood education	(1) 108,228	0	(2) 142,901	(1) 54,548	0	(1) 37,475	(5) 167,360	(10) 510,512
Full school services	(3) 29,957	(1) 443,397	(4) 81,444	(14) 1,553,297	(2) 238,810	(7) 777,156	(15) 2,051,415	(46) 5,175,476
Child advocacy	(2) 299,000	0	0	(2) 187,439	0	0	(5) 913,742	(9) 1,400,181
Career education	0	0	(4) 580,432	(3) 409,989	0	0	(5) 362,527	(12) 1,352,948
Severely handicapped	(2) 45,309	0	0	(6) 492,094	0	(1) 51,480	(1) 182,686	(10) 771,569
Personnel development	0	(1) 39,090	0	(1) 9,560	(1) 32,839	0	(10) 1,345,652	(13) 1,427,141
TOTAL	(8) 482,494	(2) 482,487	(10) 804,777	(27) 2,706,927	(3) 271,649	(9) 866,111	(42) 5,176,253	(101) 10,790,698

*( ) number of grants.

SOURCE: L. J. Glickman, Research activities for handicapped children. *American Education*, 1975, *11*(8), 30–31.

According to Krathwohl (1977):

The first federal program in educational R & D, the Cooperative Research Program of the U. S. Office of Education, was operated as an unsolicited grants program: researchers proposed the problems on which they wished to work, and were judged by a panel composed primarily of their peers. Much criticism was directed at this effort because it came to be shaped largely by the content of the proposals submitted instead of being designed to reflect priority programmatic guidelines. The research that accrued under these conditions was fragmented and projects tended to be unrelated to each other. Matters important to practitioners, the really critical problems of education, too often received too little attention.

These problems of fragmentation and insufficient concentration of resources were central considerations in the development of the National Institute of Education which assumed prime federal responsibility for educational R & D. Consequently, very little, approximately three percent, of current NIE funding goes to support unsolicited proposals. An additional 15 percent supports proposals submitted in certain targeted areas, such as selected problems in teaching basic skills. And most funds are generally distributed for projects defined by NIE through requests for proposals (RFP's). This type of procurement allows the researcher to bid for the privilege of working on a predefined scope of work, where even the approach and many of the details have sometimes already been specified. This is quite a contrast to the freedom the researchers exercised under the Cooperative Program. (pp. 8–9)

The Office of Special Education and Rehabilitative Services currently offers both contracts and grants to those interested in conducting "research in education of the handicapped" through research projects and model programs. Of course, there are priorities in funding categories, and proposals are often solicited in specified areas.

Applications (that is, proposals) usually are submitted for more funds than are available; for example, a recent form letter of rejection stated, "Applications submitted under the Field Initiated Research Program far exceeded the funds available for new projects under this program. Requests were in excess of $34 million as compared to available funds of approximately $2.5 million." The approximately 7 percent of proposed projects are selected for funding by what is essentially a peer review. As the form letter of rejection indicated, "Evaluation of applications to this program includes review by Bureau staff and panels of non-Federal experts qualified to analyze applications for research in areas of education of the handicapped. All reviews were in accordance with criteria described in the program's regulations." The selection criteria for research projects are given in Table 7.5 and are clearly quite subjective (for example, 0 to 15 points for the "potential importance of the project to

Table **7.5**   Selection Criteria for Research Projects

(a) Plan of operation.
   (1) The Commissioner reviews each application for information that shows the quality of the plan of operation for the project.
   (2) The Commissioner looks for information that shows—
      (i)   High quality in the design of the project;
      (ii) An effective plan of management that insures proper and efficient administration of the project;
      (iii) A clear description of how the objectives of the project relate to the purpose of the program;
      (iv) The way the applicant plans to use its resources and personnel to achieve each objective; and
      (v)   A clear description of how the applicant will provide equal access and treatment for eligible project participants who are members of groups that have been traditionally underrepresented, such as—
            (A) Members of racial or ethnic minority groups;
            (B) Women;
            (C) Handicapped persons; and
            (D) The elderly. (10 points)
(b) Quality of key personnel.
   (1) The Commissioner reviews each application for information that shows the quality of the key personnel the applicant plans to use on the project.
   (2) The Commissioner looks for information that shows—
      (i)   The qualifications of the project director (if one is to be used);
      (ii) The qualifications of each of the other key personnel to be used in the project;
      (iii) The time that each person referred to in paragraphs (2) (i) and (ii) of this section plans to commit to the project; and
      (iv) The extent to which the applicant, as part of its nondiscriminatory employment practices, encourages applications for employment from persons who are members of groups that have been traditionally underrepresented such as—
            (A) Members of racial or ethnic minority groups;
            (B) Women;
            (C) Handicapped persons; and
            (D) The elderly.

Table **7.5**   *(cont.)*

---

(3) To determine the qualifications of a person, the Commissioner considers evidence of past experience and training, in fields related to the objectives of the project, as well as other information that the applicant provides. (10 points)

(c) Budget and cost effectiveness.

    (1) The Commissioner reviews each application for information that shows that the project has an adequate budget and is cost effective.

    (2) The Commissioner looks for information that shows—

        (i) The budget for the project is adequate to support the project activities; and

        (ii) Costs are reasonable in relation to the objectives of the project. (10 points)

(d) Evaluation plan.

    (1) The Commissioner reviews each application for information that shows the quality of the evaluation plan for the project.

    (2) The Commissioner looks for information that shows methods of evaluation that are appropriate for the project and, to the extent possible, are objective and produce data that are quantifiable. (5 points)

(e) Adequacy of resources.

    (1) The Commissioner reviews each application for information that shows that the applicant plans to devote adequate resources to the project.

    (2) The Commissioner looks for information that shows—

        (i) The facilities that the applicant plans to use are adequate; and

        (ii) The equipment and supplies that the applicant plans to use are adequate. (5 points)

(f) The potential importance of the project to the education of the handicapped. (15 points)

(g) The probable impact of proposed research and development products and the extent to which products can be expected to have a direct influence on the handicapped or personnel responsible for the education of the handicapped. (15 points)

(h) Technical soundness of the research and development plan and adequacy of specification of procedures. (30 points)

SOURCE: U.S. Office of Special Education and Rehabilitative Services, *Research in education of the handicapped: 1981 grant announcements.* Washington, D.C.: U.S. Office of Education, 1980.

the education of the handicapped," and 0 to 15 points for the "probable impact").

The federal agencies' method of making disbursement decisions has been criticized. Donaldson and Stephens (1979a) observed that individuals who "offer" to conduct projects for the federal government assume that the Citizen's Model, or the best offer, receives the reward. But they argued that a Federal Procurement Model may be the real reason that a project receives government support. And whereas the integrity of the competitive process is the foundation for offering to do research for the government, the actual awarding of contracts or grants may be made without regard to the decisions of merit made by the review-panel experts (Donaldson & Stevens, 1979a, 1979b, 1979c).

How well does this system of peer review and awards work? When asked about the impact of federal granting intervention on the field of learning disabilities, Cruickshank (1980) replied:

I'm going to be very blunt. I think that the impact has been modest. It has been modest because the people who have the decision making in this area are not as sophisticated as they ought to be. They reinforce the point of view of the parents; they are not specialists in the field of learning disabilities; they have not read the literature fully; and they are not sophisticated in the field of neurophysiology. The kinds of proposals that have been submitted by unprepared people have been read by unprepared people on review panels, and decisions that have not been satisfactory have been made. . . . The kind of research we're funding is "Mickey Mouse" research. (p. 16)

Scriven (1980), in his presidential address to the American Educational Research Association, characterized the process of peer review as a prominent "skeleton in the closet":

I suppose my favorite entry in the Skeleton Stakes would be the continued failure to look seriously at the peer review process both in proposal and in personnel evaluation. This is not specifically an educational research problem—it affects all researchers as well as teachers—but is the key process whereby educational research is funded and rewarded, and it is still done as a group version of personal opinion instead of the highly sophisticated management process that it should and can easily be. (p. 7)

Scriven also criticized education's accreditation practices. "So the way we fund research, and the way we dispense our *professional* training are both shoddy examples of professional practice by the standards of our own textbooks" (p. 8). He proposed that "self-referent" research be conducted: "No sound-minded manufacturer would research and develop a new product with the incompetence we show in researching and developing a credentialing or research-funding process. It is at the research on research, training of trainers or research on funding—the meta-level—level that we fail" (p. 8).

So far we have discussed the nature of research and the process of its control. We now shall examine those issues that arise when we analyze the design and conduct of research.

CONSIDERATIONS IN RESEARCH DESIGN

In his lead article for a symposium in the *Journal of Special Education,* Cohen (1976) alleged that research in some areas of special education is "suffocating in correlation coefficients between fuzzies" (p. 129):

These findings contribute little to man's basic knowledge or to his theoretical models. And they contribute even less to the repertoire of materials and techniques needed by teachers who face children every Monday morning. At best these kinds of studies fill journals, feed state certifications, institutionalize subprofessions, and generally throw up a smoke screen that blocks state legislators from seeing that their appropriations have created a monstrous professional empire whose direct effect on helping children to read and write is consonant neither with its size nor its political clout. (p. 135)

Most symposium participants agreed with Cohen's allegations that research is of limited value for the improvement of practice (e.g., Anderson, 1976; Elkins, 1976; Drozda, 1976; Keogh, 1976), but few agreed with his solution, that is, that more experimental research is needed. Keogh (1976) observed that "the history of science is testimony that methodology may (and probably must) vary according to the question or problem under consideration and that differing research methods may meet the scientific criterion of 'rigor'" (p. 137). In addressing the question of how to study educational problems, it may be helpful to examine some examples of research.

HOW WE DO RESEARCH

Researchers in education (general, special, and/or remedial) have available to them a diverse collection of methodological techniques. Walker (1956), reviewing the methods used in educational research, listed as options direct observation, interviews, historical, library, case study, statistical, measurement, experimental design, action, content analysis, factor analysis, opinion poll, and survey sampling.

Ward, Hall, and Schramm (1975) systematically reviewed the articles published during 1971 in order "to determine the quality of educational research articles published in educational journals and in journals of related professions" (p. 110). Before publication, each article had been reviewed (at least allegedly) by one or more peers to evaluate the merits of the work. Ward et al. found a number of deficiencies in the articles, especially in regard to procedures, data analysis, and summaries or conclusions. The major deficiencies were as follows:

1. The validity and reliability of evidence.
2. The appropriateness of data analysis methods.
3. The substantiation of conclusions from obtained data.
4. The clarity of presentation of results.

It is also interesting to note that although the entire sample (N = 121) of articles had been published and represented accepted manuscripts, "only 8% of the research articles were rated [by the reviewers as] acceptable as is for publication, 31% were rated acceptable after minor revisions, 34% were rated acceptable only after major revisions, and 27% were rated reject" (Ward et al., 1975, p. 118). A comparison of interjudge ratings for 43 of the articles yielded a correlation of only .21 relative to the overall decision about the acceptability of the work.

Given these findings, it is little wonder that professionals are skeptical about believing research results. Educational researchers assume that there is large audience "out in the field" just dying to learn of their most recent significant finding. Much of the published research does not reliably meet the commonly accepted standards for "good" research. Our colleagues in institutions of higher education may wish to quote the previous sentence in arguing either for or against the decision to promote and grant tenure on the basis of quantity rather than quality of research.

Torgesen and Dice (1980) evaluated the "characteristics of research on learning disabilities" presented in "eight major education-psychology journals" from 1976 to 1978. They analyzed 105 articles which met the following criteria:

1. Focused primarily on children identified as learning or reading disabled.
2. Reported empirical data.
3. Examined the effectiveness of a treatment procedure (nonmedical) or attempted to provide information about the psychological characteristics of learning disabled children.
4. Studies focusing primarily on "hyperactive" children were specifically excluded.
5. Studies primarily designed to validate an instrument, or to test the rela-

Table **7.6**   Methodological Practices Characteristic of Research on Learning
Disabilities

	YES %	NO %
1. Were any measures taken to reduce the heterogeneity of the learning disabled sample?	0	100
2. Were measures of dependent variables used for the first time in this study?	41	59
3. Did experimenters directly address questions about the validity of their measures?	18	82
4. Was this the second or more study in a series by the same author(s) on the same topic?	24	76
5. Did the study manipulate an experimental variable?	61	39
6. If a study manipulated an experimental variable, was a significant interaction of subjects X experimental condition reported?	62	38

SOURCE: J. K. Torgesen & C. Dice, Characteristics of research on learning disabilities. *Journal of Learning Disabilities,* 1980, *13*(9), 5–9. Reprinted by permission of The Professional Press, Inc., 101 East Ontario St., Chicago, Illinois 60611.

tionship between two instruments and which happened to use learning
disabled children, were not included. (p. 5)

Analysis of "methodological practices was limited to studies (88) which
attempted to assess the psychological characteristics of learning disabled
children" (p. 6). The results of that analysis are presented in Table 7.6.
For example, no one attempted to reduce the heterogeneity of the LD
sample; many people used experimenter-developed tests, but few experimenters addressed the validity of the measures they used. Torgesen's and
Dice's work (1980) indicates that there are "relatively serious deficiencies" in much of the sampled research on learning-disabled children;
however, "the proportion of all data based studies, which employ true
experimental designs, is relatively high" (p. 9).

HOW CAN WE DO RESEARCH?

When considering alternative ways of doing research, the unit of analysis
is a central concern. Judgments about the appropriateness of a unit of
analysis should be made according to how representative it is of the

descriptive information being collected, analyzed, discussed, and interpreted. The researcher conducting illustrative research on the nature of
teachers' activities during the school day should be concerned with questions of how representative the sample of teacher(s) is in accordance with
the activities and school day(s) under study. The comparative researcher
investigating differences in the rates of rejection for APA and AERA journals should be concerned with how representative are the samples of articles and the years of publication being reviewed. The predictive
researcher interested in demonstrating the relation between IQ and
achievement or the effects of two reading programs usually conducts
research on a selected sample of individuals and should consider how representative the relations observed are of the larger population of individuals to whom the findings are generalized. The question of representativeness is closely tied to the concern for generalizability that permeates most
elementary discussions of educational research (cf. Dominowski, 1980;
Ferguson, 1976; Fox, 1969; Kerlinger, 1973; Tuckman, 1978; Turney &
Robb, 1971). Tuckman (1978) explained:

Specifying the group that is to constitute the population is an early step in
the sampling process that affects the nature of the conclusions that may be
drawn from a study. If the population is broadly defined (like "all teachers" . . .), external validity or generalizability will be maximized, although
such a broad definition may make obtaining a representative sample difficult
and require a large sample size. Conversely, defining the population nar-
rowly (for example, as "female, elementary school teachers") may facilitate
the selection of a suitable sample but will restrict conclusions and generalizations to the specific population used, which may be inconsistent with the
intent of the study. (p. 227)

We believe that the group being studied may be a single subject, one
group of subjects, many groups of subjects, the administrative arrange-
ment(s) (for example, classroom[s] or school[s]), bodies of knowledge (for
example, literature or a topic), or any other unit of analysis that is appropriately representative of a global entity. We also believe that the quality
of research is not a function of the "number of subjects per cell" or the
nature of the research design. In fact, the critical issue in how we do our
research (once we have identified the research topic or question) is the
unit of analysis we select.

According to Hersen and Barlow (1976), the "between-subjects
group" design for conducting both basic and applied research is popular.
In this method, the unit of analysis is groups of people, places, or things.
Hersen and Barlow listed five "objections, which tend to limit the usefulness of a group comparison approach in applied research" (p. 14): ethical

objections, practical problems in data collection, averaging results, generality of findings, and intersubject variability concerns in the discussion of the results. To combat the problems associated with group methodology, Hersen and Barlow suggested using "single-case experimental designs," which they described in some detail. In their discussion of the limitations of such designs, Hersen and Barlow focused on questions of sound fundamental practices (that is, precise variable definitions, exact measurement). It is interesting that they gave the discussion of the limits of group designs twice as much space as they gave to the others.

Whether intentional or not, the literature on design appears to have an "either-or" orientation. Single-case methodology is examined using a variety of terms, such as case study, $n = 1$, time-series, intensive, single-subject, intrasubject, and operant designs (cf. Hersen & Barlow, 1976; Howe, 1974; Kazdin, 1977; Kratochwill, 1978; Lovitt, 1975; Sidman, 1960). The terms used for group designs also vary (cf. Hays, 1973; Kerlinger, 1973; Kirk, 1968; Tuckman, 1978; Winer, 1974).

Time-series designs have become prominent in educational research because they permit the recording of changes in subjects (persons or practices) over time. They are not necessarily the best designs in all cases, however.

In their discussion of "what time-series designs may have to offer educational researchers," Kratochwill and Levin (1978) concluded:

The educational researcher has a wide range of experimental procedures from which to choose. Because time-series designs can be employed in many applied situations where more stringent experimental methodology is either inappropriate or impractical, these designs have proliferated in recent years. It should *not* be assumed that their wide applicability to many applied situations makes them a more credible form of experimentation than more conventional multisubject designs. Although the aforementioned time-series designs can advance scientific understanding of psychological and educational phenomena, they typically represent weaker procedures than conventional multisubject designs where appropriate randomization procedures are employed. However, as noted earlier, some designs (e.g., ABAB) do allow a stronger case for experimental control than, for example, the basic design. When undertaking a research project, the investigator should first consider the "best possible" design, and *only after dismissing it on the grounds of implementation implausibility or impracticability* consider the "next best possible" design. (p. 318)

We believe that the issue of design appropriateness should pertain more to the unit of analysis of interest than to the question of convenience or artificial scientific righteousness. In considering whether there needed to be any disagreement between the proponents of single-subject and of group research, Algozzine (1980) concluded:

The process of scientific inquiry is founded on the "what'll happen if . . . " form. Some researchers choose to use the form by taking repeated observations from one subject and generalizing based on the similarity of the observations under various conditions. Others choose to take one observation from many subjects and base generalizations on that unit of analysis observed under different conditions. To state that one method is better than the other seems only possible when considering the unit of analysis and generalization as the criterion of importance. Whether this is a meaningful, important difference remains in question. (p. 25)

Certainly, the access to and availability of units of analysis influence research decisions. In 1976, Gene Glass discussed *primary, secondary,* and *meta-analysis* research: decisions to conduct one of the forms could be influenced by the availability of data. According to Glass:

Primary analysis is the original analysis of data in a research study. . . . *Secondary* analysis is the re-analysis of data for the purpose of answering the original research question with better statistical techniques, or answering new questions with old data . . . and *meta-analysis* is the analysis of analyses [or] the statistical analysis of a large collection of analysis results from individual studies for the purpose of integrating the findings. (p. 3)

Others have discussed the use and importance of research analyses other than the primary one (cf. Binkley, 1980; Burstein, 1978; Cook & Gruber, 1978; Gage, 1978; Ladas, 1980; Pillemer & Light, 1980). With regard to the reviews of the literature, Ladas (1980) found that their purpose was to identify flaws in previous work and recommend improvements, to draw conclusions for practice, or to establish a rigorous demeanor in other scientists' eyes (after all, critical analysis is a hallmark of real science).

Glass (1976) noted that meta-analysis "connotes a rigorous alternative to the casual, narrative discussions of research studies which typifies our attempts to make sense of the rapidly expanding research literature" (p. 3). He added, "Most research criticism I read—and some that I've written—is airy speculation, unbefitting an empirical science" (p. 4). Ladas (1980) asserted that the verdict of many summaries of methodological weaknesses and contradictory results in research has been that "little or nothing is known and more research is needed" (p. 597), and he proposed a "microanalytic" (case study) approach to "summarizing research." Again, single-subject and group approaches appear in discussions of contemporary practice and in presentations suggesting directions for change.

There are areas in educational research that have been abundantly studied, and new questions may be addressed without collecting new data. Glass (1976) observed that integrations of the research literature on reading are rare and suggested that research on the relationship of class size to achievement or the effects of programmed instruction are relevant areas for meta-analysis. Pflaum, Walberg, and Karegianes used Glass's (1978) quantitative techniques "to synthesize the literature on instructional methods in reading" (1980, p. 13). Hammill and McNutt (1981) examined the correlates of reading. The class size–achievement literature has also been analyzed (cf. Glass & Smith, 1979; Smith & Glass, 1980).

In deciding how to study the topics that interest them, researchers can use a variety of methods. Deciding which one to use may depend more on the availability of the unit of analysis than on any scientific basis for appropriateness. For example, a researcher interested in the effects of a reading program on student performance may decide to study one subject intensively or several subjects extensively depending on subject availability, cost, and the practical importance of generalization beyond the subject(s) studied.

WHAT DETERMINES HOW WE DO RESEARCH?

In 1975, Carolyn Davis commented on a possible deterrent to research with human subjects:

A recently enacted Federal law that has received little attention in the educational research community may have the effect of greatly diminishing the amount of research that can be conducted involving the use of data on school students.

It will certainly limit the amount and types of data available to researchers and the ease with which it may be obtained. (p. 11)

In 1976, Weinberger and Michael noted that "public attention is increasingly being directed to the individual citizen's right to privacy, the treatment of research participants, confidentiality, and 'sensitive' research areas" (p. 3). They observed that the major provisions of the Family Educational Right and Privacy Act of 1974 (commonly known as the Buckley amendment) include the following:

a. Parents have a *right to inspect and review* all official files, records and data relating to their children and to have a hearing to challenge the content of the records.
b. Data may not be made available in personally identifiable manner from school records in most cases unless there is *written consent* of the parents.

c. Personal information will only be transferred to a third party on the condition that such party does *not share personally identifiable information* with any
other party without written consent of the parents. (p. 3)

Weinberger and Michael (1976) also found some exceptions to the written-consent requirements; for example, direct information (student
name, age, address, birthplace, course of study, and the like) may be
released without written permission, although parents have the right to
withhold its release. Other exceptions to the written-consent requirements are as follows:

(1) school personnel with "legitimate educational interest";
(2) school personnel in other schools in which a student seeks to enroll;
(3) in connection with a student's application for, or receipt of, financial aid;
(4) state and local officials, as required by state stature;
(5) accrediting organizations;
(6) pursuant to a court subpoena;
(7) authorized representatives of the Secretary of HEW, the U. S. Commis-
    sioner of Education, the Assistant Secretary of Education (ASE), and the
    Director of the National Institute of Education (NIE), provided access to
    student records is in connection with the audit and evaluation of fed-
    erally supported education programs or in connection with the enforce-
    ment of the federal legal requirements which relate to such programs;
(8) organizations conducting studies for, or on behalf of, local and state edu-
    cational agencies or institutions for the purpose of developing, validat-
    ing, or administering predictive tests, administering student aid pro-
    grams, and improving instruction. (Weinberger & Michael, 1976, p. 4)

Michael's and Weinberger's (1977) discussion of the Protection of
Human Subjects regulations ranged from the past to the present times.
Carter (1977) found that "Government contractors collecting information in connection with work for a Federal agency are required to have the
study's instruments reviewed by the Office of Management and Budget
(OMB)" (p. 7). Of course, no one doing educational research would
argue with the need to protect an individual's rights to confidentiality and
safety, but the net effects of these federally mandated regulations may
have gone beyond the initial intentions of safeguarding participants in
research.

Davis (1975), Weinberger and Michael (1976), and Carter (1977)
addressed the potential for and the real problems in the conduct of educational research which are created by the protection of privacy, protection
of research participants, and forms clearance. They made the following
points in their discussions and commentaries:

1. There is the possibility that schools will change their record-keeping practices and thereby make some kinds of data totally unavailable.
2. The cost of research will increase because of safeguarding procedures.
3. Research, as traditionally conducted, will become administratively cumbersome, and researchers will find new methods for making decisions.
4. The effects of assurances of confidentiality on willingness to participate in research are unknown.
5. Procedural compliance can be time consuming, costly, and often unproductive.

Michael and Weinberger (1977) argued that the model safeguarding human subjects that was adopted and applied by biomedical researchers is largely unnecessary for educational research. They added that simply obtaining consent can present problems to researchers (that is, unobtrusive study becomes impossible, and surveys of national scope become impractical). We believe that these procedural guidelines have affected (and will continue to affect) how we do our research. Because the availability of large numbers of appropriately safeguarded subjects has become an administratively rare event, intensive designs have become more prevalent, and research on research (for example, meta-analysis, secondary analysis) offers an attractive, "never-leave-the-campus" alternative. For decades, researchers have gathered data on aspects of important educational problems. But researchers currently are studying the same problems by gathering new data over and over again. The data to answer many of the questions now being asked can be found in libraries or data banks; yet researchers continue to run multiple mini-experiments, each designed to rediscover the fact that "the sun comes up in the East" or that "cutting the legs off a frog causes the frog to go deaf." Whether such research is "good" or "practical" remains to be seen, but we shall discuss the issues relating to the judgment of goodness in the next section.

EVALUATING THE "GOODNESS" OF RESEARCH

When research is carried out, we never fail to find out something. It is sometimes apparent in the discussions of the goodness of our findings that we tend to equate statistical significance or scientific rigor with importance. In fact, the magnitude of most test statistics depends on the methodological variables (for example, sample size, group variability) as well as the treatment effect. Hopkins and Kretke (1976) demonstrated that the significance of research findings could be altered simply by adding variables to be studied, and they argued that the question of a minimum number of subjects per cell is largely academic. Jones (1974) noted that we can learn as much from studying treatments that fail as from studying those that succeed. Scriven (1980) suggested that negative results may be as illuminating as positive ones, and Shaver and Norton (1980) found that the scientific canons of random assignment and replication were not evident in the research reported in the *American Educational Research Journal* from 1968–1977. In addition, some researchers (for example, Charter & Jones, 1973; Leonard & Lowrey, 1979) cautioned against accepting statistically nonsignificant results as fact without verifying that the experiment really was carried out. Cohen (1976) asserted that often the statistical representation of results is a matter of ritualistic behavior; his rule 4 for good research states, "When variables are measured with original (new, researcher-designed) instruments that yield raw scores, displaying means is a ritual, since the means are, practically speaking, meaningless" (p. 134). Recall that 41 percent of the studies evaluated by Torgesen and Dice (1980) used first-time dependent measures (see Table 7.7). Obviously, the question of goodness needs to be addressed from the standpoint of something other than what is done.

GUIDELINES FOR READING RESEARCH REPORTS

Lehmann and Mehrens (1971) urged consumers of research to be critical interpreters and evaluators. They argued that reports should be checked out as rigorously as planes are before they are flown; that readers of research should question (or challenge) "the assumptions made (or question those not made), the significance of the problem, the appropriateness of the hypotheses tested, the method of gathering the data, the reliability and the validity of the instruments used, the appropriateness of the analytical tools, the representativeness and adequacy of the sample, the conclusions drawn and the implications made" (p. 10); and they presented a check list for evaluating research articles (Table 7.7). However, their discussion of the "points to ponder when reading research" is quite general.

Tuckman (1978) took the "process of analyzing and critiquing a research study" and broke it down into the following ten steps:

1. Problem statement
2. Variables
3. Hypotheses
4. Supportive Material
5. Operational definitions
6. Measurement and manipulation of independent and dependent variables

Table **7.7**   Check List for Evaluating Research Articles

1. Is the problem clearly stated?
2. Does the problem have a theoretical rationale?
3. How significant is the problem?
4. Is there a review of literature? If so, is it relevant?
5. How clearly are hypotheses stated?
6. Are operational definitions provided?
7. Is the procedure (or method) used to attack and answer the problem fully and completely described? Was a sample used? If so, how was it selected?
8. Are there probable sources of error that might influence the results of the study? If so, how have they been controlled?
9. Were statistical techniques used to analyze the data? If so, were they appropriate?
10. How clearly are results presented?
11. Are the conclusions presented clearly? Do the data support the conclusions? Does the researcher overgeneralize his/her findings?
12. What are the limitations of the study? Are they stated?

SOURCE: From *Educational research: Readings in Focus,* Second Edition, edited by Irvin J. Lehmann and William A. Mehrens. Copyright © 1971 by Holt, Rinehart and Winston. Reprinted by permission of Holt, Rinehart and Winston.

7. Measurement and manipulation of moderator and control variables
8. Research design
9. Statistical analysis
10. Presentation and discussion of results. (p. 3)

He provided a workbook format to check out each step of the process and described it in detail. Comparable discussions of the process are found in Best (1970), Dvorak (1956), Farquhar and Krumboltz (1959), Johnson (1957), Strauss (1969), Symond (1956), and Van Dalen (1958).

We recognize the importance of critically reading research reports, but people read research reports with different degrees of interest. Regardless of one's purpose or interest in reading research reports, it is important for the reader to recognize that publication alone does not ensure research quality. In fact, as is indicated in a notice regularly printed in *Exceptional Children,* some journals receive *"many more manuscripts of interest and worth than space permits publishing in full."* Recent form letters of rejection from the editor of *Exceptional Children* explain that the decision to publish may be based on factors other than editorial review:

Thank you for submitting your manuscript to *Exceptional Children.* In recent months the journal has experienced a tremendous increase in the number of

manuscripts to be reviewed for publication; consequently it has become necessary to eliminate many *worthwhile articles*. Decisions not to publish a manuscript are based on a *number of factors*. The major consideration is the *intended
audience*. (Thomas, 1979, 1980, 1981)

Because people's reasons for reading research vary, the content of journals and publishing policies also vary. Milne and Mountain (1980),
reporting on the publishing policies of over 60 journals related to special
education, concluded:

In summary, it appears from the study that a how-to, practical-type manuscript should be well written and in APA or Chicago style. Furthermore, 2 to
3 copies, between 8 and 11 pages, aimed at the educator stand a better
chance of being published. In addition, editors suggest that manuscripts be
clear and concise and contain the latest information, including information
about successful teaching devices. (p. 125)

Given the differences in written reports of research and practice, why one
report is published but another is turned down, is interesting.

How Blind Is a Blind Review?

Many education journals that publish research on special and remedial
education require a "blind review" of their manuscripts. Despite the
temptation to argue that this practice means that reviewers are often
inadequately knowledgeable about the topics being studied or the appropriateness of the research techniques, blind review simply means the
removal of identifying information from the manuscript before it is sent
out for review. Tobias and Zibrin (1978) used papers submitted for conference presentations to conduct research on two questions:

(1) Does blind review of manuscripts result in any difference in evaluations?
(2) Does blind review interact with a number of other variables such as
    prominence of author, prominence of reviewer, and sex of author and
    reviewer? (p. 16)

The analysis of their results indicated

no difference between judgment of reviewers of manuscripts submitted to
blind review and that of reviewers of the same manuscripts with the author
identified. Furthermore, blind reviewing did not interact with any other variables in the study; [however] papers with which a prominent individual was
associated received significantly more favorable evaluations than others
[regardless of whether or not the review was blind]. (p. 16)

It appears that there may be a quality of "wiseness" that affects decisions
made about the worth of research or a presentation of it. Prominent peo-

ple achieve prominence by doing things; the disseminations of their work may make them wise to the ways of acceptance, and it certainly keeps their prominence in view. Tobias and Zibrin noted that "even when a prominent author's name is removed from a manuscript, knowledgeable reviewers can make a pretty good guess as to the identity of an author who has been affiliated with a particular type of research" (p. 16). We all know of research reports in which the author manages to cite almost every paper he or she has ever published (including those only submitted for publication); a reviewer would have to be illiterate not to recognize the author of a paper with such a reference list. Nevertheless, Lester Mann (1978), the editor of an important special education journal, explained that regardless of the vagaries of the review process, many articles are not published for other reasons:

Let me make it clear that nonacceptance of an article does not necessarily reflect on its value as a contribution to the literature. It may be that we have had too many of a similar sort, or too many in an area we believe of lesser interest to our readers. We have turned down articles that appear in other fine journals. We have also accepted ones that other journals have rejected. (p. 101)

We recognize that personal judgment greatly influences the decision to publish research. We ourselves are persistent in our attempts to find a publisher for our own work, and sometimes we shop around to find some editor or reviewer who is interested in the research that we are doing. We wonder, though, about the many "manuscripts of interest and worth" that are rejected by journals and that the authors never submit elsewhere because of their mistaken belief that the reviewer(s) knows the authors' field better or has a remarkable standard of quality. Also, we wonder about the excellent research that investigators consider unworthy of publication (for whatever reason) and never submit it for review.

The standards used by reviewers, like those used by participants on federal research proposal review panels, are generally less than objective. Some research evaluation forms with which we are familiar request a rating of the various qualities of the manuscript (for example, writing style, design, contribution); most simply request acceptability ratings (for example, reject, accept with revisions, accept); and all ask for some justification for whatever ratings or publication decisions are made. Our experience has been that the justifications usually are not very useful, especially when the manuscript falls into the "worth greater than space" category. When it is evaluated according to Ward's, Hall's and Schramm's (1975) finding of relatively low ($r = .21$) interjudge-acceptance-rating reliability, the blind review process seems to have limited value for

Table **7.8** Reasons for Classification of 153 Studies as Having High Potential for Bias and Specific Safeguards Reported to Reduce Bias

	JOURNAL				ROW TOTAL
	AJMD[a]	Ex. Child.[b]	JSE[c]	JLD[d]	
I. Reason for classification in high-potential category					153
A. Data collector aware of purpose, hypothesis group assignment of subjects, conditions, etc.	39	12	15	22	88
B. Imprecise scoring and/or classification of open-ended response	18	6	9	19	52
C. Observation of process	46	20	9	11	86
D. Retroactive observation and/or classification of behavior	10	2	5	4	21
II. Indicated safeguards					
A. Blind observation					
Reported	10	4	6	4	24
Not reported	31	11	9	18	69
B. Training of inexperienced data collectors					
Reported	10	9	4	—	23
Not reported	4	15	1	—	20
C. Interrater reliability					
Reported adequately	30	8	7	7	52
Reported inadequately	11	5	3	3	22
Not reported	26	17	10	18	61

[a] *The American Journal of Mental Deficiency.*
[b] *Exceptional Children.*
[c] *The Journal of Special Education.*
[d] *Journal of Learning Disabilities.*
SOURCE: J. A. Salvia & C. J. Meisel, Observer bias: A methodological consideration in special education research. *The Journal of Special Education*, 1980, *14*, 261–270.

judging the quality of a piece of research or for improving the state-of-the-publication art.

Bias in Research

In studying the effects of a researcher's sex on evaluations of journal articles, Mischel (1974) found that bias tended to be consistent with the perceived sex appropriateness of the contribution to the field of study (that is, women in primary education, men in law). Although this type of bias may be reduced by blind reviews, other more salient types of bias must be addressed.

Jung (1971) observed that "most published research consists of so-called *positive results,* findings which more or less support the predictions proposed by (the experimenters)" (p. 34). Most educational researchers are familiar with the "experimenter bias effect" (EBE), probably because the concept and related issues are incredibly popular topics for research (see Rosenthal & Rubin, 1978, for a review of 300 "expectancy" studies). The premise of the EBE is straightforward: experimenters who expect certain outcomes are more likely to obtain them than are experimenters who have no such expectations (Jones, 1977; Jung, 1971; Rosenthal, 1966). Salvia and Meisel (1980) analyzed how often the appropriate safeguards for observer bias were used in the research reported in several major journals in special education (that is, *American Journal of Mental Deficiency, Exceptional Children, Journal of Learning Disabilities,* and *Journal of Special Education).* Almost half (48 percent) the articles reviewed were judged to have a higher probability of observer bias: the reasons for inclusion in this group, as well as how often the various safeguards were used, are indicated in Table 7.8. Bias also may be evident in the construction of the instruments that educational researchers seem to have an affinity for constructing when they do their research. Orlich (1979) reported one such instance:

> The key item in [the] questionnaire to superintendents had an instrument bias of four positive and only one negative in the five response categories. If there were simply a random set of responses, 80% would be expected to be positive as a result of instrument bias alone! (p. 6)

SUMMARY AND PERSPECTIVES

What a mess! The models for our research lead us to conclusions that do not offer much to the practitioner. It seems that the people who do most of the research and are paid for it are those who are the least likely to cause significant changes in the schools: most of the money goes to only a few winners. We argue over how to do the research when there is not anything really to argue about. And we have generated so many contradictory ideas that we now have invented methodologies to try to describe what we really know. Finally, the standards by which we judge the importance of all of research are subjective, and the research we conduct is susceptible to many biased possibilities.

Chapter 8

Legal Regulation of Special Education

CHAPTER CONTENTS

WHAT IS AN APPROPRIATE EDUCATION?
DISCRIMINATORY ASSESSMENT
THE MAGNITUDE AND VALIDITY OF TESTING
WHAT IS AN IEP?
EDUCATION OF HANDICAPPED STUDENTS IN LEAST
    RESTRICTIVE ENVIRONMENTS

CONCLUSIONS

Educators today are as much concerned with matters of litigation and legislation as of education. During the last two decades the courts and the federal and state legislatures have become deeply involved in the process of schooling, and educators, especially special educators, have been compelled, year by year, to comply with an ever-larger number of court mandates and laws. Litigation regarding special and remedial education has focused on the extent to which the schools, by virtue of administrative arrangements and decisions, deny the equal protection of the law to many students. Earlier, litigation concentrated on the right to treatment (education) and due process, but more recently, the issues have been the assessment of students and accompanying decision-making practices. During the last 10 to 15 years, many of the methods by which educators assigned students to instructional alternatives have been challenged; school assessment practices have been cited as discriminatory; and schools have been charged with failing to provide appropriate education to handicapped and/or minority students.

These students always have been with us; it is the attention they receive from the courts and legislatures that makes them more important now. School systems that fail to comply with the mandates of federal legislation are threatened with losing the funds appropriated by Congress.

Contemporary litigation and legislation are based on efforts to clarify and, in some cases, to redefine the fundamental purposes of schooling. In Chapter 1 we observed that three ideals directed the development of American education: democracy, nationalism, and individualism. We described the four basic values and ideals of democracy: the worth of the individual, the equality of all individuals, the equality of opportunity, and faith in reason. Two of these ideals—equality of all individuals and equality of opportunity—are rights guaranteed by the equal protection clause (the Fourteenth Amendment) of the U. S. Constitution. It is the Fourteenth Amendment, which ensures equal protection, that has been cited as being violated most often when the actions of schools were tested in the courts.

THE ROLE OF LEGISLATURES IN ESTABLISHING AMERICAN EDUCATION AND THE ROLE OF COURTS IN CHANGING IT

The idea of public schooling initiated the legislative action that enabled the Commonwealth of Massachusetts to tax its citizens for the purpose of establishing schools and providing children with free education. The courts, until recently, have had a hands-off policy toward the affairs of schools. Bersoff (1979) noted:

There was a time when the behavior of school officials went virtually unexamined by the courts. Pleading lack of expert knowledge, judges were wary of interfering with the discretion of administrators to educate their students. (p. 31)

Bersoff cited a portion of the record in an 1893 case, *Watson* v. *City of Cambridge,* in which the court stated:

The management of schools involves many details, and it is important that a board of public officers . . . having jurisdiction to regulate the internal affairs of the schools should not be interfered with or have their conduct called into question before another tribunal. . . . A jury composed of men of no special fitness to decide educational questions should not be permitted to say that their answer is wrong. (*Watson* v. *City of Cambridge,* 1893, p. 864)

Bersoff (1979) also reported that as recently as 1968 the courts maintained a hands-off policy on intervention into the affairs of the school, citing a portion of the record of *Epperson* v. *Arkansas:*

Courts do not and cannot intervene in the resolution of conflicts which arise in the daily operation of school systems and which do not directly and sharply implicate basic constitutional values. (*Epperson* v. *Arkansas,* 1968, p. 104)

The courts' hands-off policy could be said to have ended with the Supreme Court's declaration in *Tinker* v. *Des Moines Independent Community School District* (1969) that "students in school as well as out of schools are persons under our Constitution . . . possessed of fundamental rights which the State must respect." Since 1969, according to Bersoff (1979):

[The Supreme Court] . . . has decided such issues as the reach of compulsory education laws, the requirements of due process prior to infliction of disciplinary and academic sanctions, the immunity of school officials from

money damage liability for violations of students' civil rights, the allocation
of financial resources to pupils in poor school districts, the education of non-
English speaking children, the permissibility of sex-separate high schools, the
legality of special admissions programs for minorities, the obligation of colleges and universities to admit handicapped students, and most recently, the
validity of system-wide remedies to reduce school segregation. (p. 33)

Table 8.1 lists 23 court cases that have significant implications for special
education. Although many of these cases contain more than one provision,
we attempted in each instance to identify the primary findings that had
direct relevance to special and remedial education. (For a thorough review
of the litigation and legislation that relates to psychological testing, see
Bersoff, 1979).

LITIGATION RELEVANT TO SPECIAL
AND REMEDIAL EDUCATION

Inasmuch as most of the litigation relating to special and remedial education alleged denial of equal protection, it is clear that a substantive issue
in many of these very important cases was abuse in the process of assessment. This litigation provided the basis for contemporary special education legislation.

AMERICA'S SCHOOLS ARE FOR EVERYONE

The cornerstone for subsequent litigation was set when the Supreme
Court, in the landmark decision in *Brown* v. *Board of Education* (1954),
declared separate schools for black and white students to be unconstitutional. As we shall see, the Court's decision in *Brown* was not lost on the
parents of handicapped students, who later sued school systems for the
denial of equal protection in the assessment and assignment of their handicapped children to allegedly inferior educational settings.

ABILITY GROUPING BASED ON TEST PERFORMANCE
IS RULED UNCONSTITUTIONAL

An important decision was rendered by Judge Skelley Wright in 1967 in
in the case of *Hansen* v. *Hobson*. A suit was brought on behalf of black students who were assigned in disproportionate numbers to lower ability
groups or lower tracks in the Washington, D. C., schools. The chief argument was against the practice of using pupil performance on standardized
aptitude and achievement tests to make grouping or placement decisions.
Judge Wright ruled:

Table **8.1**   Primary Rulings in Court Cases Relevant to Special and Remedial Education

COURT CASE	RULINGS
Watson v. *City of Cambridge* (1893)	A student could be expelled for "disorderly conduct or imbecility."
Beattie v. *State Board of Education* (1919)	Physically handicapped students could be excluded from school because their presence was said to have a "depressing and nauseating effect" on other students.
Brown v. *Board of Education* (1954)	The Supreme Court ruled that school segregation is illegal and said that it denies equal protection and equal opportunity.
Hobson v. *Hansen* (1967)	Ability grouping (tracking) based on pupil performance on standardized tests, as employed in the Washington, D.C., schools, was ruled unconstitutional. Tracking was said to violate both due process and equal protection.
Tinker v. *Des Moines Independent School District* (1969)	Children are "persons" under the Constitution and have civil rights independent of their parents.
Diana v. *State Board of Education* (1970)	In a consent decree, the state of California agreed: 1. to test all children whose primary language was not English in both their primary language and English, 2. to eliminate "unfair verbal items" from tests, 3. to re-evaluate all Mexican-American and Chinese students enrolled in EMR classes by using only nonverbal items and testing them in their primary language, 4. to develop IQ tests reflecting Mexican-American culture and standardized only on Mexican Americans.
Covarrubias v. *San Diego Unified School District* (1971)	A consent decree established the right of plaintiffs to monetary damages for misclassification.
Lemon v. *Bossier Parish School Board* (1971)	Ability grouping was ruled unconstitutional.

Table **8.1**   *(cont.)*

COURT CASE	RULINGS
Ordway v. *Hargraves* (1971)	Exclusion from school of pregnant students was ruled unconstitutional.
Martarella v. Kelley (1972)	The right to treatment for juveniles held in noncriminal custody was upheld.
Mills v. *Board of Education* (1972)	1. The exclusion of students labeled as behavior problems, mentally retarded, emotionally disturbed, or hyperactive is unconstitutional. 2. Any handicapped child has a right, under equal protection, to a "constructive education," including appropriate specialized instruction. 3. Due process of law requires a hearing prior to exclusion from, termination of, or classification into a special program.
Pennsylvania Association for Retarded Children v. *Commonwealth of Pennsylvania* (1972)	By means of a consent decree, the state of Pennsylvania was enjoined from excluding mentally retarded students from the state's schools. The state agreed to engage in extensive child-find activities.
Meriken v. *Cressman* (1973)	1. The use of personality tests in a study of potential drug abusers was ruled an invasion of privacy. 2. Personality tests were said to lack the necessary technical adequacy to identify "the right students."
Goso v. *Lopez* (1974)	Due process is required prior to suspension or exclusion of students from school.
Hairston v. *Drosick* (1974)	The exclusion of handicapped children from the regular classroom without procedural safeguards is a violation of constitutional rights as well as of the Rehabilitation Act of 1973.
Wyatt v. *Stickney* (1971)	The right to adequate treatment (education) for mentally retarded individuals committed to a state school was established.
Washington v. *Davis* (1976)	When actions result in discriminatory outcomes, one may assume discriminatory intent.

Table **8.1** *(cont.)*

COURT CASE	RULINGS
Panitch v. *State of Wisconsin* (1977)	A long delay in implementing a state law designed to give equal education to the handicapped was sufficient indication of "intentional discrimination" in violation of the equal protection clause.
Frederick L. v. *Thomas* (1977)	The court ruled that the Philadelphia schools must engage in massive screening and follow-up evaluation designed to locate and serve learning-disabled students.
Lora v. *New York City Board of Education* (1978)	1. The process of evaluating students to determine whether they should enter "special day schools" for emotionally disturbed students violated the students' right to treatment and due process. 2. Because students were referred to largely racially segregated schools, there was a denial of equal opportunity in violation of Title VI. 3. New York City's monetary problems did not excuse the violation of the students' rights.
Larry P. v. *Riles* (1979)	1. The California State Department of Education was enjoined from using intelligence tests to place black students in EMR classes. 2. Schools in California were ordered to take steps to eliminate disproportionate placement of black students in EMR classes. 3. Schools in California were ordered to reevaluate all black students currently enrolled in EMR classes.
PASE v. *Hannon* (1980)	It was ruled that intelligence tests were not biased against black students and that they were appropriate for use in deciding placement of black students in EMR classes.

The evidence shows that the method by which track assignments are made depends essentially on standardized aptitude tests which, although given on a system-wide basis, are completely inappropriate for use with a large segment of the student body. Because these tests are standardized primarily on and are relevant to a white middle class group of students, they produce inaccurate and misleading test scores when given to lower class and Negro students. (*Hansen* v. *Hobson,* 1967, p. 514)

Bersoff (1979) noted that after *Hansen* v. *Hobson,* both ability grouping and testing "came under intense judicial scrutiny." The courts have been able, repeatedly, to demonstrate that educational placements based on pupil performance on ability or achievement tests result in the disproportionate placement in lower tracks of minority students and those from lower socioeconomic backgrounds. In Chapter 1 we observed that students with minority and/or low socioeconomic backgrounds fail more often to meet the objectives of schools than do other students. We also observed that minority and low socioeconomic students earn lower scores on measures of ability and achievement than do white middle-class students. The courts, in cases like *Hansen* v. *Hobson,* have ruled that these readily observable instances constitute a denial of equal protection of the law.

CHILDREN ARE DECLARED "PERSONS"

An important court decision, primarily because it, like *Brown,* set the stage for later litigation, was *Tinker* v. *Des Moines Independent Community School District* (1969). The issue it addressed was the right of students to wear black armbands to protest the Vietnam War. The court ruled that children are "persons" under the Constitution and have first amendment rights independent of their parents, and it reaffirmed that children do not lose their civil rights when they attend school. The establishment of the principle that children are persons who have rights was later cited in many judicial rulings relating to special education.

SCHOOLS MAY NOT EXCLUDE HANDICAPPED STUDENTS

The courts' decisions in *Brown* and *Hobson* attacked segregated schools and segregated classes. In *Mills* v. *Board of Education* (1972), the court addressed the exclusion of handicapped students from educational programs, asserted the right of students to due process prior to exclusion, and asserted the right of handicapped students to an "appropriate education." The court, in *Mills,* ruled on three principles:

1. The exclusion of students labeled as behavior problems, mentally retarded, emotionally disturbed, or hyperactive is unconstitutional.

2. Any handicapped child has a right, under equal protection, to a "constructive education," including appropriate specialized instruction.
3. Due process of law requires a hearing prior to exclusion from, termination of, or classification into a special program.

MISCLASSIFICATION OF MINORITY AND
NON-ENGLISH SPEAKING STUDENTS

At the time of the *Mills* v. *Board of Education* case, the courts and school systems entered into a number of consent decrees that have important implications for special education. In a consent decree reached as part of *Diana* v. *State Board of Education* (1970), the state of California agreed to (1) test all children whose primary language was not English in both their primary language and English, (2) eliminate "unfair verbal items" from tests, (3) re-evaluate all Mexican-American and Chinese students enrolled in EMR classes by using only nonverbal items and testing them in their primary language, and (4) develop IQ tests that reflect Mexican-American culture and are standardized only on Mexican Americans. *Diana* arose when the parents of Mexican-American students entered into a class action suit against the state, arguing that the assignment of Mexican-American students to EMR classes on the basis of their performances on standardized intelligence tests was discriminatory. In *Covarrubias* v. *San Diego Unified School District* (1971), a consent decree established the right of the plaintiffs and only those plaintiffs to monetary damages as a result of their misclassification as handicapped.

THE RIGHT OF RETARDED STUDENTS TO A
FREE AND APPROPRIATE PUBLIC EDUCATION

Contrary to the 1893 decree regarding the exclusion from schools of children for imbecility, the Pennsylvania Association for Retarded Children (PARC) in 1971 entered into a class action suit against the commonwealth of Pennsylvania, arguing that mentally retarded students had the right to a free and appropriate education and that the exclusion of these students from school constituted a denial of equal protection. The state was enjoined from excluding mentally retarded students and, in a consent decree (1972), agreed to engage in extensive efforts to identify all mentally retarded students in the state and to re-evaluate all those then attending public school classes for the mentally retarded.

SUMMARY

Litigation during the late 1960s and early 1970s set restraints on and guidelines for the states' rights to educate students. Students were defined as persons under the Constitution, and constitutional guarantees were extended to students attending school. Schools are designed to educate students, but the courts became involved when it was clear that the U. S. Constitution was being violated.

We have one important note regarding recent litigation: It nearly always has focused on the margins; that is, it has addressed the rights of marginal populations. Although the courts sometimes intervene in school affairs regarding policies and procedures for educating all students—less often for normal students—their involvement in the education of handicapped students has been rapidly growing. Litigation has led to legislation, and the federal government has taken an ever-increasing role in mandating what it is the states must do.

LEGISLATION FOR THE HANDICAPPED: 1966–1974

Early litigation regarding equal protection, the right to treatment, the right to an appropriate education, and the right to due process set the stage for much legislation concerning the education of handicapped students. Bersoff (1979) observed that the motivation for legislative involvement in special education came about only because the problems brought to the attention of the courts required broad intervention:

Courts develop rules of conduct in piecemeal fashion and only after litigants have presented legally cognizable issues. Rulemaking bodies such as legislatures and government agencies, on the other hand, need not wait for complaining litigants. When, among other reasons, problems need a broader solution than courts can provide, or they affect many people, lawmakers enact statutes and administrators promulgate regulations that have comprehensive effect. This process is evident with regard to special education and psychological testing. Legislation for the handicapped and those misclassified as handicapped directly affects the assessment practices of psychologists. The involvement of the federal government in the education of handicapped children began in 1966 but did not become intensive until 1974, when Congress passed the Education of the Handicapped Amendments, more commonly known to educators as Public Law 93–380. (Bersoff, 1979, p. 77)

Congress initially considered the special problems in the education of handicapped students in 1966 when it added Title VI to the Elementary and Secondary Education Act. Title VI established the Bureau of Education for the Handicapped, an agency whose first purpose was to conduct research on the education of handicapped students. Title VI was repealed in 1970 when Congress created the Education of the Handicapped Act, Public Law 91–230. That law expanded the powers of the Bureau of Education for the Handicapped, giving the agency authority to disburse grants to support both training in and research on the education of handicapped students. In 1973, Congress amended the Education of the Handicapped Act by establishing new legislation under Public Law 93–380. Public Law 93–380 is of historical interest only because it was significantly amended in Public Law 94–142, the Education for All Handicapped Children Act. The basis for Public Law 94–142 is found in the Senate report on the statute:

Congress found that . . . of the more than eight million children (between birth and twenty-one years of age) with handicapping conditions requiring special education and related services, only 3.9 million such children are receiving appropriate education. 1.75 million handicapped children are receiving an inappropriate education. (U. S., Congress, Senate, Report no. 94–168, 94th Cong., 1st sess., p. 8)

PUBLIC LAW 94–142: THE EDUCATION FOR ALL HANDICAPPED CHILDREN ACT OF 1975

The Education for All Handicapped Children Act of 1975 significantly expanded the earlier Education of the Handicapped Act. It is described in considerable detail here because of its importance to current practice and because of the significant issues relating to it. In the earlier legislation (Public Law 93–380), schools for the first time were told that they could lose federal financial assistance if they failed to have a state plan that specified a goal of full educational opportunity for handicapped students and a means of ensuring procedural safeguards in identification, evaluation, and educational placement. Parents were given the right to examine all records relevant to classification or placement and the right to an independent evaluation.

Preceding Public Law 94–142 was the Rehabilitation Act of 1973, which is important because it mandated nondiscrimination against the handicapped. Section 504 of that law is important to our concerns in this chapter, and it later became a part of Public Law 94–142. In section 504 of the Rehabilitation Act of 1973, Congress stated that "no otherwise qualified handicapped individual in the United States . . . shall, solely by reason of his handicap, be excluded from participation in, be denied the benefits of, or be subjected to discrimination under any program or activity receiving Federal financial assistance."

The Context for Public Law 94–142

Public Law 94–142 is designed to meet four major purposes, which were described by Ballard and Zettel (1977) as follows:

1. to guarantee that special educational services are available to children who need them,
2. to assure that decision making regarding provision of services to handicapped students is both fair and appropriate,
3. to establish clear management and auditing requirements and procedures for special education at all levels of government, and
4. to provide federal funds to assist states in educating handicapped children and youth.

Public Law 94–142 was enacted in response to several congressional findings. Nine of these findings are specifically identified in the act as follows:

(1) there are more than eight million handicapped children in the United States today;
(2) the special educational needs of such children are not being fully met;
(3) more than half of the handicapped children in the United States do not receive appropriate educational services which would enable them to have full equality of opportunity;
(4) one million of the handicapped children in the United States are excluded entirely from the public school system and will not go through the educational process with their peers;
(5) there are many handicapped children throughout the United States participating in regular school programs whose handicaps prevent them from having a successful educational experience because their handicaps are undetected;
(6) because of lack of adequate services within the public school system, families are often forced to find services outside the public school system, often at great distance from their residence and at their own expense;
(7) developments in the training of teachers and in diagnostic and instructional procedures and methods have advanced to the point that, given appropriate funding, State and local educational agencies can and will provide effective special education and related services to meet the needs of handicapped children;
(8) State and local educational agencies have a responsibility to provide education for all handicapped children, but present financial resources are inadequate to meet the special educational needs of handicapped children; and
(9) it is in the national interest that the Federal government assist State and local efforts to provide programs to meet the educational needs of handi-

capped children in order to assure equal protection of the law (U. S. Congress, 89 Stat., pp. 774–775).

Congress mandated that each state, if it were to receive federal funds, must meet the following requirements:

A. Each state had to show that it had in effect a policy assuring all handicapped students the right to a free appropriate public education.
B. Each state plan had to include a detailed description of the policies and procedures that had been, or would be, undertaken to assure that:
 1. it had an established goal of providing full educational opportunities for every handicapped child, a timetable for doing so, and the necessary facilities, personnel, and services to meet that goal;
 2. a free appropriate education would be available to all handicapped students between the ages of 3 and 18 not later than September 1, 1978, and all handicapped students between the ages of 3 and 21 not later than September 1, 1980;
 3. procedures were in place for identifying all handicapped students; and
 4. parents and guardians of handicapped students were given an opportunity to review the state plan 30 days prior to its submission.
C. The state had established priorities for providing a free appropriate education, first to those out of school and second to the most severely handicapped within each disability area.
D. The state would maintain records of the individual educational plan for each handicapped student.
E. The state had established
 1. procedures to assure that, to the maximum extent appropriate, handicapped children would be educated with children who were not handicapped and that special classes, separate schools, or other removal of handicapped students from the regular education environment would occur only when the nature or severity of the handicap was such that education in regular classes with supplementary aids could not be achieved satisfactorily; and
 2. procedures to assure that testing and evaluation materials and procedures used for the evaluation and placement of handicapped students would be selected so as not to be racially or culturally discriminatory.
F. All educational programs for handicapped students were under the supervision of special educational personnel in the state agency and met the general educational standards of the state educational agency.
G. The general public, including the parents of handicapped students, must be given an opportunity to consult on the development of state

plans and must be given an opportunity for a public hearing before policies and procedures are developed.

Four provisions of Public Law 94–142 deserve special attention (1) due process, (2) protection in evaluation procedures, (3) least restrictive environment, and (4) individual educational programs.

DUE PROCESS

The provision for due process is clearly specified in Public Law 94–142. The law states that handicapped children's parents, guardians, or parent surrogates have the right to examine all pupil records and the right to secure independent evaluations of their children. Whenever a school proposes or refuses to initiate or change the identification, evaluation, or placement of a child, the parents must be given written prior notice. Such notice must be in their native language "unless it is clearly not feasible to do so." Parents have a right to complain at the time they are notified, and those who complain have the right to an impartial due process hearing at which they may challenge the school's decision. Parents who are not satisfied with the findings of the due process hearing may (in most states) appeal the decision to the state education agency. Either party not satisfied with the actions taken by the state education agency may appeal the decision to the civil courts. When the due process hearings are held, parents have several rights: the right to be accompanied by counsel and/or experts in the education of handicapped students; the right to present evidence, cross-examine, and compel the attendance of witnesses; the right to an independent evaluation; and the right to a written or electronic verbatim recording of the hearing.

PROTECTION IN EVALUATION PROCEDURES (PEP)

The PEP provisions of Public Law 94–142 address fairness in assessment. The law specifies the procedures that state and local education agencies are expected to develop:

Procedures to assure that testing and evaluation materials and procedures utilized for the purposes of evaluation and placement of handicapped children will be selected and administered so as not to be racially or culturally discriminatory. Such materials or procedures shall be provided and administered in the child's native language or mode of communication, unless it clearly is not feasible to do so, and no single procedure shall be the sole criterion for determining an appropriate educational program for a child. (Section 615–5C)

Specific rules and regulations for the implementation of the PEP provisions were published in the *Federal Register,* August 23, 1977 (pp. 42474–42518). These rules and regulations are as follows:

1. A "full and individual evaluation" of a child's needs must be made prior to initial placement of that child in a special educational program.
2. Tests used must be administered in the child's native language or other mode of communication.
3. Tests that are used must have been validated for the specific purpose for which they are used.
4. Tests are administered by "trained personnel" in conformance with instructions provided by their producer.
5. Tests and other evaluation materials must include those intended to assess specific areas of educational need and not merely those designed to yield a single general I.Q.
6. When tests are administered to students who have impaired sensory, manual, or speaking skills, the results must reflect aptitude or achievement rather than the impairment.
7. No single procedure is to be the sole criterion on which special education placement is determined.
8. Evaluations for special education placement are made by a multidisciplinary team, including at least one teacher or other specialist with "knowledge in the area of suspected disability."
9. Children are to be assessed in all areas related to a suspected disability, including when appropriate, health, vision, hearing, social emotional functioning, general intelligence, motor abilities, academic performance, and communicative status. (20 U.S.C. 1415 (b)(2)(B)(121a532a-f)

LEAST RESTRICTIVE ENVIRONMENT

Public Law 94–142 also specifies that handicapped students are to be educated in the "least restrictive environment." States were mandated to have in place policies and procedures to assure that

all handicapped students, including those in public or private institutions or other care facilities, are educated with children who are not handicapped, and that special classes, separate schooling, or other removal of handicapped children from the regular education environment occurs only when the nature or severity of the handicap is such that an education in regular classes with the use of supplementary aids and services cannot be achieved satisfactorily (Section 612-5)

INDIVIDUALIZED EDUCATIONAL PROGRAMS

This fourth regulation is most commonly referred to as the IEP provision. In Public Law 94–142, Congress mandated each local education agency in each state to "maintain records of the individualized educational program for each handicapped child and each such program shall be established, reviewed, and revised" in accordance with procedures specified in the law.

LITIGATION SUBSEQUENT TO PUBLIC LAW 94–142

Bersoff (1979) observed that "legislation itself may serve as a springboard to future litigation, as parties seek to define, implement, and enforce its provisions. Federal and state statutes may evoke what may be called 'second generation' issues" (p. 103). We shall review here four legal cases that followed the enactment of Public Law 94–142, each of which challenged the procedures by which schools assessed and made placement decisions regarding handicapped and/or potentially handicapped students.

THE USE OF INTELLIGENCE TESTS TO PLACE
MINORITY STUDENTS IN PROGRAMS FOR THE HANDICAPPED

The best-known court decision subsequent to Public Law 94–142 was rendered in 1979 in response to a California case that began in 1971: *Larry P.* v. *Riles*. The plaintiffs in that case represented the class of black children in California who had been or in the future might be wrongfully placed and maintained in special classes for the educable mentally retarded. The plaintiffs challenged the placement process and, specifically, the use of standardized intelligence tests in the decision-making process. The plaintiffs contended that the IQ tests were biased and discriminated against black children and cited as evidence the disproportionate placement of black students in EMR classes. The defendant in the case was Wilson Riles, superintendent of public instruction in California.

The initial complaint in *Larry P.* v. *Riles* was filed in November 1971. In June 1972 the court ruled that the case could proceed as a class action suit on behalf of all black San Francisco schoolchildren who had been classified as mentally retarded on the basis of IQ test results. School personnel in California were, at that time, restrained from placing black students in EMR classes using criteria based primarily on IQ test results.

The defendants appealed the court's decision, and in 1974 the circuit court of appeals upheld the lower court's injunction. Following that action, the plaintiffs moved and were granted permission to expand the case to a class action suit on behalf of all black schoolchildren in California who had been or might be classified as mentally retarded on the basis of their performance on IQ tests. In 1974, the court restrained educational and psychological personnel in California from administering to black students standardized ability or achievement tests that did not properly consider cultural background, listing as approved tests that did not take cultural differences into account, and placing black children in EMR classes based on the results of tests that did not properly evaluate their cultural background.

In January 1975 the California State Department of Education voluntarily imposed a moratorium on IQ testing for all children, regardless of race. In January 1977 the plaintiffs filed an amended complaint, reflecting recent legislative concerns, and in August 1977 the U.S. Department of Justice entered the case as *amicus curiae,* contending that provisions of the Education for All Handicapped Children Act and section 504 of the Rehabilitation Act of 1973 had been violated. The Justice Department contended that intelligence tests had not been validated for diagnosing mental retardation and that the use of such tests had a disproportionate impact on black children.

The court decided this case in favor of the plaintiffs. In outlining his solution for the plaintiffs, Judge Robert F. Peckham addressed two specific problems: abuses in testing and the disproportionate enrollment of black children in special EMR classes:

1. The state of California was enjoined from using, permitting the use of, or approving the use of any standardized intelligence test for identifying black EMR children or placing them in special classes for the educable mentally retarded.
2. Defendants were ordered to monitor or eliminate the disproportionate placement of black students in California's EMR classes.
3. Defendants were ordered to re-evaluate every black child currently identified as an EMR pupil, without using standardized intelligence tests.

Judge Peckham concluded his opinion by stating:

Whatever the future, it is essential that California's educators confront the problem of the widespread failure to provide an adequate education to underprivileged minorities such as the black children who brought this lawsuit. Educators have too often been able to rationalize inaction by blaming educational failure on an assumed intellectual inferiority of disproportionate numbers of black children. That assumption without validation is unacceptable, and it is made all the more invidious when "legitimized" by ostensibly neutral, scientific I.Q. scores. (pp. 109–110)

The issue of bias in assessment clearly was not settled by the *Larry P.* case because the issue continues to be debated in the nation's courtrooms.

A case of significant note, *PASE* v. *Hannon* (1980), was a class action suit brought by Parents in Action on Special Education on behalf of "all black children who have been or will be placed in special classes for the educably mentally handicapped in the Chicago school system" (*PASE* v. *Hannon,* 1980, p. 1). The plaintiffs observed that although 62 percent of the enrollment of the Chicago public schools was black, black students comprised 82 percent of the enrollment in classes for the educable mentally handicapped. The plaintiffs claimed that the misassessment of children as retarded was caused by racial bias in the standardized intelligence tests they were given, causing them to achieve low scores.

At issue in *PASE* v. *Hannon,* as in the *Larry P.* case, was the detrimental effect on students of placement in classes for educable mentally handicapped (EMH):

An erroneous assessment of mental retardation, leading to an inappropriate placement of a child in an EMH class, is nearly an educational tragedy. However beneficial such classes may be for those who truly need them, they are likely to be almost totally harmful to those who do not. (*PASE* v. *Hannon,* 1980, p. 4)

Judge John Grady, who presided in this case, took a unique approach to addressing the issues. He systematically examined each item on the Stanford-Binet and the WISC-R tests, reading every item into the court record and expressing his own opinion on how much each item was biased against Blacks. Judge Grady said:

It is obvious to me that I must examine the tests themselves in order to know what the witnesses are talking about. I do not see how an informed decision on the question of bias could be reached in any other way. For me to say that the tests are either biased or unbiased without analyzing the test items in detail would reveal nothing about the tests but only something about my opinion of the tests. (*PASE* v. *Hannon,* 1980, p. 8)

The judge ruled in favor of the defendants, stating that he could identify little evidence that the tests, in fact, were biased. The ruling was clearly contrary to that in *Larry P.* Judge Grady addressed this fact, stating:

As is by now obvious, the witnesses and the arguments which persuaded Judge Peckham have not persuaded me. Moreover, I believe the issue in the case cannot properly be analyzed without a detailed examination of the items on the tests. It is clear that this was not undertaken in the *Larry P.* case. (*PASE* v. *Hannon,* 1980, p. 108)

Judge Grady found only eight items on the WISC or WISC-R test and one item on the Stanford-Binet test to be biased against black children.

He stated further that poor performance on these items alone was not sufficient to result in the misclassification of black students as educable mentally handicapped.

FAILURE TO PROVIDE AN APPROPRIATE EDUCATION

Two other postlegislation court cases (*Frederick L.* v. *Thomas,* 1978 and *Lora* v. *New York City Board of Education,* 1978) concerned legal issues particularly important to special and remedial education. *Frederick L.* v. *Thomas* was a class action suit in which the Philadelphia school district was charged with failing to provide learning-disabled students with appropriate education, that is, with denying services to significant numbers of learning-disabled students. Using as a criterion a 3 percent incidence of learning disabilities, the plaintiffs charged that the schools were serving too few learning-disabled children. Regarding the 3 percent criterion, the plaintiffs said that 7,900 students should be identified as learning disabled, although only 1,300 students were being served in special programs for the learning disabled. The schools argued that other students had not been referred and that they were being served appropriately in regular classrooms. The court ordered the school district to engage in "massive screening and follow-up individual psychological evaluations" which were designed to identify learning-disabled students.

Lora v. *New York City Board of Education* (1978) was a class action suit brought by black and Hispanic students. They asserted that students' constitutional and statutory rights were being violated by the procedures and facilities used by New York City for educating children whose emotional problems had led to severe acting out and aggression in school. Judge Weinstein held the opinion that (1) the process of evaluating students to determine whether they should enter "special day schools" violated the students' right to treatment and due process; (2) because students were referred to largely racially segregated schools, there was a denial of equal educational opportunity in violation of Title VI; and (3) New York City's monetary problems did not excuse the violation of the students' rights.

In both *Lora* and *Frederick L.,* the schools were mandated to make more extensive assessments and evaluations.

ISSUES ARISING FROM LEGAL INTERVENTION IN EDUCATION

An entire text could be written on the issues arising from legal intervention into the affairs of schools. Each court case described in this chapter addressed one or more legal problems. In response to judicial decisions, legislatures have tried to provide special education services to the students who need them by resolving these issues in all their complex interaction. The most salient of these issues are examined in this section.

TO WHAT EXTENT CAN THE SCHOOLS BE EXPECTED TO EDUCATE ALL STUDENTS?

Public Law 94–142 is entitled the Education for All Handicapped Children Act and specifies that all handicapped students have the right to free and appropriate public education. The schools are expected to educate all students, though one must question the extent to which this expectation is feasible, practical, and/or possible. We are aware of instances in which schools, in order to provide a free, appropriate education to an individual handicapped student, have found it necessary to hire a special teacher for that one student. This situation has occurred in rural areas when a student demonstrated such unusual needs that he or she did not fit into any existing program. To provide the appropriate program, the school was forced to design one and to hire a teacher for the student. When this happens, the costs for educating that one student can run as much as $30,000 over the usual costs. Early compulsory education laws were passed in the belief that attendance alone guaranteed education. Special education came about when that belief did not bring results. Will compulsory special education evolve from the failure to meet the mandate of Public Law 94–142 that all handicapped children be educated?

School personnel often argue that it is almost impossible to educate certain kinds of students. Parents or advocacy groups bring lawsuits against school districts when the schools fail to provide an appropriate education for students who are very, very difficult to teach. Many students enter school with such severe physical, neurological, or medical problems that the schools have trouble designing instructional interventions to meet their needs. Or many have had deficient or debilitating early experiences that suppress their ability to profit from educational programs as they are designed. Finally, many have severe emotional problems that prevent them from responding to education and will not be able to do so until those problems are alleviated or the educational programs are changed significantly to accommodate the children.

Although there may be some students for whom it is difficult to envision an appropriate education, at the same time it is true that educational personnel grossly overestimate the number of students who may be handicapped. Ysseldyke, Algozzine, and Richey (in press) asked a group of 224 Minnesota teachers, school psychologists, and educational support personnel how many students they thought were mentally retarded or emotionally disturbed or had severe academic difficulties. Their estimates were 6 to 25 times the actual incidence figures. Educators believe that many more students are handicapped than is indicated by actual statistics.

Public Law 94–142 states that "developments in the training of teachers and in diagnostic and instructional procedures and methods have advanced to the point that, given appropriate funding, State and local education agencies can and will provide effective special education and related services to meet the needs of handicapped students" (p. 776). This, in essence, asserts that if the schools had the necessary funds they could provide "effective special education and related services" for all handicapped students. This claim is analogous to the one made for automobile manufacturers: given adequate funding they could produce an automobile that meets federal emission control standards or one that gets 96 miles per gallon of gasoline.

There are instances in which the courts and legislatures have mandated schools to provide services that technically cannot be achieved. Schools obviously do not now have the technological expertise to educate effectively every handicapped student. The current research on assessment and intervention does not support the contention that our technology is adequately developed to offer an effective education to all handicapped students.

WHAT IS AN APPROPRIATE EDUCATION?

The substantive issue in much of the litigation discussed in this chapter is the failure of schools to provide handicapped students with an appropriate education. Indeed, since Public Law 94–142 mandated this, much of the later litigation has tried to clarify the meaning of appropriate.

The U. S. Department of Health, Education and Welfare, in 1977, defined appropriate education as "the provision of regular or special education and related aids and services that . . . are designed to meet individual educational needs of handicapped persons as adequately as the needs of nonhandicapped persons" (H. E. W. Regulations, Supplementary information, 42 *Fed. Reg.* no. 86, 22676, 1977).

This definition does not help us identify the actual or intended meaning of the term appropriate. Would an adequate education be appropriate? If so, how do we define adequate? Inasmuch as no one ever has seen an appropriate education, it is necessary to define what is meant by the term. An operational definition would require a statement of the goals of education. But what are these, and specifically, what are the goals of education for handicapped students?

Educators often argue about the goals of education and just as often differ in their responses. When educational objectives are stated, they usually become more nebulous and nonoperational as they rise in the educational administrative hierarchy. State education agencies usually articulate goals like "teaching responsibility for engaging in civic actions" or "developing the worth of the individual." In Chapter 1 we listed the educational goals or objectives advanced by the National Education Association. But how do schools demonstrate that they are educating students? How do they demonstrate that students are being educated appropriately? How do the goals of education differ for handicapped and for nonhandicapped students? To what extent are the goals of education attainable?

DISCRIMINATORY ASSESSMENT

In many court cases, the litigants contended that school system assessment practices and the outcomes of those practices were discriminatory. Schools and state education agencies have been charged with discriminatory intent when their assessment practices resulted in the disproportionate assignment of Blacks and minority students to special education classes.

For decades, educators and psychologists have argued about how fair specific tests are for use with specific groups of students. Two facts are clear: First, educators and psychologists have been unable to agree on how fair specific tests are. Elaborate models for ascertaining fairness have been proposed by such eminent psychologists as Clearly, Thorndike, Linn, Guion, Cole, Peterson, and Novick. The use of alternative models results in different decisions on the fairness of using specific tests with specific groups. Second, educators and psychologists have been unable to agree on the concept of fairness.

Although educators and psychologists have been unable to reach a consensus on the meaning of nondiscriminatory assessment, Public Law 94–142 now mandates schools to select and administer assessment devices in a way that will be racially and culturally nondiscriminatory. As early as 1967, Judge Wright, in *Hansen* v. *Hobson,* ruled that the standardized tests employed by the Washington, D. C., schools for making tracking decisions were inappropriate for use with black students because they were both developed and standardized on white middle-class students. In *Lora* v. *New York City Board of Education* (1978), the assessment procedures of the school district were cited as inadequate and discriminatory. But contrast the decisions in the *Larry P.* and *PASE* cases: Whereas in *Larry P.* v. *Riles* (1979), the Court declared discriminatory the IQ tests that were used to place black students in EMR classes; in *PASE* v. *Hannon* (1980), Judge Grady ruled that two standard intelligence tests were not biased against black chidren. Without a clear definition of terms like bias, discriminatory, and nondiscriminatory, decisions on whether tests exhibit these characteristics are, at best, problematic. There still are several questions regarding the recent litigation and legislation:

1. How big a difference may (or must) one observe in the test performance of Blacks and Whites before concluding that the test is biased?
2. If intelligence tests are banned, how does one go about deciding MR placement?
3. What is race?
4. To what extent are classes for handicapped students a dead end?
5. Does recent litigation mean the end of EMR classes?

THE MAGNITUDE AND VALIDITY OF TESTING

Recent court cases have mandated that testing be limited (*Larry P.* v. *Riles,* 1979) and expanded (*Frederick L.* v. *Thomas,* 1978; *Lora* v. *New York City Board of Education,* 1978). What, then, should educators do? Should intellectual assessment be discontinued, or should more and better intelligence tests be administered in order to identify the increasing numbers of handicapped students? What are the standards for better tests of intelligence?

Public Law 94–142 also states that tests must be validated for the purposes for which they are used. Judge Peckham, in *Larry P.* v. *Riles,* ruled that school personnel could use intelligence tests to make EMR placement decisions regarding black students only if, before doing so, they could demonstrate that the tests they planned to use were valid for making EMR placement decisions for black students. Sarason and Doris (1979) pointed out, however:

Anyone who sets for himself the task of collecting, describing, and criticizing intelligence tests either currently in use or advertised for use has staked out at least half a career. In the face of such a bewildering array of tests, conceptions, and criticisms, it is understandable if one concludes that far from being naked the emperor not only has a surfeit of clothes but he is wearing them all at the same time. This is said to suggest that as one gets overwhelmed pursuing test after test and tries to organize the various underlying conceptions into some coherent framework, one may well conclude that the concept of intelligence has all the characteristics of an inkblot onto which people have projected meanings on the basis of which they wish to urge other people to see what they see, to "measure" it in the same way they do. (p. 30)

Courts and legislatures have ordered that tests be validated for the purposes for which they are used. Yet the examination of some of the purposes for which tests are employed in special and remedial education reveals that we cannot achieve compliance with the mandate. Tests are

used to differentiate individuals, to identify those who are mentally
retarded, learning disabled, and emotionally disturbed, and to spot those
who have incipient learning disabilities. They are used to identify children who have limited intelligence, body image problems, auditory
sequential memory deficits, figure-ground pathology, or who suffer from
hysteria, hypochondriasis, and depression. But, we are not certain what
those terms mean and what those conditions are, and we have no idea of
what to do (with any degree of validity) when we find them. Sarason and
Doris (1979) observed that definitions of such conditions as mental retardation, learning disabilities, and emotional disturbance are constantly
shifting because they reflect changing societal values and attitudes:

Why define intelligence and mental retardation? Why measure them? We
can now formulate an answer: in the realm of human behavior and actions,
the need to define and measure always reflects dominant social needs as the
society at the time perceives them, and these perceptions are inevitably col-
ored by moral or value judgments. Neither the substance of definitions nor
the types of measuring devices to which they give rise are neutral, dispassion-
ate affairs, although the effectiveness with which the culture transmits these
dominant perceptions to us ordinarily obscures how rooted in the culture we
and the definitions are. What we take to be "natural" and objective is not
free from the influences of social time and place. (p. 36)

How can we demonstrate the validity of tests for measuring things we
can neither define or conceptualize? Current measures of traits, aptitudes, and abilities do not provide empirical evidence for their validity as
measures of those traits, aptitudes, and abilities.

WHAT IS AN IEP?

Entire volumes have been written on IEP development. Yet, in school districts across the country, a particular district's IEPs look very much alike.
How does a school system know when it has a valid IEP for a student?
The recent extensive reviews of diagnostic-prescriptive teaching (Arter &
Jenkins, 1979; Ysseldyke, 1973; Ysseldyke & Mirkin, 1981) all state that
there is little empirical support for the contention that test data can be
used to decide how to teach students. Test data are helpful in deciding
what to teach, but not how to teach. We believe that any IEP is a set of
hypotheses about what might work in teaching a youngster and that the
only valid IEP is one that has been carried out and has demonstrated its
effectiveness.

EDUCATION OF HANDICAPPED STUDENTS
IN LEAST RESTRICTIVE ENVIRONMENTS

Federal law mandates that handicapped students be educated in least restrictive environments. What is a least restrictive environment, and how does one know when placement is in one? The determination of what is least restrictive is so dependent on the particular child that it is impossible to make any general conclusions. In many, if not most, school districts, least restrictive is interpreted for the convenience of the system rather than of the student's needs. The interpretation of least restrictive may be one of the most outstanding failures of Public Law 94–142 because it leads to dumping students in regular classes, eliminating the hiring of special education teachers, and devising phony individualized educational plans.

CONCLUSIONS

Judicial and legislative mandates enunciate society's ideals for the education of America's students. But these mandates, because they are based on or derived from ideals, often require schools to demonstrate compliance with pie-in-the-sky requirements in the absence of a knowledge base and/or the technical expertise to meet the letter, let alone the intent, of the law. Recent litigation and legislation have created much conceptual confusion in education, and educators have responded by doing some absurd things under the belief that "it is the law."

Bensky et al., (1980) found that the disparity between what educators are able to accomplish and what others expect them to accomplish leads to considerable stress. Individual teachers report frustration in achieving instructional objectives for students, as well as lowered self-esteem and self-confidence (Weiskopf, 1980). Public Law 94–142 has led to an incredible paper chase and paper shuffle in special and remedial education. In response to the demands that schools educate all children and that they produce for each handicapped student a written record of the student's individualized educational program, we witness a veritable inundation by paper. Meanwhile, valuable time that could be devoted to students is devoted, instead, to paperwork.

In order to determine how to comply with the requirements of Public Law 94–142 and the judicial determinations in their states, school districts have assigned task forces to formulate necessary procedures. These task forces try to develop lists of tests that are fair for use with groups of students, check lists of instructional objectives matched to test items and minute pieces of curricula, and extensive inservice training which is designed to facilitate compliance.

The demand that students receive an appropriate education leads to the increasing generation of bandwagons and a smorgasbord of interventions from which teachers may sample in trial-and-error fashion.

Reynolds (1975a) expressed an omnipresent danger:

I fear that in the press to achieve compliance, at least on paper, with the right-to-education directives, many state and school districts may initiate programs for handicapped children which provide neither education nor recognition of the child's individuality. (p. 61)

He also spoke of legislative directives fostering an atmosphere of "more process than is due" and of bureaucratic excesses in the name of bureaucratic preservation:

I believe we are facing currently some rather strong tendencies to create a strongly hierarchical, bureaucratic, detailed, rule-making system by which special educators will be expected to operate. These bureaucratic excesses appear to reflect a hostile vision of the whole field. It involves a dangerous degree of distrust: by legislators, who distrust bureaucrats and virtually all professionals; by central office bureaucrats, who distrust local bureaucrats and professionals; by legalists, who take their court-won victories as a mandate for excessive regulation-writing; by local bureaucrats and professionals, who distrust national leaders who may write unnecessary restrictions into programs; and by parents who distrust all professionals in the schools. (Reynolds, 1975a, p. 68).

Chapter 9

The Issues As Reflected
in Current Practice

In the preceding chapters, we discussed several critical issues in personnel preparation, identification, assessment, intervention, litigation, legislation, and research. The issues are not isolated from one another but interact in complex patterns to influence current practice: indeed, they are readily evident in nearly all aspects of practice today. In this chapter, we examine how these issues affect current administrative arrangements and instructional practices in special and remedial education.

CURRENT CHANGES IN SPECIAL AND REMEDIAL EDUCATION

Reynolds (in press) argued that a profound change is taking place in the administrative arrangements for educating all students in America and

237

that special and remedial educational services are delivered in a very complex environment, one that is significantly changed from that of our recent past:

The semi-autonomous characteristics of neighborhood schools in recent years have been overwhelmed by mandates emanating from national social policies, federal and state legislation, judicial interpretations, teachers' associations, and professional developments. As a result, public education has changed: Student bodies have become more heterogeneous, new structures have begun to appear, and new functions and roles are demanded of teachers, building principals, school psychologists, and other specialists. Most of the changes derive from the mandated provision of services to populations that, heretofore, were considered marginal, that is, the handicapped, minority, economically disadvantaged, bilingual, migrant, and other children and youth who have been systematically set aside or excluded from the mainstream of society and the schools. (p. 1)

The recent revisions of public policy on the education of handicapped students are reflected in the provisions of Public Law 94–142. The law requires the delivery of appropriate education for every handicapped student in the least restrictive environment. An individual educational plan must be devised for each such student, one that is tailored to the individual's specific needs as ascertained by a comprehensive individual assessment and negotiated by a multidisciplinary team of school professionals and the student or the student's biological or surrogate parents. Assessments must be so conducted that they are racially and culturally nondiscriminatory.

But will change really occur? Special and remedial education have been given the "hard sell" in this country. To muster public support for handicapped children, the early pioneers drew heavily on the religious beliefs, community morality, political philosophy, and social conscience of the American people. If the result initially was the practice of institutionalizing handicapped children, it was because at that time institutionalization was the only acceptable alternative to neglect and/or exploitation. These institutions, like all residential communities that operate within the strictures of inadequate budgets and social isolation, functioned by de-individualizing their residents, such as using inmate numbers rather than names in prisons (see Wolfensberger, 1971).

We believe that society is permeated by an institutional mentality characterized by the belief that the important differences that require special or remedial education exist within individuals. The net result of this kind of thinking is to de-emphasize an individual's worth (the de-individualizing phenomenon). We (that is, society) started with the belief that there are important differences among individuals; we proved that they were there and created explanations for them; and then we organized a special system to deal with them. To paraphrase Dybwad (1980), the message of Public Law 94–142 and recent public policy is that it is normal to be different. The existing system and the attitudes, beliefs, and expectations it has created, we believe, are too ingrained to be easily altered.

Public Law 94–142 was passed in 1975, but school districts were not expected to be in full compliance until 1980. Nonetheless, the school districts are scrambling to live up to the provisions of the law. Many educators argue that Public Law 94–142 is here to stay and that it will greatly affect all of education. Such arguments are based on the beliefs that people actually are committed to the ideals expressed in the law and that with the law we have finally achieved equality of educational opportunity for all children and youth. Reynolds (in press) presented the most cogent reasons to support the notion that Public Law 94–142 is here to stay.

Reynolds (in press) believes that the changes occurring in response to Public Law 94–142 are "openers for major revisions of schooling that will affect all categorical programs and, eventually, all programs for all students" (p. 5), and that "two decades of activity at the 'margins' has finally been recognized as having profound implications for all students" (p. 5). The provisions of Public Law 94–142 are not going to go away, he asserted, they are too ingrained in state legislation. These provisions "reflect a major social change in the policy-ruling institutional commitment" (p. 7); the policies are supported by strong advocacy groups; the origins of the concept of mainstreaming are educational as well as legal or political; and the principles of the law are being incorporated into teacher-education programs.

With all due respect to Reynolds's views, we cannot at this point support his contention that real change is taking place. Rather, we believe that Public Law 94–142 is another in a series of compulsory education laws and is likely to go the way of previous such enactments. Public Law 94–142 and educational change are merely correlated, and one cannot conclude that the law caused the currently observed change. Indeed, it well may be that change brought about Public Law 94–142. One can argue that a more inclusive kind of change was in process in the schools before the passage of Public Law 94–142 and that if the schools had been left alone, they would have adopted inclusive provisions for handicapped students without the law. It also can be argued that no real change has taken place, that handicapped students have been moved about by the administration but are not receiving better education or equal educational opportunities, and that they are not better off today than they were prior to the passage of Public Law 94-142. Although real change may not be occurring, resistance to change certainly is.

In the same way, it is difficult to support the contention that the changes brought about by Public Law 94–142 will not go away. A quick look at educational history leads us to believe otherwise: Public Law 94–142 comes up for reauthorization in 1982. If the funding associated with the law is significantly reduced, the economic and political incentives for compliance will have been removed. Except in those states whose schools are under relevant court orders, schools may well see no benefit in compliance. They probably will continue to change, but not in response to Public Law 94–142; they will change simply because education today is going so badly.

PARALLELS TO EARLY COMPULSORY EDUCATION

In many ways, Public Law 94–142 is a new compulsory education act. We can expect that future developments in response to the law will parallel the developments observed in responses to earlier concepts of compulsory education. Tyack (1976) distinguished two phases in his analysis of the history of compulsory education in America: the symbolic stage and the bureaucratic phase.

The symbolic stage (from about 1852 to 1890) was characterized by ideological disagreement over the nature and form of compulsory education laws. During this period, however, the implementation or enforcement of those laws was not emphasized (Sarason & Doris, 1979; Tyack, 1976). The bureaucratic phase of compulsory education (from about 1900 to the present) was evidenced by an increase in the size and power of the American education system and the development of techniques for control. Compulsory education laws were strengthened and increasingly enforced.

We believe that Public Law 94–142—if not in name, surely in intent—represents a restatement of the symbolic era of compulsory education. The intent and purpose of the Education for All Handicapped Children Act of 1975 was to guarantee access to education. Harvey (1978a) stated that it "stipulates that all handicapped children 3 through 21 years of age shall receive a free, appropriate public education with (a) first priority to children who are not receiving an education and (b) second priority to children inadequately served with the most severe handicaps" (pp. 234–235). Because of inadequacies in the first legislative enactments, a rebirth of compulsory education was necessary. The history of this new compulsory special education act likely will parallel that of general compulsory education acts. We believe that we can expect a period of ideological transition that will be characterized by considerable professional discourse on the merits and limitations of Public Law 94–142 before full implementation is realized. In fact, the discourse has already begun (Abeson & Zettel, 1977; Reynolds, 1975, in press).

The state of the art in treatment must be considered in any discussion of changes. At the same time, the alleged changes must be viewed historically with full consideration for our track record in serving handicapped students and students who fail in both institutional and noninstitutional environments. The failure of America's schools to educate a significant number of students is addressed in Chapters 1 and 2. In an analysis of the 1970 census data completed by the Children's Defense Fund (Washington Research Project, 1978), the conclusion was that "out of school children share a common characteristic of *differentness* by virtue of race, income, physical, mental, or emotional handicap and age" (p. 4). Compulsory school attendance laws permitted the exclusion of children who could not profit from instruction or who had learned all they could (Abeson & Zettel, 1977). Yet, clearly, the exclusion of children from school is counter to the ideals of compulsory education. In examining treatments, it is important to consider the varieties offered to students who actually or functionally have been excluded from school.

Institutional Care

The treatment of the different individuals in institutions always has been a topic of considerable public concern. When the harshness of early (prior to the 1800s) treatments (for example, boring holes in the head [trephining] or burning at the stake for being a witch) was criticized, "moral" treatment was instituted (Ullman & Krasner, 1969). Bockoven (1963) noted:

Moral treatment was never clearly defined, possibly because its meaning was self-evident during the era in which it was used. It meant compassionate and understanding treatment of innocent sufferers. Even innocence was not a prerequisite to meriting compassion. Compassion extended to those whose mental illness was thought due to willful and excessive indulgence in the passions. (p. 12)

Ullmann and Krasner (1969) pointed out that moral treatment represented "the first effort to provide systematic and responsible care for large numbers of deviant people" (p. 126). Certainly, Dorothea Dix's (1843) plea to the Massachusetts legislature for better treatment of "insane" persons, whom she described as "in cages, closets, cellars, stalls, pens! chained, naked, beaten with rods, and lashed into obedience," can be viewed as a plea for more humane treatment of the insane. However, Bockoven (1963) noted that Dix's interest in providing facilities for treatment may have been responsible for the false notion that "institutional treatment is better treatment."

Her immense emphasis on eliminating gross abuse of the insane had the most unfortunate effect of driving into the background any serious considerations of the requirements to be met in securing positive treatment. The inundation of mental hospitals with long-standing chronic cases ruined moral treatment. (Bockoven, 1963, p. 38)

The same perspective is shown in a historical analysis of American institutions for mentally defective people. In describing two stages in the development of these institutions, Davies (1925) wrote:

These early institutions were in a sense a branch of the public school system, boarding schools having for their purpose the education of the mentally defective. . . . When these early education methods proved less fruitful than had been anticipated in the intellectual rehabilitation of the mentally defective, the institutions . . . were forced to face reality in the demands made upon them for the custodial care of many relatively unimprovable cases, and they entered upon that second and familiar stage in which custodial care and segregation were most prominent. (p. 210)

Davies added that the custodial-care stage arose because of society's fears about the freedom of defective persons. We would add that custodial, rather than therapeutic, care was probably all that could be expected, considering the growing mass of so-called deviant persons in need of treatment, and we agree with Bockoven's analysis of Dorothea Dix's contribution.

To say that the effects of institutionalization have been less than favorable is probably a great understatement. Goffman (1961) vividly described the depersonalization and degrading experiences (for example, assignment of number instead of name) that often accompany entrance to an institution. And although Roos (1966) was optimistic about the changing roles of residential institutions for mentally retarded persons, Blatt (1970, 1975, 1976) described the deplorable conditions extant in the contemporary treatment facilities available to them. A poignant record of his views (and their similarity to those seen by Dix in different settings) is available in *Christmas in Purgatory: A Photographic Essay on Mental Retardation* (Blatt & Kaplan, 1966).

Zigler and Baller (1977) summarized 25 years of research on the impact of institutionalization on the people who are called retarded. Several conclusions of the two investigators reflect contemporary opinions on the value of institutional care. One is that the nature of stimulation before institutionalization can affect behavior after institutionalization. In addition, family relationships are very important during institutionalization:

The retarded individuals who maintained contact with their parents or parent-surrogates either by being visited at the institution or by going home on vacations were more likely to display the type of autonomous behavior characteristic of nonretarded children. Thus, we found clear empirical evidence that an institutional *policy of encouraging many contacts with the community* does promote psychological growth. (p. 4)

Zigler and Baller (1977) also reported a surprising lack of association among administrative factors (for example, cost per resident per day, number of staff per resident) and the effects of the institutional experience.

In 1969 Wolfensberger predicted that the traditional institution would gradually fade away, and in 1971 he argued that changes in the incidence (that is, occurrence of new cases) and prevalence (that is, ratio of cases in the population) of different levels of mental retardation would determine the degree to which institutions disappear. Wolfensberger has supported the principles of normalization and advocacy for the retarded (see Wolfensberger, 1972; Wolfensberger & Kurtz, 1969). Historical and contemporary analyses of the effects of institutional care have led other theorists in the same direction.

Noninstitutional Care

Certainly the traditional institutional facility is not the only domain that treats difference; it is not even the predominant one. The historical development of the special class in the public schools is discussed in Chapter 2, and the nature and effectiveness of special interventions is addressed in Chapter 6. A contemporary issue that must be examined is mainstreaming: in our opinion, the belief that handicapped children should, to the maximum extent feasible, be educated in the mainstream is directly related to the issue of institutional vs. noninstitutional care. Reynolds (in press) stated that "the 'mainstream' movement in communities is based on the same principles that govern deinstitutionalization" (p. 7).

Efforts to evaluate the success of children placed in special classrooms are often referred to as efficacy studies, and they have been amply discussed (see Cegelka & Tyler, 1970; Goldstein, 1967; Guskin & Spicker, 1968; Kirk, 1964; MacMillan, 1971; Quay, 1963). Meyers, MacMillan, and Yoshida (1980) critically reviewed and analyzed the sampling procedures, outcome measures, and nature of treatments in the studies of the efficacy of special classrooms. They indicated that uncritical interpretation has led some people to believe that placement in a regular classroom (that is, a form of mainstreaming) is a good alternative to special class education. In their discussion of legal issues in the education of handicapped children, Abeson and Zettel (1977) presented evidence that the exclusion of children with handicaps, incorrect or inappropriate classification or programming, and/or capricious educational decision making was the basis for changes in public policy relating to the education of handi-capped students (that is, Public Law 94–142). See Chapter 8 for addi-tional discussion of the implications of these legal issues. Coupled with the failure of special education to demonstrate significant effects from special class placement, legal challenges to intraschool segregation based on arbi-trary classification (for example, ability grouping) has led to an interest in a new kind of compulsory education. How well compulsory special educa-tion will achieve bureaucratic rather than ideologic prominence depends on the changes in two main areas (that is, teacher attitudes toward and public policies on special education): we shall discuss the state of the art of each area after a brief digression on the subject of mainstreaming.

THE HOPE OF MAINSTREAMING

Mainstreaming does not mean that all handicapped children will be retained in or returned to regular classrooms, but it does represent one aspect of the general principle of normalization, or the idea that the expe-riences of handicapped children should be as much like those of their nor-mal peers as possible. The mechanism through which proponents of mainstreaming hope to achieve normalized school experiences is the least restrictive environment (LRE). Dybwad (1980) indicated that "in the field of special education hardly anything provokes heated controversy as surely as the use of the new catchwords: *mainstreaming, normalization,* and *the least restrictive environment*" (p. 85). Put simply, each aspect contributed to and is part of the notion that the education and life experiences of handicapped individuals should be no more different than necessary.

With the enactment of Public Law 94–142, free, appropriate education became a handicapped individual's right. Abeson and Zettel (1977) pointed out that

[T]o deal with the past problems of inappropriate educational services being provided to children who have handicaps, the Congress included as a major component of P. L. 94–142 a requirement that each child be provided with a written individualized education program known as the IEP. (p. 123)

They also noted that each state must establish

procedures to insure that, to the maximum extent appropriate, handicapped children, including children in public and private institutions or other care facilities, are educated with children who are not handicapped and that spe-cial classes, separate schooling, or the removal of handicapped children from the regular education environment occurs only when the nature or severity of the handicap is such that education in regular classes with the use of supplementary aids and services cannot be achieved satisfactorily (Public Law 94–142, 1975, sec. 612,5,B). (p. 125)

Not only is free education for handicapped children compulsory, but the law now mandates that that education also must be appropriate to the maximum extent possible with regard to normalization, mainstreaming, and least restrictive placements. And although we do not disagree with the educational mainstreaming ideal represented by Public Law 94–142, we do recognize that there are serious obstacles in the way of full, bureaucratic implementation of that ideal.

FACTORS THAT IMPEDE THE SUCCESS OF MAINSTREAMING

With the enactment of Public Law 94–142, several educational ideals moved from the realm of preferred or best practice to the arena of public policy. In addition to the right to a free, appropriate education, the rights to a nondiscriminatory evaluation and due process are mandated by the Education for All Handicapped Children Act of 1975 (Abeson & Zettel, 1977). The legal basis for these best practices is discussed in Chapter 8. The shift in emphasis from preferred practice with regard to these ideals to educational policy has profound implications for full and complete compliance with the law.

The direct instruction of all school children is the responsibility of classroom teachers. Implementation of educational policy is usually the responsibility of administrative staff members. Education is a "loose coupled" system; that is, the extent to which the behaviors of subordinates (for example, teachers) are directly influenced by the desires, wishes, behaviors, and policies of supraordinates (for example, principals, curriculum coordinators, directors) is marginal. A few "tight couplings" make teachers extensions of administrators. How closely the ideals embodied in Public Law 94–142 represent the dreams of individuals removed from teaching will determine how well the ideals will be realized, and in fact, we have few models for the implementation of major innovations (for example, compulsory special education).

Baker and Gottlieb (1980) believe that the principal concern of Public Law 94–142 is the notion of mainstreamed education, and they wrote that "perhaps more than any other aspect of [the law], the mandate to place handicapped children in the least restrictive environment has caused teachers and administrators to be wary of forthcoming trends in special education and to close their eyes to the problem in the hope that it will disappear" (p. 4). An innovative aspect of compulsory special education is the notion that it should be provided, as much as possible, in the mainstream. Of importance, then, in the implementation of Public Law 94–142, is how well its ultimate goal and/or purpose is realized.

In determining any program or implementing any policy, various levels of achievement are possible. Hall and Loucks (1977) introduced the concept of levels of use as a means of evaluating the extent to which an educational innovation or treatment is implemented. In their model they identified and defined eight levels of use indicators, as well as observable activities that offer cues for evaluating decisions to innovate or implement at various levels. For example, the state in which "the user has little or no knowledge of the innovation" (p. 266) was identified as the Nonuse level; taking "action to learn more detailed information about the innovation" (p. 266) was considered evidence of a decision to alter one's level of use (in this case, nonuse). Similarly, the state in which "changes in use are made more to meet user needs than client needs" (p. 266) was defined as the Mechanical Use level; changing use to increase client outcomes was listed as evidence of a decision to change use levels. Hall and Loucks also described their research on the utility of the level of use indicators and their model.

Public Law 94–142 represents an intended major educational innovation, and its effects are presumed to be far-reaching and profound. As with any innovation, however, different levels of implementation are possible. To determine the extent to which the components of Public Law 94–142 are being developed and carried out, it is necessary to evaluate the levels of use among different groups of individuals. We believe that teacher attitudes and expectancies, as well as several dimensions of public policy, impede the full implementation of the innovative concepts of normalization, mainstreaming, and least restrictive environments embodied in the law.

TEACHER ATTITUDES

In a review of the implications of mainstreaming, Abramson (1980) found that the results of studies designed to determine how regular educators perceive children with handicaps have not been encouraging:

The results of these studies . . . suggest that teacher attitudes and instructional practices in regard to handicapped children are unfavorable (for example, Palmer, 1979; Parish & Copeland, 1978; Parish & Dyck, 1979).
    Although there is some evidence indicating that regular education teachers are favorably inclined toward integrating handicapped children (Guerin & Szatlocky, 1974), the vast majority of studies have demonstrated no such favoritism. Regular classroom teachers have consistently indicated lack of

support for the integration of exceptional children in the regular classroom (Gickling & Theobald, 1975; MacMillan et al., 1978; Moore & Fine, 1978; Shotel et al., 1972; Vacc & Kurst, 1977). . . .

There is some evidence to indicate that many of the attitudes seen in regular classroom teachers may be formed before the actual teaching process begins. (pp. 326–327)

Baker and Gottlieb (1980) reviewed attitudes of teachers toward mainstreaming retarded children and discussed factors "likely to underlie teachers' feelings about integration in their classes" (p. 206). They included the following factors in that discussion:

1. Knowledge of the behaviors of retarded children
2. Feelings about their own competence with retarded children
3. Expectations of supportive service assistance
4. Beliefs concerning advantages and disadvantages of different placements for retarded children
5. Attitudes toward other teaching-related matters

The two investigators also reported that the attitudes of many teachers are unfavorable because of these factors. They went on to explain that "knowing that a classroom teacher harbors negative attitudes tells us little about his behavior toward the handicapped child" (p. 206). Of equal importance are the kinds of behaviors that teachers exhibit and their influence on the behaviors of handicapped children.

TEACHER EXPECTANCIES

In 1968, Robert Rosenthal and Lenore Jacobsen published *Pygmalion in the Classroom,* whose basic premise was that teacher expectations were influential in student performances. Algozzine and Mercer (1980) suggested that "one's expectations (or expectancies in general) may be defined as the predicted probability of the occurrence of a future event" (p. 290). To Brophy and Good (1974), "the idea that teacher expectations can function as self-fulfilling prophesies appears to be an established fact rather than a mere hypothesis" (p. 77). They found that the expectation of low achievement by a youngster may result in interactions different (that is, teacher behaviors) from those resulting from the expectation of high achievement.

Reviewing expectancies in special education, Algozzine and Mercer (1980) presented the case as follows:

A variety of factors have been shown to influence teachers' predictions of the future performance (i.e., expectations) of their children; actual interactions with those children as well as their classroom achievements have also been shown to be differentially effected by teachers' expectancies (Baker & Crist, 1971; Brophy & Good, 1974; Dusek, 1975). Within this context, the biasing factors may be thought of as naturally-occurring or experimentally-induced. Organismic characteristics upon which individuals may be sorted and which result in differential predictions of future performances have been shown to have powerfully biasing effects. In fact, such naturally-occurring factors as appearance (Algozzine, 1975; Berscheid & Walster, 1974; Ross & Salvia, 1975; Salvia, Sheare, & Algozzine, 1975), race (Coates, 1972; Datta, Schaefer, & Davis, 1968; Rubovits & Maehr, 1973), sex of the child (Carter, 1952; Jackson & Lahaderne, 1967; Lippett & Gold, 1959; Meyer & Thompson, 1956; Palardy, 1969), behavior (Algozzine, 1977; Algozzine, Mercer, & Countermine, 1977; Curran, 1977), and achievement level of older siblings (Seaver, 1973) have been shown to differentially effect the formation and transmission of classroom teachers' expectations.

Experimentally-induced expectations differ from naturally-occurring ones in that the former are manipulated by the researcher in an attempt to bring about differential outcomes for different levels of the expectancy biaser. . . . [A] number of investigators have shown that teachers hold differential expectations and/or perform differently with children for whom they hold high or low expectations (Beez, 1970; Brophy & Good, 1974; Dusek, 1975; Medinnus & Unruh, 1971; Meichenbaum, Bowers, & Ross, 1969; Rothbart, Dalfen, & Barrett, 1971; Rubovits & Maehr (1971). (pp. 293–294)

PUBLIC POLICY

A Massive System of Identification

We observed in Chapter 2 that according to a recent survey conducted by the National Education Association, 95 percent of all classroom teachers believed that students' academic and social difficulties were caused by (1) home and family problems and (2) deficits and disabilities within the student. We noted in Chapter 5 that the prevalent orientation in assessment is one designed to find out what is wrong with students. School personnel have developed a massive system to support the identification of handicaps, disabilities, dysfunctions, and disorders in students. The size of this system is evidenced by the fact that the public schools employ as many as 15,000 school psychologists, and despite their competence in other areas, those school psychologists are used as gatekeepers for special education. There are currently more than 1,500 published tests (Buros, 1978), each designed to identify specific traits, skills, or characteristics and to promote the identification of differences in students. Testing is big business, and the special education system supports it.

A Massive System of Funding

Regardless of the educator's perennial excuse of lack of funding when asked why the field has not produced more answers than questions, a great deal of money has been spent in special and remedial education. As Donaldson and Stevens (1979a) explain:

Special Education is BIG business. Calculation of the total amount of funding directed into special education programs in one form or another is not a simple task. The enormous sum, however can be scoped somewhat by assuming that projections for support of Public Law 94–142, the Education for All Handicapped Children Act of 1975, will become in-fact appropriations, thus pass the $1 billion threshold within the next few years. (p. 213)

As we have indicated previously, the federal government does not give away money. The millions of dollars in government support for special and remedial education reaches practitioners in one of two ways. It is either distributed according to congressionally mandated formulas or allocated through special projects judged appropriate for support (Donaldson & Stevens, 1979a). In either case, the federal influence in education (though a state's right) is obvious in the guidelines, mandates, procedures, priorities and categories that must be met if educational agencies are to receive federal dollars.

The Office of Special Education and Rehabilitation Services (OSERS) of the Department of Education is a primary source through which federal support for failing children is channeled. To facilitate the administration of its programs and the distribution of some of its funds, OSERS utilizes categories such as mentally retarded, hearing impaired, seriously emotionally disturbed, and specific learning disabilities. Estimates of the numbers of such children serve, in part, as the basis for requesting funds from Congress and distributing them to educational professionals. Gallagher, Forsythe, Ringelheim, and Weintraub (1976) indicate that in order to guarantee that federal funds were spent appropriately, "strict requirements were established that forced some type of labeling to ensure that only handicapped children were benefited" (p. 441).

Of course, federal support is not the only basis for funding special and remedial education. Gallagher and his colleagues (1976) report that "nonfederal expenditures (for the education of handicapped children) are of an order of fifteen to twenty times that of the federal expenditures. . . ." (p.441). They add that several several different methods (for example, weighted formulas, unit financing, percentage reimbursements) are used to determine the actual distribution of all funds for handicapped children. In general, these disbursements for special and remedial education are made according to the numbers of children served, the number of trained professionals working with such children, or the type of treatment they receive (Gallagher et al., 1976).

There obviously is a lot of money at stake when we ask a question such as "Who should be paid for educating handicapped children?" and no special education administrator can dismiss this question easily. Similarly,

the question of who receives funding for educating the handicapped children in the mainstream has far-reaching implications, as does that of
deciding who shall receive money to train professionals to work with
handicapped children in any setting.

In the past, the work of training professionals to work with special children began separate from regular education in isolation (often in the base-
ments of colleges of education). Special educators became accustomed to
working alone. To compensate for the professional loneliness, they formed
professional organizations within professional organizations: the Council
for Exceptional Children has over ten divisions, some of which have separate meetings to discuss important, topical issues. Handicapped children
also used to be educated apart from regular children. The establishment of
this "separate, but unequal" system has cost money, and special educators have become accustomed to receiving additional money to provide
services for handicapped children. That they are concerned about the
potential loss of this money is evidenced in the discussion of the results of
a survey conducted by Gallagher and his colleagues (1976). They indicated that "special education administrators at the state level have generally
shown concern that sudden changes in existing patterns of labels may
cause a sharp decrease in resources for special programs for handicapped
children. . . ." (pp. 460–461).

The federal government does not give away money; no one gives away
money. But everyone would be willing to take it. To believe that significant numbers of school children will move from special to least restrictive
regular education without deciding who will pay is naive. Like asking oil
companies to distribute windfall profits to consumers, expecting mainstreaming to happen without concern for finances is absurd. The hope of
mainstreaming cannot be fulfilled without considering the disbursement
of special education's money. Unfortunately, much of that money is
appropriated and allocated through a system bound, at least in principle,
to the integrity of a categorical approach to providing services.

CURRENT INSTRUCTIONAL PRACTICE IN
SPECIAL AND REMEDIAL EDUCATION

In their work "Educating a Profession," Howsam, Corrigan, Denemark,
and Nash (1976) explained that "teaching is a decision-making and a
decision-implementing process" (p. 36). They added that engagement in
this process requires that "teachers study each learning case and identify
learning needs. Then they consider alternative strategies and decide
which ones to use. Implementing the strategy requires highly professional

skills; no two learning cases are ever exactly the same" (Howsam et al., 1976, p. 36). Current instructional practices in all of education are based, in most cases, on the belief that children do have important differences, which are the reason for the successful implementation of particular strategies of interventions.

Special and remedial education teachers often are trained in diagnostic-prescriptive teaching strategies, that is, the "practice of formulating instructional prescriptions on the basis of differential diagnostic results" (Arter & Jenkins, 1979, p. 518). A differential diagnosis is often made by assessing an individual's learning characteristics so that teaching strategies and learning needs can be matched to them (Arter & Jenkins, 1979; Kirk & Kirk, 1971). The practice of assessing an individual's abilities and prescribing subsequent teaching strategies (labeled differential diagnosis-prescriptive teaching by Arter & Jenkins, 1979) has been the "majority position within the field of learning disabilities over the past 20 or 30 years" (Haring & Bateman, 1977, p. 130).

Teaching is a decision-making–decision-implementing process, and as such, it may defy scientific definition because the exact ingredients of teaching have not been precisely identified. In special and remedial education, the attempts to define the components of successful learning (and teaching) have not had overwhelming acceptance or success.

Ysseldyke and Salvia (1974) found two models of diagnostic prescriptive teaching (DPT): task analysis and ability training, and they described the underlying assumptions and relative efficacy of each. Arter and Jenkins (1979) discussed and analyzed six assumptions underlying the Differential Diagnosis-Prescriptive Teaching (DD-PT) practice as follows:

1. Educationally relevant psychological abilities exist and can be measured. (p. 521)
2. Existing tests used in differential diagnosis are reliable. (p. 522)
3. Existing tests used for differential diagnosis are valid. (p. 524)
4. Prescriptions can be generated from differential diagnosis to remediate weak abilities. (p. 537)
5. Remediation of weak abilities improves academic achievement. (p. 540)
6. Prescriptions can be generated from ability profiles to improve academic achievement, with no direct training of weak abilities. (p. 542)

In their analysis of the literature supporting these assumptions, Arter and Jenkins concluded:

It is not surprising that DD-PT has not improved academic achievement, since most ability assessment devices have inadequate reliability and suspect validity. Moreover, abilities themselves have resisted training, and given the low correlations between ability assessments and reading achievement, it is not surprising that modality-instructional matching has failed to improve achievement.

The repeated failure to support the basic assumptions underlying the DD-PT model casts doubt on the model's validity. We do not intend to suggest that the model is theoretically untenable, or that it may not one day be effectively implemented. Rather, we believe that with the current instructional programs and tests, this model is not useful. (p. 549)

Although not all professionals in special and remedial education agree with Arter and Jenkins (see Kirk, Senf, & Larsen, 1981), no comparable, comprehensive analysis of research supporting DD-PT is available. It appears that the assessment of youngsters so as to identify appropriate alternative instructional strategies is more art than skill, more folklore than science. The popularity of the notion is shown in the results of a statewide survey that examined the benefits and prevalence of modality considerations in special education (Arter & Jenkins, 1977):

1. A majority (87%) of the teachers surveyed reported that they were familiar with the modality model [modifying instructional methods and materials relative to a child's strengths and weaknesses]. . . . (p. 293)
2. Of those familiar with the model, ninety-nine percent agreed that information about modality is one of the major outcomes of diagnosis. (p. 293)
3. Teachers familiar with the model attribute their information regarding the model to experience and coursework rather than books and journals. (p. 294)
4. Ninety-five percent of the teachers familiar with the model believed that research supports the use of the model to improve learning and ninety-six percent believed they obtained better results when instruction was modified based on ability assessment. (p. 294)

Arter and Jenkins (1977) concluded that "although research has not supported the practice of modality/instructional matching, teachers feel that the model is correct, and they attribute this judgment, in large part, to their personal experience" (p. 295). In addition, their findings suggest:

Relying on standardized norm-referenced ability tests for planning instruction must be seriously questioned. Among the problems with differential diagnosis and instruction are the questionable validity of the standardized instruments in measuring educationally relevant behaviors: the one-shot nature of these tests, which raises concerns over sources of unreliability both within the child and within the test instrument; the tendency to generalize findings based on group averages to the behavior of specific children; and the added inference that is required when using norm-referenced measures to choose instructional materials. (Arter & Jenkins, 1977, p. 296)

It appears, then, that the practices followed in much instructional decision making in special and remedial education are limited and in fact are part of a system recognized as essential to all teaching (see Howsam et al., 1976, p. 36). We believe that these practices are prevalent for two reasons:

1. The differences that exist in and among individuals are perceived as important sources of problems rather than as unique features on which to structure learning.
2. The study of teaching has focused on the wrong set of variables.

From the beginning of organized education, children who were expected to profit from schooling have differed. Educators concentrated too heavily on determining the reason for individual differences and spent too little time on how these differences should affect instructional practice or how to teach children despite their differences.

The first explanations for why individuals differed were based on belief systems that put faith in morality and the good life. Violations of natural laws were blamed for the observed abnormalities in people. With the help of psychologists and other social scientists, educators looked to intelligence to explain children's educational problems. Rather than being viewed as a difference (much like achievement), intelligence was seen as a source of diffference, and in this regard, intelligence became more an explanation than an observation of differences. Consistent with this social scientific trend, a variety of other observed differences (for example, memory, eye-hand coordination) among individuals acquired significance as explanations for other observed differences (for example, achievement). Thus, an elaborate, psychometrically inadequate system of identifying and explaining the extent of presumed important differences among individuals has evolved. In fact, special and remedial educators are easily overwhelmed by the vast array of standardized tests available for identifying the reason for a student's problems.

Unfortunately, once the reason is identified (and right or wrong, it almost always is), little is known about how to alleviate the problem. We believe that educators are searching an empty field and expect to find solutions to problems they have created without recognizing the error of their omission. The differences among individuals are not the reasons children are not learning in school but are merely symptoms we have chosen to analyze, and they have not fared well in the analysis. That is, the differences appear to be important, though educators have failed to analyze their universal and specific natures. For example, it is true not only that individuals identified as retarded score poorly on intelligence tests but also that individuals who are native Spanish speakers also may score poorly on intelligence tests. Similarly, individuals whose cultural back-grounds differ from that of the population on whom the particular intelli-gence test was normed also may do poorly on such tests. It is true that poor readers reverse letters, but some good readers reverse letters and some poor readers do not. The importance of differences, like beauty, is in the eye of the beholder.

The search for underlying causes for observed differences in individu-als has been largely fruitless, insofar as improving instructional practice is concerned. In the same way, our identification of functionally important components of teaching is marginal at best. We know little about how teachers spend their time with children or about how differences in the time spent influence how different children learn.

It is not surprising that teachers practice and believe in diagnostic-pre-scriptive teaching: their teachers or trainers had little other information that could be translated into sound educational practice. Teaching is a decision-making, decision-implementing process. Unfortunately, it appears to be a process about which precious little is known.

The challenge that faces special educators is formidable and goes beyond the development of manuals for writing IEPs or the question of whether our research should be basic or applied. We are faced with deci-sions greater than the appropriate content and form of inservice or preser-vice training. In fact, we must question the basis for the existence of spe-cial education, which is the belief that being different is somehow a problem. To survive and to continue to prosper, we must derive new views and perspectives, not regarding why differences exist and what to do about them, but how education and difference can coexist.

PERSPECTIVES ON THE FUTURE OF
SPECIAL AND REMEDIAL EDUCATION

Like the driver who puts a new set of Michelin tires on his 1951 Desoto and believes he has a new vehicle, we have been led to believe that schools are undergoing significant change. But that change is more superficial than substantive. There are major inconsistencies in current practice. Children with minimal differences from normal or average behavior are still being removed from regular classrooms. Students are still being given special education services in isolated settings. Students are still sitting in regular classrooms without taking part in the learning and social activi-ties. Regular classroom teachers are still looking for differences in stu-dents in order to refer them out of the classroom for assessment and other placement. How we address these inconsistencies will influence future practice in special and remedial education.

Public education in America, although legally for all and based on a number of democratic ideals, is not now designed to reach all students. In many ways the public education of today is as elitist as it always has been. Although we espouse the ideal of educating each individual to his or her full potential and set as a goal education for the realization of the enjoyment of life, it is clear that children are and always have been educated for social purposes. Schools continue to perform a sorting function for society, although the function loses its viability when there are no longer jobs for the illiterate. Education will change, but it will change more in response to economic needs than to legal mandates.

Chapter 10

The Critical Issue

A number of social, political, economic, and educational considerations guide and influence contemporary American education. Society sets the goals for its schools and, through its political and legal structures, establishes ideals for meeting these goals. Society and its members also decide how much they are willing to pay for the education of their children and youth, and how much more they are willing to pay to educate those who do not profit from the schools' standard offerings. Educators are left to devise administrative structures, educational environments, and technologies to achieve society's goals according to its ideals. That task is a formidable one.

Throughout this text we have described a number of critical issues in personnel preparation, identification of children with differences, assessment, intervention, and research. In approaching the conclusion of the text, we felt obligated to propose specific solutions to the many problems we discussed. Indeed, readers of prepublication copies of the chapters repeatedly asked for the delineation of solutions to the specific issues we had mentioned. As we began preparing our list of the ways to do things, we soon recognized the sheer foolishness of the endeavor. We found ourselves in the same trap that has snared so many before us—the trap of presuming that we did have the solutions to the difficult problems faced by educators who attempt to provide special and remedial education.

The critical issue in special and remedial education seems to be the demand for instant, simple solutions to incredibly complex problems. We believe that it is presumptious for anyone today to believe that he or she does have the answers to the problems we face, but the demand for instant simple solutions has been so strong that it has created a receptive natural environment for those people who believe that they do have those answers. But there are no simple solutions to the problems and issues we examine in this book.

An interesting marketing enterprise has developed around special and remedial education. Workshops and inservice training programs promise step-by-step directives, and publishers and developers claim to have *the* intervention to assist handicapped or failing students. Educators have demanded, and have been provided with, *the* treatment or intervention that works. We have not only demanded *the* programs, but we have given

Table **10.1**   Claims for Specific Tests and Instructional Programs Found in
Advertisements in Major Professional Journals

"Widely field tested and found to be effective when implemented with normal as well
as handicapped and gifted students."

"_____ is the one program that works. It works for *you!* It works for pupils of *every
age!*"

"_____ is the one program so thoroughly researched and concisely planned that it
gives you every element you need to help pupils achieve a level of reading success
never before attained."

"All the instruments you'll ever need for evaluation and testing."

"Need an individual test which *quickly* provides a stable and reliable estimate of
intelligence in 4 or 5 minutes per form? Has three forms?"

"For the special child you can now diagnose specific Language and Auditory
Processing problems—and then prescribe the correct materials for remediation—
A great help when making IEPs."

"You can teach the obese mentally retarded person to lose weight—and keep it
off—in just 19 weeks."

"Our products and services help you detect the handicapped, identify their particular
difficulties, and provide remedial action."

"Can your students become confident spellers in only 15 minutes per day? YES,
when you fill the time with lessons from _____ ."

"With this text, your students will be able to identify appropriate and effective
methods for helping children with emotional and behavioral problems."

---

them widespread use without examining our assumptions and/or requiring evidence of the safety or efficacy of the interventions.

The professional literature in special and remedial education also
publishes examples of instant, easy solutions to problems in the education
of handicapped and failing students. A perusal of several of the most
recent issues of the major professional publications in this field was
revealing.

Table 10.1 lists the claims made for special and remedial education
products. The claims are verbatim extracts from advertisements for specific tests or instructional programs in the 1980 issues of *Exceptional Children, Teaching Exceptional Children, Journal of School Psychology,* and *Journal of
Learning Disabilities*. The claims made in these advertisements, along with
claims made for the benefits of specific workshops and inservice training

sessions, illustrate vividly the Madison Avenue approach that has come to characterize the products developed for this profession. Repeatedly, claims are made for a program as *the* answer, *the* solution to complex problems.

In education, there currently is no equivalent to the Federal Food and Drug Administration, although perhaps there should be. But at least we can learn from the history of efforts by the pharmacological profession to control both prescription and over-the-counter medication. Until 1906 there were few, if any, regulations controlling the over-the-counter sale of drugs. In 1906 the Pure Food and Drug Act was passed, specifying that drugs must meet the standards of strength and purity claimed by their manufacturer. The Sherley amendment to the Pure Food and Drug Act, passed in 1912, specified that manufacturers were not to make false and fraudulent claims for products and left enforcement in the hands of government officials. The safety of drugs was not addressed until 1938 when the Food, Drug, and Cosmetic Act was passed, in which Congress specified that new drug products had to be approved as safe prior to marketing. In 1951, the Durham-Humphrey amendments to the Food, Drug, and Cosmetic Act divided drugs into two classes, prescription and nonprescription, and in 1962 the Kefauver-Harris amendments ruled that manufacturers must specify both the safety and effectiveness of all drugs marketed after 1938. In 1966 a joint committee of the National Academy of Sciences and the National Research Council began a study of 3,400 drugs that had entered the market between 1938 and 1962. Of 512 over-the-counter drugs studied, only 15 percent were judged to be effective for their specified uses. In 1972, the Food and Drug Administration began a study of the safety and effectiveness of over-the-counter medications. Today, drug manufacturers are required to demonstrate that their products are both safe and effective. The present federal regulations certainly are not without problems (see Mirkin, 1980), but they are a long step ahead of the current provisions for the regulation of the assessment-intervention enterprise in special and remedial education.

We noted earlier that we cannot tell educators specifically what is right or what the definitive solution is to the issues we face. We can, however, suggest some ways to look at the problems.

The first step in addressing critical issues in special and remedial education is to define the issues, and we have attempted to do so throughout this text. We believe that educators must examine their assumptions regarding students, how students learn (or why they fail to learn), and our current knowledge base in special and remedial education. Samuels (1981) illustrated the importance of two assumptions: (1) that schools can have a significant impact on students' academic achievement and (2) that most students are capable of learning basic skills (that is, the "cultural imperatives").

It is important that educators both examine the match between their assumptions and the assumptions underlying the development of commonly used tests and recognize that tests may provide information on what to teach but not on how to teach. Assessment is simply a behavior-sampling process, and as such, it should be used only when one wants to sample behaviors to enable making specific decisions more easily. Improving assessment will require much hard work and will begin when assessors stop asking, "What specific test should I give?" and instead address the decisions to be made, the behaviors to be sampled, the relevance of testing to planning interventions, and the technical adequacy of the tests they use.

Improvements in intervention will begin when educators start evaluating their assumptions regarding what students need and recognize that there are no magic ways of providing appropriate education for all students, and when they stop demanding an intervention that will work for all students. Drucker (1981) observed that "for too long, educators have insisted that there is one best way to teach and learn, even though they have disagreed about what that way is" (p. 20). There is no way, at present, to decide specifically how to teach students.

What can we do? We can collect data on the effectiveness of different interventions with different children and then use these data as the basis of future intervention decisions. In other words, by considering every intervention as a hypothesis and testing it under the best possible conditions, we will find out what works best with what child, which, after all, is the reason for education.

Cases and Statutory Materials

Beattie v. Board of Education, 169 Wis. 231, 233, 172 N. W. 153, 154 (1919).

Brown v. Board of Education, 347 U. S. 483 (1954).

Covarrubias v. San Diego Unified School District, Civ. No. 70–394–S (S. D. Cal., filed Feb. 1971) (settled by consent decree, July 31, 1972).

Diana v. State Board of Education. C. A. No. C–70–37 R. F. P. (N. D. Cal. filed Feb. 3, 1970).

Epperson v. Arkansas, 393 U. S. 97, 104 (1968).

Frederick L. v. Thomas, 419 F. Supp. 960 (E. D. Pa. 1976), aff'd, 57 F. 2a 373 (3d Cir. 1977).

Goso v. Lopez, 419 U. S. 565 (1975).

Hairston v. Drosick, 423 F. Supp. 180 (S.D. W. Va. 1974).

Hansen v. Hobson, 269 F. Supp. 401 (D. D. C. 1967).

Larry P. v. Riles, 343 F. Supp. 1306 (N. D. Cal. 1972), aff'd, 502 F. 2d. 963 (9th Cir. 1974)

Lemon v. Bossier Parish School Board, 444 F. 2d 1400 (5th Cir. 1971).

Lora v. New York City Board of Education, 456 F. Supp. 1211, 1275 (E. D. N. Y. 1978).

Martarella v. Kelley, 359 F. Supp. 478 (S.D. N.Y. 1972).

Merriken v. Cressman, 364 F. Supp. 913 (E. D. Pa. 1973).

Mills v. Board of Education, 348 F. Supp. 866, 880 (D. D. C. 1972).

Ordway v. Hargraves, 323 F. Supp. 1155 (D. Mass. 1971).

Panitch v. State of Wisconsin, 451 F. Supp. 132 (E. D. Wis. 1978).

PASE v. Hannon, 74C3586, (N. D. Ill. 1980).

Pennsylvania Association for Retarded Children v. Commonwealth of Pennsylvania, 334 F. Supp. 1257 (E. D. Pa. 1971); 343 F. Supp. 279 (E. D. Pa. 1972).

Pub. L. No. 94–142, 89 Stat. 773 (1975) (codified at 20 U. S. C. 1401–1461 (1978)).

Rehabilitation Act of 1973, 29 U. S. C., 701–794 (1975).

Tinker v. Des Moines Ind. Community School Dist., 393 U. S. 503, 511 (1969).

Washington v. Davis, 426 U. S. 229 (1976).

Watson v. City of Cambridge, 157 Mass. 561, 563, 32 N. E. 864, 864-65 (1893).

Wyatt v. Stickney, 325 F. Supp. 781 (M. D. Ala. 1971).

References

Abeson, A., & Zettel, J. The end of the quiet revolution: The Education for All Handicapped Children Act of 1975. *Exceptional Children,* 1977, *44,* 115–128.

Abramson, M. Implications of mainstreaming: A challenge for special education. In L. Mann & D. A. Sabatino (Eds.), *Fourth review of special education,* New York: Grune & Stratton, 1980.

Algozzine, B. *Attractiveness as a biasing factor in teacher-pupil interactions.* Unpublished doctoral dissertation, The Pennsylvania State University, 1975.

Algozzine, B. The emotionally disturbed child: Disturbed or disturbing? *Journal of Abnormal Child Psychology,* 1977, *5,* 205–211.

Algozzine, B. Single-subject or group research: Is any controversy necessary? *Educational Researcher,* 1980, *9*(4), 24–25.

Algozzine, B., & Mercer, C. D. Labels and expectancies for handicapped children and youth. In L. Mann and D. A. Sabatino (Eds.), *Fourth review of special education.* New York: Grune & Stratton, 1980.

Algozzine, B., Mercer, C. D., & Countermine, T. The effects of labels and behavior on teacher expectations. *Exceptional Children,* 1977, *44,* 131–132.

Algozzine, B., Schmid, R., & Mercer, C. D. *Childhood behavior disorders: Applied research and educational practice.* Rockville, Md.: Aspen Systems Corp., 1981.

Algozzine, B., & Stoller, L. *Effects of labels and competence on teachers' attributions for a student.* Research Report No. 43. Minneapolis: University of Minnesota Institute for Research on Learning Disabilities, 1980.

Algozzine, B., Ysseldyke, J. E., & Shinn, M. R. *Identifying children with learning disabilities: When is a discrepancy severe?* Research Report No. 47. Minneapolis: University of Minnesota Institute for Research on Learning Disabilities, 1980.

Alley, G., Snider, W., Spencer, J., & Angell, R. Reading readiness and the Frostig training program. *Exceptional Children,* 1968, *35,* 68.

Almanza, H. P., & Mosley, W. J. Curriculum adaptations and modifications for culturally diverse handicapped children. *Exceptional Children,* 1980, *46,* 608–614.

Aloia, G. F. Effects of physical stigmata and labels on judgments of subnormality by preservice teachers. *Mental Retardation,* 1975, *13,* 17–21.

American Psychiatric Association. Committee on Nomenclature and Statistics of the American Psychiatric Association. *Diagnostic and statistical manual of mental disorders.* Washington, D. C.: American Psychiatric Association Mental Hospital Service, 1952.

American Psychiatric Association. *Diagnostic and statistical manual of mental disorders: Second edition.* Washington, D. C.: American Psychiatric Association, 1968.

American Psychiatric Association. *Diagnostic and statistical manual of mental disorders: Third edition.* Washington, D. C.: American Psychiatric Association, 1980.

American Psychological Association. American Educational Research Association, & National Council on Measurement in Education. *Standards for educational and psychological tests.* Washington, D. C.: American Psychological Association, 1974.

Anderson, D. O. Pruning the fuzziness and flab from learning disabilities research. *The Journal of Special Education,* 1976, *10,* 157–161.

Angoff, W. H., & Ford, S. F. *Item-race interaction on a test of scholastic aptitude.* Princeton, N. J.: ETS, 1971.

Arena, J. J. *Teaching through sensory-motor experiences.* San Rafael, Calif.: Academic Therapy Publications, 1969.

Arter, J. A., & Jenkins, J. R. Examining the benefits and prevalence of modality considerations in special education. *The Journal of Special Education,* 1977, *11,* 281–298.

Arter, J. A., & Jenkins, J. R. Differential diagnosis-prescriptive teaching: A critical appraisal. *Review of Educational Research,* 1979, *49,* 517–555.

Baca, L. Issues in the education of culturally diverse exceptional children. *Exceptional Children,* 1980, *46,* 583.

Baer, D., & Bushell, D. The future of behavior analysis in the school? Consider its recent past, and then ask a different question. In J. Ysseldyke & R. Weinberg (Eds.), *The future of psychology in the schools: Proceedings of the Spring Hill Symposium. School Psychology Review, A Special Issue,* 1981, *10,* 2.

Baker, J. L., & Gottlieb, J. Attitudes of teachers toward mainstreaming retarded children. In J. Gottlieb (Ed.), *Educating mentally retarded persons in the mainstream.* Baltimore: Md.: University Park Press, 1980.

Baker, J. P., & Crist, J. L. Teacher expectancies: A review of the literature. In J. D. Elashoff & R. E. Snow (Eds.), *Pygmalion reconsidered.* Worthington, Ohio: Jones, 1971.

Ballard, J., & Zettel, J. Public Law 94–142 and Sec. 504: What they say about rights and protections. *Exceptional Children,* 1977, *44,* 177–185.

Barsch, R. H. *A movigenic curriculum.* Madison, Wis.: Bureau for Handicapped Children, 1965.

Barsch, R. H. *Achieving perceptual-motor efficiency.* Seattle: Special Child Publications, 1967.

Barsch, R. H. *Enriching perception and cognition.* Seattle: Special Child Publications. 1968.

Bayley, N. Consistency and variability in the growth of intelligence from birth to 18 years. *Journal of Genetic Psychology,* 1965, *75,* 96.

Beez, W. V. Influence of biased psychological reports on "teacher" behavior and pupil performance. Unpublished doctoral dissertation, Indiana University, 1970.

Belch, P. J. Toward noncategorical teacher certification in special education—myth or reality? *Exceptional Children*, 1979, *46*, 129–131.

Bensky, J. M., Shaw, S. F., Gouse, A. S., Bates, H., Dixon, B., & Beane, W. E. Public Law 94–142 and stress: A problem for educators. *Exceptional Children*, 1980, *47*, 24–29.

Bereiter, C. The future of individual differences. *Harvard Educational Review*, 1969, *39*, 162–170.

Berger, J., Cohen, B., & Zelditch, M. Status characteristics and expectations status: A process model. In J. Berger, M. Zelditch, & B. Anderson (Eds.), *Sociological theories in progress* (Vol. 1). Boston: Houghton Mifflin, 1966.

Berman, P., & McLaughlin, M .W. *Federal programs supporting educational change, Vol. VIII: Implementing and sustaining innovations.* Washington, D. C.: Department of Health, Education & Welfare, 1978.

Berry, G. L., & Lopez, C. A. Testing programs and the Spanish-speaking child: Assessment guidelines for school counselors. *School Counselor*, 1977, *24*, 261–269.

Berscheid, E., & Walster, E. Physical attractiveness. In L. Berkowitz (Ed.), *Advances in experimental social psychology* (Vol. 7). New York: Academic Press, 1974.

Bersoff, D. N. Regarding psychologists testily: Legal regulation of psychological assessment in the public schools. *Maryland Law Review*, 1979, *39*, 27–120.

Best, J. W. *Research in education.* Englewood Cliffs, N. J.: Prentice-Hall, 1970.

Bijou, S. W. Environment and intelligence: A behavioral analysis. In R. Cancro (Ed.), *Intelligence: Genetic and environmental contributions.* New York: Grune & Stratton, 1971.

Binet, A., & Simon, J. *The development of intelligence in children.* Baltimore: Md.: Williams & Wilkins, 1916.

Binkley, J. R. Viewpoints. *Journal of Reading*, 1980, *24*, 69–70.

Blackhurst, A. E., & Hofmeister, A. M. Technology in special education. In L. Mann & D. A. Sabatino (Eds.), *Fourth review of special education.* New York: Grune & Stratton, 1980.

Blanton, R. L. Historical perspectives on classification of mental retardation. In N. Hobbs (Ed.), *Issues in the classification of children* (Vol. 1). San Francisco: Jossey-Bass, 1976.

Blatt, B. *Exodus from pandemonium.* Boston: Allyn & Bacon, 1970.

Blatt, B. *Souls in extremis.* Boston, Allyn & Bacon, 1975.

Blatt, B. *The revolt of the idiots.* Glen Ridge, N. J.: Exceptional Press, 1976.

Blatt, B., & Kaplan, F. *Christmas in purgatory: A photographic essay on mental retardation.* Boston: Allyn & Bacon, 1966.

Bloom, B. S. *Stability and change in human characteristics*. New York: John Wiley, 1964.

Bockoven, J. S. *Moral treatment in American psychiatry*. New York: Springer, 1963.

Bogdan, R., & Taylor, S. The judged, not the judges: An insider's view of mental retardation. *American Psychologist, 1976, 31,* 47–52.

Bourne, W. O. *History of the public school society*. New York: W. Wood & Co., 1870.

Bower, E. M. *Early identification of emotionally handicapped children in schools* (2nd ed.). Springfield, Ill.: Chas. C Thomas, 1969.

Brolin, D. E., & D'Alonzo, B. J. Critical issues in career education for handicapped students. *Exceptional Children, 1979, 46,* 246–253.

Brophy, J. E., & Good, T. L *Teacher-student relationships: Causes and consequences*. New York: Holt, Rinehart & Winston, 1974.

Broudy, H. S. Conflicts in school programs. *Today's education, 1978, 67,* 24–27.

Brown, D. T. Issues in accreditation, certification, and licensure. In G. Phye & D. Reschly (Eds.), *School psychology: Perspectives and issues,* New York: Academic Press, 1979.

Burke, P. J. Personnel preparation: Historical perspective. *Exceptional Children, 1976, 43,* 144–147.

Burkhead, J., Fox, T. G., & Holland, J. W. *Input and output in large-city high schools*. Syracuse; N. Y.: Syracuse University Press, 1967.

Buros, O. *Eighth mental measurements yearbook*. Highland Park, N. J.: Gryphon Press, 1978.

Burstein, L. Secondary analysis: An important resource for educational research. *Educational Researcher, 1978, 7*(5), 9–12.

Bush, R. N., & Enemark, P. Control and responsibility in teacher education. In K. Ryan (Ed.), *Teacher education: The seventy-fourth yearbook of the National Society for the Study of Education* (Part 2). Chicago: University of Chicago Press, 1975.

Bush, W. J., & Waugh, K. W. *Diagnosing learning disabilities*. Columbus, Ohio: Chas. E. Merrill, 1976.

Callahan, R. E. *An introduction of education in American society*. New York: Knopf, 1961.

Carnine, D. Direct instruction: A successful system for educationally high-risk children. *Journal of Curriculum Studies, 1979, 7,* 29–45.

Carter, L. Federal clearance of educational evaluation instruments: Procedural problems and proposed remedies. *Educational Researcher, 1977, 6*(6), 7–12.

Carter, R. How invalid are marks assigned by teachers? *Journal of Educational Psychology, 1952, 45,* 213–228.

Cegelka, W. J. Competencies of persons responsible for the classification of mentally retarded individuals. *Exceptional Children, 1978, 45,* 26–31.

Cegelka, W. J., & Tyler, J. L. The efficacy of special class placement for the mentally retarded in proper perspective. *Training School Bulletin, 1970, 65,* 33–65.

Charter, W. W., & Jones, J. E. On the risk of appraising non-events in program evaluation. *Educational Researcher,* 1973, *2*(11), 5–7.

Clark, D. L., & Marker G. The institutionalization of teacher education. In K. Ryan (Ed.), *Teacher education: The seventy-fourth yearbook of the National Society for the Study of Education* (Part 2). Chicago: University of Chicago Press, 1975.

Cleary, T. A. Test bias: Prediction of grades of Negro and white students in integrated colleges. *Journal of Educational Measurement,* 1968, *5,*115–124.

Coates, B. White adult behavior toward black and white children. *Child Development,* 1972, *43,* 143–154.

Cohen, S. A. The fuzziness and the flab: Some solutions to research problems in learning disabilities. *The Journal of Special Education,* 1976, *10,* 129–136.

Cohen, S., Semmes, M., & Guralnick, M. J. Public Law 94–142 and the education of preschool children. *Exceptional Children,* 1979, *45,* 279–285.

Cole, N. S. Bias in selection. *Journal of Educational Measurement,* 1973, *10,* 237–255.

Coleman, H. M., & Dawson, S. T. Educational evaluation of visual-perceptual-motor dysfunction. *Journal of Learning Disabilities,* 1969, *2,* 242–251.

Coleman, J. *Equality of educational opportunity.* Washington, D. C.: U. S. Government Printing Office, 1966.

Cone, J. D., & Hawkins, R. P. (Eds.), *Behavioral assessment: New directions in clinical psychology.* New York: Brunner/Mazel, 1977.

Connor, F. P. The past is prologue: Teacher preparation in special education. *Exceptional Children,* 1976, *42,* 365–378.

Cook, T. D., & Gruber, C. L. Meta evaluation research. *Evaluation Quarterly,* 1978, *2,* 5–49.

Cooper, C. L., & Marshall, J. Occupational sources of stress: A review of literature relating to coronary heart disease and mental ill health. *Journal of Occupational Psychology,* 1976, *49,* 11–28.

Cooper, H. M. Pygmalion grows up: A model for teacher expectation communication and performance influence. *Review of Educational Research,* 1979, *49,* 389–410.

Copperman, P. *The literacy hoax: The decline of reading, writing, and learning in the public schools and what we can do about it.* New York: Morrow, 1978.

Craig, S. B. Fifty years of training teachers of the deaf. *School and Society,* 1942, *56,* 301–303.

Cremin, L. A. *The transformation of the school.* New York: Knopf, 1961.

Cromwell, R. I., Blashfield, R. K., & Strauss, J. S. Criteria for classification systems. In N. Hobbs (Ed.), *Issues in the classification of children* (Vol. 1). San Francisco: Jossey-Bass, 1975.

Cronbach, L. J. Heredity, environment, and educational policy. *Harvard Educational Review,* 1969, *39,* 190–199.

Cronbach, L. J. Five decades of public controversy over mental testing. *American Psychologist,* 1975, *30,* 1–14.

Cruickshank, W. M. An interview with. . . . *The Directive Teacher,* 1980, *16,* 18.

Cubberley, E. P. *Readings in public education in the United States.* Boston: Houghton Mifflin, 1934.

Curran, T. *Mainstreaming attitudes as a function of behavioral expectations.* Unpublished doctoral dissertation, Pennsylvania State University, 1977.

Datta, L., Schaefer, E., & Davis, M. Sex and scholastic aptitude as variables in teachers' ratings of the adjustment and classroom behavior of Negro and other seventh-grade students. *Journal of Educational Psychology,* 1968, *59,* 94–101.

Davies, S. P. The institution in relation to the school system. *Journal of Psycho-Asthenics,* 1925, *30,* 210–226. Reprinted in M. Rosen, G. R. Clark, & M. S. Kivitz (Eds.), *The history of mental retardation* (Vol. 2). Baltimore: University Park Press, 1976.

Davis, C. R. The Buckley regulations: Rights and restraints. *Educational Researcher,* 1975, *4*(2), 11–13.

Dearman, N. B., & Plisko, V. W. *The condition of education.* Washington, D. C.: National Center for Education Statistics, 1979.

Deno, E. Special education as developmental capital. *Exceptional Children,* 1970, *37,* 229–240.

Deno, S., & Mirkin, P. *Data-based program modification: A manual.* Reston, Va.: The Council for Exceptional Children, 1977.

DeWeerd, J., & Cole, A. Handicapped children's early childhood program. *Exceptional Children,* 1976, *43,* 155–157.

Dilbard, J. D., Houghton, D. W., & Thomas, D. G. The effects of optometric care on educable mentally retarded children. *Journal of Optometric Vision Therapy,* 1972, *3,* 35–57.

Dix, D. Memorial to the legislature of Massachusetts, 1843. Reprinted in M. Rosen, G. R. Clark, & M. S. Kivitz (Eds.), *The history of mental retardation* (Vol. 1). Baltimore: University Park Press, 1976.

Doll, E. Current problems in mental diagnosis. *Journal of Psycho-Asthenics,* 1924, *29,* 298-308.

Dominowski, R. L. *Research methods.* Englewood Cliffs, N. J.: Prentice-Hall, 1980.

Donaldson, W. S., & Stephens, T. M. Service delivery to the handicapped: The role of the federal procurement process. Part I. Defining and funding programs in special education. *Journal of Learning Disabilities,* 1979, *12,* 212–221. (a)

Donaldson, W. S., & Stephens, T. M. Service delivery to the handicapped: The role of the federal procurement process. Part II. Selecting contractors by competitive award. *Journal of Learning Disabilities,* 1979, *12*(5), 12–23. (b)

Donaldson, W. S., & Stephens, T. M. Service delivery to the handicapped: The role of the federal procurement process. Part III. Appealing contract award. *Journal of Learning Disabilities,* 1979, *12*(6), 9–20. (c)

Drozda, D. G. Scientific research: An aid, not a cure, for the malaise that currently characterizes LD practice and research. *The Journal of Special Education,* 1976, *10,* 141–148.

Drucker, P. The coming changes in our school systems. *Wall Street Journal,* 1981, *61,* 20.

Drummond, W. H., & Andrews, T. E. The influence of federal and state governments on teacher education. *Phi Delta Kappan,* 1980, *62,* 97–100.

Dunn, L. M. Special education for the mildly retarded—Is much of it justifiable? *Exceptional Children,* 1968, *35,* 5–22.

Dusek, J. Do teachers bias children's learning? *Review of Educational Research,* 1975, *45,* 661–684.

Dvorak, E. A. General guide to a study of research reports. *Peabody Journal of Education,* 1956, *34,* 141–144.

Dwyer, C. A. *Test content in mathematics and science: The consideration of sex.* Paper presented at the annual meeting of the American Educational Research Association, 1976.

Dybwad, G. Avoiding misconceptions of mainstreaming, the least restrictive environment, and normalization. *Exceptional Children,* 1980, *47,* 85–88.

Educational Policies Commission. *The purposes of education in American democracy.* Washington, D. C.: National Education Association of the United States and American Association of School Administrators, 1938.

Elkind, D. Piagetian and psychometric conceptions of intelligence. *Harvard Educational Review,* 1969, *39,* 171–189.

Elkins, J. Learning disability research: Structured reactions to random thoughts about a fuzzy subject. *The Journal of Special Education,* 1976, *10,* 149–155.

Englemann, S., Granzin, A., & Severson, H. Diagnosing instruction. *The Journal of Special Education,* 1979, *13,* 355–365.

Entwistle, D., & Webster, M. Raising children's performance expectations. *Social Science Research,* 1972, *1,* 147–158.

Esquirol, J. E. D. Mental maladies. (E. K. Hunt trans.). Philadelphia: Lea and Blanchard, 1845. (Originally published as *Maladies mentales,* 1838.)

Estes, W. K. *Learning theory and mental development.* New York: Academic Press, 1970.

Farquhar, W. W., & Krumboltz, J. D. A checklist for evaluating experimental research in psychology and education. *Journal of Educational Research,* 1959, *52,* 353–354.

Farrell, E. E. Special classes in the New York City schools. *Journal of Psycho-Asthenics*, 1908–1909, *13*, 91–96.

Ferguson, G. A. *Statistical analysis in psychology & education* (3rd ed.). New York: McGraw-Hill, 1976.

Filler, J. W., Jr., Robinson, C. C., Smith, R. A., Vincent-Smith, L. J., Bricker, D. D., & Bricker, W. A. *Mental retardation*. In N. Hobbs (Ed.), *Issues in the classification of children* (Vol. 1). San Francisco: Jossey-Bass, 1976.

Finn, J. Expectations and the educational environment. *Review of Educational Research*, 1972, *42*, 387–410.

Fishbein, R. L. *An investigation of the fairness of the items of a test battery*. Paper presented at the annual meeting of the National Council on Measurement in Education, Washington, D. C., April 1975.

Flesch, R. F. *Why Johnny can't read*. New York: Harper, 1955.

Florio, D. H. Fiscal year 1981 education research/studies budget request: An underlying plan. *Educational Researcher*, 1980, *9*,(3), 19–21, 26, 35.

Foley, J. M. Effect of labeling and teacher behavior on children's attitudes. *American Journal of Mental Deficiency*, 1978, *83*, 380–384.

Forrest, E. B. Approaching vision training. *Academic Therapy*, 1968, *3*, 155–161.

Foster, G. G. *Expectancy and halo effects as a result of artificially induced teacher bias*. Unpublished doctoral dissertation, Pennsylvania State University, 1976.

Fox, D. J. *The research process in education*. New York: Holt, Rinehart & Winston, 1969.

Freudenberger, J. J. Burn-out: Occupational hazard of the child care worker. *Child Care Quarterly*, 1977, *6*, 90–98.

Frost, J. L. *Early childhood education rediscovered*. New York: Holt, Rinehart & Winston, 1968.

Frostig, M., & Horne, D. *The Frostig program for development of visual perception*. Chicago: Follett, 1964.

Fuller, F. F., & Bown, D. H. Becoming a teacher. In K. Ryan (Ed.), *Teacher Education: The seventy-fourth yearbook of the National Society for the Study of Education* (Part 2). Chicago: University of Chicago Press, 1975.

Gage, N. L. The yield of research on teaching. *Phi Delta Kappan*, 1978, *60*, 229–235.

Gallagher, J. J. The sacred and profane uses of labeling. *Mental Retardation*, 1976, *14*, 3–7.

Gallagher, J. J., Forsythe, P., Ringelheim, D., & Weintraub, F. J. Funding patterns and labeling. In N. Hobbs (Ed.), *Issues in the classification of children* (Vol. 2). San Francisco: Jossey-Bass, 1976.

Gardner, W. I. *Learning and behavior characteristics of exceptional children and youth*. Boston: Allyn & Bacon, 1977.

Getman, G. N. Pre-school perceptual skills: An aid to first grade achievement. *Optometric Weekly,* 1962, *53,* 1749–1753.

Getman, G. N. *How to develop your child's intelligence* (6th ed.). Luverne, Minn.: Announcer Press, 1966. (a)

Getman, G. N. The visuomotor complex in the acquisition of learning skills. In J. Hellman (Ed.), *Learning Disabilities* (Vol. 2). Seattle: Special Child Publications, 1966. (b)

Getman, G. N. The mileposts to maturity. *Optometric Weekly,* 1972, *63,* 321–331.

Getz, D. J. *Vision and perception training.* Chula Vista, Calif.: College of Optometrists in Vision Development, 1973.

Gickling, E. E., & Theobald, J. T. Mainstreaming: Affect or effect. *The Journal of Special Education,* 1975, *9,* 317–328.

Glass, G. V. Primary, secondary, and meta-analysis of research. *Educational Researcher,* 1976, *5,*(10), 3–8.

Glass, G. V. Integrating findings: The meta-analysis of research. In L. S. Shulman (Ed.), *Review of research in education* (Vol. 5), Itasca, Ill.: F. E. Peacock, 1978.

Glass, G. V., & Smith, M. L. Meta-analysis of the research on class size and achievement. *Education Evaluation and Policy Analysis,* 1979, *1,* 2–16.

Glatthorn, A. A. *Alternatives in education: School and programs.* New York: Dodd, Mead, 1975.

Glickman, L. J. Research activities for handicapped children. *American Education,* 1975, *11*(8), 30–31.

Goddard, H. H. *Juvenile delinquency.* New York: Dodd, Mead, 1921.

Goffman, E. *Asylums.* New York: Anchor-Doubleday, 1961.

Goldman, R. D., & Hewitt, B. N. Predicting the success of black, chicano, oriental, and white college students. *Journal of Educational Measurement,* 1976, *13,* 107–117.

Goldstein, H. The efficacy of special classes and regular classes in the education of educable mentally retarded children. In J. Zubin & G. A. Jervis (Eds.), *Psychopathology of mental development.* New York: Grune & Stratton, 1967.

Golladay, M. A. *The condition of education.* Washington, D. C.: National Center for Education Statistics, 1977.

Golladay, M. A., & Noell, J. *The condition of education.* Washington, D. C.: National Center for Education Statistics, 1978.

Goodenough, F. L. Racial differences in the intelligence of school children. *Journal of Experimental Psychology,* 1926, *9,* 388–397.

Goodlad, J. I. (Ed.). *Alternatives in education.* San Francisco: Jossey-Bass, 1973.

Goodlad, J. I. *What schools are for.* Bloomington, Ind.: Phi Delta Kappa Education Foundation, 1979.

Goodlad, J. I. How fares the common school? *Today's Education*, 1980, *69*, 37–40.

Goodman, L., & Hammill, D. The effectiveness of the Kephart-Getman activities in developing perceptual-motor cognitive skills. *Focus on Exceptional Children*, 1973, *9*, 1–9.

Gordon, E. W. Methodological problems and pseudo issues in the nature-nurture controversy. In R. Cancro (Ed.), *Intelligence: Genetic and environmental contributions*. New York: Grune & Stratton, 1971.

Gorham, K. A., Des Jardins, C., Page, R., Pettis, E., & Scherber, B. Effect on parents. In N. Hobbs (Ed.), *Issues in the classification of children* (Vol. 2). San Francisco: Jossey-Bass, 1976.

Gottlieb, J. Attitudes toward retarded children: Effects of labeling and academic performance. *American Journal of Mental Deficiency*, 1974, *79*, 268–273.

Gould, L. N. Optometry as a discipline in the educational complex. *Optometric Weekly*, 1962, *53*, 1665–1668.

Greenspan, S. B. The pediatric optometrist as a coordinator of multi-disciplinary care. *Journal of the American Optometric Association*, 1973, *44*, 149–151.

Grossman, H. (Ed.), *Manual on terminology and classification in mental retardation, 1973 revision*. Washington, D. C.: American Association on Mental Deficiency, 1973.

Group for the Advancement of Psychiatry. *Psychopathological disorders in childhood: Theoretical considerations and a proposed classification*. Formulated by the Committee on Child Psychiatry, 1966, *6*(62), 173–343.

Gubser, L. NCATE's director comments on the Tom critique. *Phi Delta Kappan*, 1980, *62*, 117–119.

Guerin, G. R., & Szatlocky, K. Integration programs for the mentally retarded. *Exceptional Children*, 1974, *41*, 173–177.

Guion, R. Employment tests and discriminatory hiring. *Industrial Relations*, 1966, *5*, 20–37.

Guskin, S. L., Bartel, N. R., & MacMillan, D. L. Perspective of the labeled child. In N. Hobbs (Ed.), *Issues in the classification of children* (Vol. 2). San Francisco: Jossey-Bass, 1976.

Guskin, S. L., & Spicker, H. H. Educational research in mental retardation. In N. R. Ellis (Ed.), *International review of research in mental retardation* (Vol. 3), New York: Academic Press, 1968.

Hall, G. E., & Loucks, S. F. A developmental model for determining whether the treatment is actually implemented. *American Educational Research Journal*, 1977, *14*, 263–276.

Hall, V., Greenwood, C., & Delquadri, J. *The importance of opportunity to respond to children's academic success*. Unpublished manuscript, Kansas City, Kans., 1979.

Hallahan, D. P., & Cruickshank, W. M. *Psychoeducational foundations of learning disabilities*. Englewood Cliffs, N.J.: Prentice-Hall, 1973.

Hallahan, D. P., & Kauffman, J. M. Labels, categories, behaviors: ED, LD, and EMR reconsidered. *The Journal of Special Education,* 1977, *11,* 139–149.

Halliwell, J. W., & Solan, H. A. The effects of a supplemental perceptual program on reading achievement. *Exceptional Children,* 1972, *39,* 613–621.

Hammill, D. D., & Larsen, S. C. The relationship of selected auditory perceptual skills and reading ability. *Journal of Learning Disabilities,* 1974, *7,* 429–435.

Hammill, D. D., Larsen, S. C., Parker, R., Bagley, M. T., & Sanford, H. G. *Perceptual and conceptual correlates of reading.* Unpublished manuscript, 1974. 1505 Sunny Vale, #217, Austin, Tex.

Hammill, D. D., & McNutt, G. *The correlates of reading.* Austin, Tex.: Pro-Ed, Monograph #1, 1981.

Hammill, D. D., & Wiederholt, J. L. Review of the Developmental Test of Visual Perception and the related training program. In L. Mann & D. A. Sabatino (Eds.), *First Review of Special Education.* New York: Grune & Stratton, 1973.

Haring, N. G., & Bateman, B. *Teaching the learning disabled child.* Englewood Cliffs, N.J.: Prentice-Hall, 1977.

Harmon, L. W. Sexual bias in interest measurement. *Measurement and Evaluation in Guidance,* 1973, *5,* 496–501.

Harrington, M. *The other America.* Baltimore: Penguin, 1962.

Harvey, J. Future trends in personal preparation. *Exceptional Children,* 1976, *43,* 148–150.

Harvey, J. Legislative intent and progress. *Exceptional Children,* 1978, *44,* 234–237. (a)

Harvey, J., Regional collaboration. In J. Smith (Ed.), *Personnel preparation and Public Law 94–142: The map, the mission and the mandate.* (2nd ed.). Boothwyn, Pa.: Educational Resources Center, 1978. (b)

Hatlin, P. H., Hall, A. P., & Tuttle, D. Education of the visually handicapped: An overview and update. In L. Mann & D. A. Sabatino (Eds.), *Fourth review of special education.* New York: Grune & Stratton, 1980.

Hays, W. L. *Statistics for the social sciences* (2nd ed.). New York: Holt, Rinehart & Winston, 1973.

Haywood, H. C. Editorial: What happened to mild and moderate mental retardation? *American Journal of Mental Deficiency,* 1979, *83,* 429–431.

Hazard, W. R., & Stent, M. D. Cultural pluralism and schooling: Some preliminary observations. In M. D. Stent, W. R. Hazard, & H. N. Rivlin (Eds.), *Cultural pluralism in education.* New York: Appleton-Century-Crofts, 1973.

Heath, R. W., & Nielson, M. A. The research basis for performance-based teacher education. *Review of Educational Research,* 1974, *44,* 463–484.

Hennessy, J. J., & Merrifield, P. R. A comparison of the factor structures of mental abilities in four ethnic groups. *Journal of Educational Psychology,* 1976, *68*(6), 754–759.

Hersen, M., & Barlow, D. H. *Single case experimental designs: Strategies for studying behavior change.* New York: Pergamon Press, 1976.

Hilliard, A. G. Cultural diversity and special education. *Exceptional Children,* 1980, *46,* 584–588.

Hirsch, J. Behavior-genetic analysis and its biosocial consequences. In R. Cancro (Ed.), *Intelligence: Genetic and environmental contributions.* New York: Grune & Stratton, 1971.

Hirsch, N. D. M. A study of natio-racial mental differences. *Genetic Psychology Monographs,* 1926, *1,* 231–406.

Hirshoren, A., & Umansky, W. Certification for teachers of preschool handicapped children. *Exceptional Children,* 1977, *44,* 191–193.

Holt, J. *How children fail.* New York: Dell, 1964.

Hopkins, K. D., & Kretke, G. L. n/cell considerations: Asking the wrong question for the right reason. *The Journal of Special Education,* 1976, *10,* 321–324.

Howe, M. W. Casework self-evaluation: A single-evaluation: A single-subject approach. *Social Science Review,* 1974, *48,* 11-23.

Howe, S. G. Report of commission to inquire into the conditions of idiots of the Commonwealth of Massachusetts. Boston: Senate Document No. 51, 1848, 1–37.

Howsam, R. B. The workplace: Does it hamper professionalization of pedagogy? *Phi Delta Kappan,* 1980, *62,* 93–96.

Howsam, R. B., Corrigan, D. C., Denemark, G. W., & Nash, R. J. *Educating a profession: Report of the bicentennial commission on education for the profession of teaching of the American Association of Colleges for Teacher Education.* Washington, D. C.: American Association of Colleges of Teacher Education, 1976.

Hunt, J. M. Psychological assessment in education and social class. In B. Z. Friedlander, G. M. Sterritt, & G. Kirk. *Exceptional infant* (Vol. 3). New York: Brunner/Mazel, 1975.

Hunter, J. E., & Schmidt, F. L. Critical analysis of the statistical and ethical implications of various definitions of test bias. *Psychological Bulletin,* 1976, *83,* 1053–1071.

Hurley, R. *Poverty and mental retardation: A causal relationship.* New York: Random House, 1969.

Hyman, I. A. Will the real school psychologist please stand up? III. A struggle of jurisdictional imperialism. *School Psychology Digest,* 1979, *8,* 174–180.

Irvin, T. The Education for All Handicapped Children Act of 1975: Public Law 94–142 regulations. In J. Smith (Ed.), *Personnel preparation and Public Law 94–142: The map, the mission and the mandate.* Boothwyn, Pa.: Educational Resources Center, 1978.

Jackson, P., & Kieslar, S. B. Fundamental research and practice. *Educational Researcher,* 1977, *6*(8), 13–18.

Jackson, P., & Lahaderne, H. Inequalities of teacher-pupil contracts. *Psychology in the Schools,* 1967, *4,* 204–211.

Jensen, A. R. Estimation of the limits of heritability of traits by comparison of monozygotic and dizygotic twins. *Proceedings of the National Academy of Sciences,* 1967.

Jensen, A. R. Patterns of mental ability and socio-economic status. *Proceedings of the National Academy of Sciences,* 1968, *60,* 1330–1337. (a)

Jensen, A. R. Social class, race, and genetics: Implications for education. *American Educational Research Journal,* 1968 *5,* 1–42. (b)

Jensen, A. R. How much can we boost IQ and scholastic achievement. *Harvard Educational Review,* 1969, *39,* 1–123. (a)

Jensen, A. R. Reducing the heredity-environment uncertainty. *Harvard Educational Review,* 1969, *39,* 209–243. (b)

Jensen, A. R. Test bias and construct validity. *Phi Delta Kappan,* 1976, *58,* 340–346.

Jensen, A. R. *Bias in mental testing.* New York: Free Press, 1979.

John-Steiner, V. P., & Souberman, E. Perspectives on bilingual education. In B. Spodek & H. J. Walberg (Eds.), *Early childhood education: Issues and insights.* Berkeley, Calif.: McCutchan, 1977.

Johnson, D. J., & Myklebust, H. R. *Learning disabilities: Educational principles and practices.* New York: Grune & Stratton, 1967.

Johnson, G. B. A method for evaluating research articles in education. *Journal of Educational Research,* 1957, *51,* 149–151.

Johnstone, E. R. The functions of the special class. *National Education Association Journal of Proceedings and Address of the 46th Annual Meeting,* 1908, pp, 114–118.

Johnstone, E. R. The summer school for teachers of backward children. *Journal of Psycho-Asthenics,* 1909–1910, *14,* 122–130.

Jones, R. A. *Self-fulfilling prophecies.* Hillsdale, N.J.: Lawrence Erlbaum Associates. 1977.

Jones, R. R. Design and analysis problems in program evaluation. In P. O. Davidson, F. W. Clark, & L. A. Hammerlynck (Eds.), *Evaluation of behavioral programs.* Champaign, Ill.: Research Press, 1974.

Joyce, B., & Weil, M. *Models of teaching.* Englewood Cliffs, N.J.: Prentice-Hall, 1972.

Jung, J. *The experimenter's dilemma.* New York: Harper & Row, Pub., 1971.

Kamin, L. J. *The science and politics of I.Q.* Hillsdale, N. J.: Lawrence Erlbaum Associates, 1974.

Kane, M. Summary report: Experimental program—transitional first grade. *Journal of Optometric Vision Therapy,* 1972, *3,* 23–29.

Karnes, M. B., & Zehrbach, R. R. Early education of the handicapped: Issues and alternatives. In B. Spodek & H. J. Walberg (Eds.), *Early childhood education.* Berkeley, Calif.: McCutchan, 1977.

Kauffman, J. M. Where special education for disturbed children is going: A personal view. *Exceptional Children,* 1980, *46,* 522–527.

Kazdin, A. E. Methodology of applied behavior analysis. In T. A. Brigham & A. C. Catania (Eds.), *Social and instructional process: Foundations and application of a behavioral analysis.* New York: Irvington/Naiburg–Wiley & Sons, 1977.

Keogh, B. K. Optometric vision training programs for children with learning disabilities: Review of issues and research, *Journal of Learning Disabilities,* 1974, *7,* 36–48.

Keogh, B. K. Another way to drown in the name of science: A response to S. Alan Cohen's proposed solution to research problems in learning disabilities. *The Journal of Special Education,* 1976, *10,* 137–139.

Kephart, N. C. *The slow learner in the classroom* (2nd ed.). Columbus, Ohio: Chas. E. Merrill, 1971.

Kerlinger, F. N. *Foundations of behavioral research* (2nd ed.). New York: Holt, Rinehart & Winston, 1973.

Kerlinger, F. N. The influence of research on practice. *Educational Researcher,* 1977, *6*(8), 5–12.

Kinney, L. B. *Certification in education.* Englewood Cliffs, N.J.: Prentice-Hall, 1964.

Kirk, R. E. *Experimental design: Procedures for behavioral sciences.* Belmont, Calif.: Brooks/Cole, 1968.

Kirk, S. *Educating exceptional children.* Boston: Houghton Mifflin, 1962.

Kirk, S. A. Research in education. In H. A. Stevens & R. Heber (Eds.), *Mental retardation: A review of research.* Chicago: University of Chicago Press, 1964.

Kirk, S. A. General and historical rationale for early education of the handicapped. In N. E. Ellis & L. Cross (Eds.), *Planning programs for early education of the handicapped,* New York: Walker, 1977.

Kirk, S., & Kirk, W. D. Psycholinguistic learning disabilities: Diagnosis and remediation. Urbana: University of Illinois Press, 1971.

Kirk, S. A., Senf, G. M. & Larsen, R. P. Current issues in learning disabilities. In W. M. Cruickshank & A. A. Silver (Eds.), *Bridges to tomorrow* (Vol. 2), *The best of ACLD.* Syracuse, N.Y.: Syracuse University Press, 1981.

Kirshner, A. J. Visual training and motivation. *Journal of the American Optometric Association,* 1967, *38,* 641–645.

Knight, E. W., & Hall, C. L. *Readings in American educational history.* New York: Appleton-Century-Crofts, 1951.

Kozol, J. *Death at an early age.* Boston: Houghton Mifflin, 1967.

Krathwohl, D. Improving educational research and development. *Educational Researcher,* 1977, *6*(4), 8–14.

Kratochwill, T. R. Foundations of time-series research. In T.R. Kratochwill (Ed.), *Single subject research: Strategies for evaluating change.* New York: Academic Press, 1978.

Kratochwill, T. R., & Levin, J. R. What time-series designs may have to offer educational researchers. *Contemporary Educational Psychology,* 1978, *3,* 273–329.

Kunzelmann, H. P., Cohen, M. A., Hulten, W. J., Martin, G. L., & Mingo, A. R. *Precision teaching.* Seattle: Special Child Publications, 1970.

Kurtz, P. D., Harrison, M., Neisworth, J. T., & Jones, R. T. Influence of "mentally retarded" label on teachers' nonverbal behavior toward preschool children. *American Journal of Mental Deficiency,* 1977, *82,* 204–206.

Ladas, H. Summarizing research: A case study. *Review of Educational Research,* 1980, *50,* 597–624.

Lambert, N. School psychology training for the decades ahead. In J. Ysseldyke & R. Weinberg (Eds.), *The future of psychology in the schools: Proceedings of the Spring Hill symposium. School Psychology Review, A Special Issue,* 1981, *10,* 2.

Landsman, L. Teacher burnout. *Instructor,* 1979, *88,* 56–62.

Larsen, S. C., & Hammill, D. D. The relationship of selected visual perceptual abilities to school learning. *The Journal of Special Education,* 1975, *9,* 281–291.

LaVor, M. Economic Opportunity Amendments of 1972, Public Law 92–424. *Exceptional Children,* 1972, *39,* 249–253.

LaVor, M., & Harvey, J. Headstart, Economic Opportunity, Community Partnership Act of 1974. *Exceptional Children,* 1976, *42,* 227–230.

Laycock, S. R. Every teacher a diagnostician. *Exceptional Child Review,* 1934, *2,* 47.

Lehmann, I. J., & Mehrens, W. A. (Eds.). *Educational research: Readings in focus.* New York: Holt, Rinehart & Winston, 1971.

Leonard, W. H., & Lowry, L. F. Was there really an experiment? *Educational Researcher,* 1979, *8*(6), 4–7.

Lessen, E. I., & Rose, T. L. State definitions of preschool handicapped populations. *Exceptional Children,* 1980, *46,* 467–469.

Levy, L., & Rowitz, L. *The ecology of mental disorders.* New York: Behavioral Publications, 1973.

Lincoln, D. F. Special classes for feeble-minded children in the Boston public schools. *Journal of Psycho-Asthenics,* 1903, *7,* 83–93.

Lindsey, M. (Ed.), *New horizons for the teaching profession.* Washington, D. C.: National Commission on Teacher Education and Professional Standards, National Education Association, 1961.

Lindsey, M. Teacher education: Reflections. *Journal of Teacher Education,* 1978, *29*(4), 5–9.

Linn, R. L., & Werts, C. E. Considerations for studies of test bias. *Journal of Educational Measurement,* 1971, *8,* 1–4.

Lippett, R., & Gold, M. Classroom social structure as a mental health problem. *Journal of Social Issues,* 1959, *15,* 40–49.

Lockheed-Katz, M. *Sex bias in educational testing: A sociologist's perspective.* Research Memorandum No. 74–13. Princeton, N. J.: ETS, 1974.

Lord, F. E. A realistic look at special classes. *Exceptional Children,* 1956, *22,* 321–325.

Lord, F. M. *A study of item bias using characteristic curve theory.* New York: College Entrance Examination Board, 1977.

Lovitt, T. T. Characteristics of ABA part 1: General recommendations and methodological limitations. *Journal of Learning Disabilities,* 1975, *8,* 432–433.

Lovitt, T. *Reactions to planned research.* Paper presented at the Roundtable Conference on Learning Disabilities. Minneapolis: Institute for Research on Learning Disabilities, 1978.

Lund, K. A., Foster, G. E., & McCall-Perez, F. C. The effectiveness of psycholinguistic training: A reevaluation. *Exceptional Children,* 1978, *44,* 310–319.

Lynn, R. *Learning disabilities.* New York: Free Press, 1979.

Macht, J. *The slaying of the dragons within.* Littleton, Colo.: JEM, 1980.

MacMillan, D. L. Special education for the mildly handicapped—Servant or savant? *Focus on Exceptional Children,* 1971, *2,* 1–11.

MacMillan, D. L., Jones, R. L., & Aloia, G. F. The mentally retarded label: A theoretical analysis and review of research. *American Journal of Mental Deficiency,* 1974, *79,* 241–261.

MacMillan, D. L., Meyers, C. E., & Yoshida, R. K. Regular class teachers' perceptions of transition programs for EMR students and their impact on the students. *Psychology in the Schools,* 1978, *15,* 99–103.

Mann. L. Are we fractionating too much? *Academic Therapy,* 1970, *5,* 85–91.

Mann, L. Psychometric phrenology and the new faculty psychology: The case against ability assessment and training. *The Journal of Special Education,* 1971, *5,* 3–14.

Mann, L. Divagations II. *The Journal of Special Education,* 1978, *12,* 100–101.

Mann, L. *On the trail of process.* New York: Grune & Stratton, 1979.

Mann. L. M., & Phillips, W. A. Fractional practices in special education: A critique. *Exceptional Children,* 1967, *33,* 311–317.

Maslach, C. Burned-out. *Human Behavior,* 1976, *5,* 16-22.

Maslach, C., & Pines, A. The burn-out syndrome in the day care setting. *Child Care Quarterly,* 1977, *6,* 100–113.

Matluck, J. H., & Mace, B. J. Language characteristics of Mexican-American children: Implications for assessment. *Journal of School Psychology,* 1973, *11,* 365–386.

Matluck, J. H., & Mace-Matluck, B. J. Language and culture in the multi-ethnic community: Spoken-language assessment. *Modern Language Journal,* 1975, *59,* 250–255.

Mattingly, M. Sources of stress and burn-out in professional child care work. *Child Care Quarterly,* 1977, *6,* 127–137.

Matuszek, P., & Oakland, T. *A factor analysis of several reading readiness measures for different socioeconomic and ethnic groups.* Paper presented at the annual meeting of the American Educational Research Association, 1972.

Maxwell, W. H. *Fourth Annual Report of the City Superintendent of Schools for the Year Ending July 31, 1902,* Department of Education, City of New York.

Mayer, M. *The Schools.* New York: Harper & Row, Pub., 1961. In B. Johnston (Ed.), *Issues in education.* Boston: Houghton Mifflin, 1964.

McGuire, W. Personality and susceptibility to social influence. In E. G. Borgatta & W. W. Albert (Eds.). *Handbook of personality theory and research.* New York: Appleton-Century-Crofts, 1966.

McGuire, W. H. Teacher burnout. *Today's Education,* 1979, *68,* 5.

McNemar, Q. On so-called test bias. *American Psychologist,* 1975, *30,* 848–851.

Medinnus, G., & Unruh, R. *Teacher expectations and verbal communication.* Paper presented at the annual meeting of the Western Psychological Association, 1971.

Mehrabian, A. *Nonverbal communication.* Chicago: Aldine-Atherton, 1972.

Meichenbaum, D., Bowers, H., & Ross, R. A behavioral analysis of teacher expectancy effect. *Journal of Personality and Social Psychology,* 1969, *13,* 306–316.

Menges, R. J. Assessing readiness for professional practice. *Review of Educational Research,* 1975, *45,* 173–207.

Mercer, C. D., Forgnone, C., & Wolking, W. D. Definitions of learning disabilities used in the United States. *Journal of Learning Disabilities,* 1976, *9,* 376–386.

Mercer, J. R. Sociological perspectives on mild mental retardation. In H. C. Haywood (Ed.), *Socio-cultural aspects of mental retardation.* New York: Appleton-Century-Crofts, 1970.

Mercer, J. R. *Labeling the mentally retarded.* Berkeley and Los Angeles: University of California Press, 1973.

Mercer, J. Psychological assessment and the rights of children. In N. Hobbs (Ed.), *Issues in the classification of children.* San Francisco: Jossey-Bass, 1976.

Mercer, J., & Ysseldyke, J. E. Designing diagnostic-intervention programs. In T. Oakland, *Psychological and educational assessment of minority children.* New York: Brunner/Mazel, 1977.

Meyer, C. E., MacMillan, D. L., & Yoshida, R. K. Regular class education of EMR students, from efficacy to mainstreaming. In J. Gottlieb (Ed.), *Educating mentally retarded persons in the mainstream.* Baltimore: University Park Press, 1980.

Meyer, W., & Thompson, G. Sex differences in the distribution of teacher approval and disapproval among sixth grade children. *Journal of Educational Psychology,* 1956, *47,* 385–396.

Michael, J. A., & Weinberger, J. A. Federal restrictions on educational research: Protection for research participants. *Educational Researcher,* 1977, *6*(1), 3–7.

Miller, H. A. *The school and the immigrant.* Cleveland: Survey Committee of the Cleveland Foundation, 1916.

Miller, S. R., Ewing, N. J., & Phelps, L. A. Career and vocational education for the handicapped: A historical perspective. In L. Mann & D. A. Sabatino (Eds.), *Fourth review of special education.* New York: Grune & Stratton, 1980.

Milne, N. M., & Mountain, L. Publishing policies of special-education-related journals. *The Journal of Special Education,* 1980, *14,* 121–125.

Minskoff, E. Research on psycholinguistic training: Critique and guidelines. *Exceptional Children,* 1975, *42,* 136–144.

Mirkin, B. Evaluation of drugs in children and pregnant women: An ineluctable conundrum? *Trends in Pharmacological Science,* 1980, *2,* 1–3.

Mirkin, P. K. Conclusions. In J. Ysseldyke & M. Thurlow (Eds.), *The special education assessment and decision-making process: Seven case studies.* Minneapolis: University of Minnesota Institute for Research on Learning Disabilities, 1980.

Mischel, H. Achievements. *Journal of Educational Psychology,* 1974, *66,* 157–166.

Moore, J., & Fine, M. J. Regular and special class teachers' perceptions of normal and exceptional children and their attitudes toward mainstreaming. *Psychology in the Schools,* 1978, *15,* 253–259.

Moores, D. F. *Educating the deaf: Psychology, principles and practices.* Boston: Houghton Mifflin, 1978.

Morse, W., Cutler, R., & Fink, A. *Public school classes for the emotionally handicapped: A research analysis.* Washington, D. C., CEC, 1964.

Mueller, M. Research and education of the handicapped, *Exceptional Children,* 1976, *43,* 151–153.

Mueller, M. Personal communication to J. Ysseldyke, June 22, 1981.

Mullins, J. B. A rationale for vision training. *Journal of the American Optometric Association,* 1969, *40,* 139–142.

Nairn, A. & Associates. *The reign of ETS: The corporation that makes up minds.* Washington, D. C., 1980.

National Education Association. Teacher opinion poll. *Today's Education,* 1979, *68,* 10.

National Education Association, Department of Superintendence. *Ideals of public education.* Chicago: National Education Association, 1922.

National Education Association, National Committee of the Project on Instruction. *Deciding what to teach.* Washington, D. C.: National Education Association, 1963.

National Society for the Prevention of Blindness. *Estimated statistics on blindness and vision problems.* New York: National Society for the Prevention of Blindness, 1966.

Neisser, U. *Cognitive psychology.* New York: Appleton-Century-Crofts, 1967.

Neisworth, J. T., & Greer, J. G. Functional similarities of learning disability and mild retardation. *Exceptional Children,* 1975, *42,* 17–21.

Newcomer, P., & Hammill, D. D. The ITPA and academic achievement: A survey. *The Reading Teacher,* 1975, *28,* 731–741.

Newland, T. E. Assumptions underlying psychological testing. *Journal of School Psychology,* 1973, *11,* 316–322.

Newland, T. E. Psychological assessment of exceptional children and youth. In W. Cruickshank (Ed.), *Psychology of Exceptional Children and Youth.* Englewood Cliffs, N.J.: Prentice-Hall, 1980.

Orlich, D. C. Federal educational policy: The paradox of innovation and centralization. *Educational Researcher,* 1979, *8*(7), 4–9.

Palardy, J. What teachers believe — What children achieve. *Elementary School Journal,* 1969, *69,* 370–374.

Palmer, D. Regular classroom teachers' attributions and instructional prescriptions for handicapped and nonhandicapped pupils. *The Journal of Special Education,* 1979, *13,* 325–337.

Pancrazio, S. B. State education agencies as research arenas. *Educational Researcher,* 1978, *7*(1), 5–10.

Parish, T. S., & Copeland, R. F. Teachers' and students' attitudes in mainstreamed classrooms. *Psychological Reports,* 1978, *43,* 54.

Parish, T. S., & Dyck, N. *Stereotypes of normal and handicapped children: A stumbling block for mainstreaming.* Paper presented at the meeting of the American Educational Research Association, San Francisco, April 1979.

Petersen, N. S., & Novick, M. R. An evaluation of some models for culture-fair selection. *Journal of Educational Measurement,* 1976, *13,* 3–29.

Pflaum, S. W., Walberg, H. J., Karegianes, M. L., & Rasher, S. P. Reading instruction: A quantitative analysis. *Educational Researcher,* 1980, *9*(7), 12–18.

Phillips, L., Draguns, J. G., & Bartlett, D. P. Classification of behavior disorders. In N. Hobbs (Ed.), *Issues in the classification of children* (Vol. 1). San Francisco: Jossey-Bass, 1976.

Pillemer, D. B., & Light, R. J. Synthesizing outcomes: How to use research evidence from many studies. *Harvard Educational Review,* 1980, *50,* 176–195.

Pintner, R. *Intelligence testing: Methods and results* (2nd ed.). New York: Henry Holt, 1932.

Poland, S., Thurlow, M., Ysseldyke, J., & Mirkin, P. Current psychoeducational decision-making practices as reported by directors of special education. *Journal of School Psychology,* in press.

Prehm, H. J. Special education research: Retrospect and prospect. *Exceptional Children,* 1976, *43,* 10–19.

Quay, H. C. Special education: Assumptions, techniques, and evaluative criteria. *Exceptional Children,* 1973, *40,* 165–170.

Quay, L. C. Academic skills. In N. R. Ellis (Ed.), *Handbook of mental deficiency.* New York: McGraw-Hill, 1963.

Raywid, M. A. The first decade of public school alternatives. *Phi Delta Kappan,* 1981, *62,* 551–554.

Redden, M. R., & Blackhurst, A. E. Mainstreaming competency specification for elementary teachers. *Exceptional Children,* 1978, *45,* 615–617.

Reinert, H. C. *Children in conflict.* St. Louis: C. V. Mosby, 1967.

Reisler, R. F. An education agenda for the eighties. *Phi Delta Kappan,* 1981, *62,* 413–414, 435.

Report to Congress. Menlo Park, Calif.: SRI International, 1979.

Reschly, D. J., & Lambrecht, M. J. Expectancy effects of labels: Fact or artifact? *Exceptional Children,* 1979, *46,* 55–58.

Reynolds, M. C. More process than is due. *Theory into practice,* 1975, *14,* 61–68. (a)

Reynolds, M. C. Trends in special education: Implications for measurement. In M. Reynolds & W. Hively (Eds.), *Domain-referenced testing in special education.* Minneapolis: University of Minnesota Leadership Training Institute/Special Education, 1975. (b)

Reynolds, M. C. Final notes. In J. Grosenick & M. Reynolds (Eds.), *Teacher education.* Minneapolis: University of Minnesota Leadership Training Institute/Special Education, 1978.

Reynolds, M. C. (Ed.). *A common body of practice for teachers: The challenge of Public Law 94-142 to teacher education.* Washington, D. C.: American Association of Colleges of Teacher Education, 1980.

Reynolds, M. C. The rights of children: A challenge to school psychologists. In T. Kratochwill, *Advances in School Psychology.* Hillsdale, N.J.: Lawrence Erlbaum Associates, in press.

Rhodes, W. C. The disturbing child: A problem of ecological management. *Exceptional Children,* 1967, *33,* 449–455.

Rhodes, W. C. A community participation analysis of emotional disturbance. *Exceptional Children,* 1970, *37,* 309–314.

Rhodes, W. C., & Sagor, M. Community perspectives. In N. Hobbs (Ed.), *Issues in the classification of children* (Vol. 1). San Francisco: Jossey-Bass, 1976.

Richey, L. S., Ysseldyke, J. E., Potter, M., Regan, R. R., & Greener, J. *Teachers' attitudes and expectations for siblings of learning disabled students.* Research Report #39. Minneapolis: University of Minnesota Institute for Research on Learning Disabilities, 1980.

Riese, W. *A history of neurology.* New York: M. D. Publications, 1959.

Robbins, M., & Glass, G. V. The Doman-Delacato rationale: A critical analysis. In J. Hellmuth (Ed.), *Educational therapy* (Vol. 2). Seattle: Special Child Publications, 1969.

Robinson, N. M., & Robinson, H. B. *The mentally retarded child* (2nd ed.). New York: McGraw-Hill, 1976.

Rosenshine, B. Classroom instruction. In *The psychology of teaching methods: The seventy-fifth yearbook of the National Society for the Study of Education.* Chicago: University of Chicago Press, 1976.

Rosenshine, B., & Furst, N. Research on teacher performance criteria. In B. O. Smith (Ed.), *Research in teacher education: A symposium.* Englewood Cliffs, N.J.: Prentice-Hall, 1971.

Rosenthal, R. *Experimenter effects in behavioral research.* New York: Appleton-Century-Crofts, 1966.

Rosenthal, R., & Jacobsen, L. *Pygmalion in the classroom: Teacher expectation and pupils' intellectual development.* New York: Holt, Rinehart & Winston, 1968.

Rosenthal, R., & Rubin, D. B. Interpersonal expectancy effects: The first 345 studies. *Behavioral and Brain Sciences,* 1978, *3,* 377–415.

Rosner, J. The philosophy of developmental vision. *Journal of the American Optometric Association,* 1963, *34,* 550–556.

Ross, M. B., & Salvia, J. Attractiveness as a biasing factor in teacher judgments. *American Journal of Mental Deficiency,* 1975, *80,* 96–98.

Roth, R. A. Certifying teachers: An overhaul is underway. *The Clearinghouse,* 1973, *47,* 287–291.

Rothbart, M., Dalfen, S., & Barrett, R. Effects of teachers' expectancy on student-teacher interaction. *Journal of Educational Psychology,* 1971, *62,* 49–54.

Rubin, R., & Balow, B. Learning and behavior disorders. A longitudinal study. *Exceptional Children,* 1971, *38,* 293–299.

Rubovitz, P., & Maehr, M. Pygmalion analyzed: Toward an explanation of the Rosenthal-Jacobsen findings. *Journal of Personality and Social Psychology,* 1971, *19,* 197–203.

Rubovitz, P., & Maehr, M. Pygmalion black and white. *Journal of Personality and Social Psychology,* 1973, *25,* 210–218.

Rutter, M. Diagnosis and definition. In M. Rutter & E. Schopler (Eds.), *Autism: A reappraisal of concepts and treatment.* New York: Plenum, 1978.

Ryan, K., Applegate, J., Flora, V. R., Johnston, J., Lasley, T., Mager, G., &

Newman, K. "My teacher education program? Well. . . . ": First year teachers reflect and react. *Peabody Journal of Education,* 1979, *56,* 267–271.

Sabatino, D. A. Auditory perception: Development, assessment, and intervention. In L. Mann & D. A. Sabatino (Eds.), *First review of special education.* New York: Grune & Stratton, 1973.

Salvia, J., Algozzine, R., & Sheare, J. Attractiveness and school achievement. *Journal of School Psychology,* 1977, *15,* 60–67.

Salvia, J. A., & Meisel, C. J. Observer bias: A methodological consideration in special education research. *The Journal of Special Education,* 1980, *14,* 261–270.

Salvia, J., & Podol, J. Effects of visibility of a prepalatal cleft on the evaluation of speech. *Cleft Palate Journal,* 1976, *13,* 361–366.

Salvia, J., Sheare, J., & Algozzine, B. Facial attractiveness and personal social development. *Journal of Abnormal Child Psychology,* 1975, *3,* 171–178.

Salvia, J., & Ysseldyke, J. E. *Assessment in special and remedial education* (2nd ed.). Boston: Houghton Mifflin, 1981.

Sameroff, A. J., & Zax, M. Schizotaxia revisited: Model issues in the etiology of schizophrenia. *American Journal of Orthopsychiatry,* 1973, *43,* 744–754.

Samuels, S. J. Characteristics of exemplary reading programs. In J. Guthrie (Ed.), *Comprehension and teaching: Reviews of research.* Newark, Del.: International Reading Association, 1981.

Sarason, S. B., Davidson, K., & Blatt, B. *The preparation of teachers: An unstudied problem in education.* New York: John Wiley, 1962.

Sarason, S. B., & Doris, J. *Educational handicap, public policy, and social history.* New York: Free Press, 1979.

Sax, G. *Empirical foundations of educational research.* Englewood Cliffs, N.J.: Prentice-Hall, 1968.

Schain, S. *Learning of low ability children and tutor behavior as a function of self-fulfilling prophecy.* Unpublished doctoral dissertation, University of Illinois, 1972.

Scheyneman, J. *Validating a procedure for assessing bias in test items in the absence of an outside criterion.* Paper presented at the annual meeting of the American Educational Research Association, 1976.

Schleier, L. M. *Problems in the training of certain special class teachers.* New York: Bureau of Publications, Teachers College, Columbia University, 1931.

Schofer, R. C., & Lilly, M. S. Personnel preparation in special education. In L. Mann & D. A. Sabatino (Eds.), *Fourth review of special education.* New York: Grune & Stratton, 1980.

Schubert, W. H. Recalibrating educational research: Toward a focus on practice. *Educational Researcher,* 1980, *9*(1), 17–24, 31.

Scriven, M. Self-referent research. *Educational Researcher,* 1980, *9,*(4), 7–11.

Seaver, W. B. Effects of naturally induced teacher expectancies. *Journal of Personality and Social Psychology,* 1973, *28,* 333–342.

Shane, H. Editorial: The renaissance of early childhood education. *Phi Delta Kappan,* 1969, *50,* 369, 412–413.

Sharp, L. M., & Frankel, J. Organizations that perform educational R & D: A first look at the universe. *Educational Researcher,* 1979, *8*(11), 6-11.

Shaver, J. P. The productivity of educational research and the applied-basic research distinction. *Educational Researcher,* 1979, *8*(1), 3–9.

Shaver, J. P., & Norton, R. S. Randomness and replication in ten years of the American Educational Research Journal. *Educational Researcher,* 1980, *9*(1), 9–15.

Shea, T. M. *Teaching children and youth with behavior disorders.* St. Louis: C. V. Mosby, 1978.

Shores, R., Cegelka, P., & Nelson, C. M. A review of research on teacher competencies. *Exceptional Children,* 1973, *40* 192–197.

Shotel, J. R., Iano, R. P., & McGettigan, J. F. Teacher attitudes associated with the integration of handicapped children. *Exceptional Children,* 1972, *38,* 677–683.

Shutz, R. E. Where we've been, where we are, and where we're going in educational R & D. *Educational Researcher,* 1979, *8*(8), 6–8, 24.

Siantz, J., & Moore, E. Inservice programming and preservice priorities. In J. Smith (Ed.), *Personnel preparation and Public Law 94–142: The map, the mission and the mandate* (2nd Ed.). Boothwyn, Pa.: Educational Resources Center, 1978.

Sidman, M. *Tactics of scientific research.* New York: Basic Books, 1960.

Silberman, C. E. *Crisis in the classroom: The remaking of American education.* New York: Random House, 1970.

Sloat, R. S. Optometry: What is it worth to education. *Optometric Weekly,* 1971, *62,* 40–51.

Smith, B. O. Pedagogical education: How about reform? *Phi Delta Kappan,* 1980, *62,* 87–91.

Smith, D. C., & Street, S. The professional component in selected professions. *Phi Delta Kappan,* 1980, *62,* 103–107.

Smith, M. L., & Glass, G. V. Meta-analysis of research on class size and its relationship to attitudes and instruction. *American Educational Research Journal,* 1980, *17,* 419–433.

Smith, V., Barr, R., & Burke, D. *Alternatives in education: Freedom to choose.* Bloomington, Ind.: Phi Delta Kappa Education Foundation, 1976.

Stebbins, L., St. Pierre, R., Proper, E., Anderson, R., & Cerva, T. *Education as experimentation: A planned variation model.* Cambridge, Mass.: Abt Associates. 1977.

Stephens, T. M., Hartman, A. C., & Lucas, V. H. *Teaching children basic skills: A curriculum handbook.* Columbus, Ohio: Chas. E. Merrill, 1978.

Stinnett, T. M. Teacher education, certification and accreditation. In E. Fuller & J. B. Pearson (Eds.), *Education in the states: Nationwide development since 1900.* Washington, D. C.: National Education Association, 1969.

Stinnett, T. M. *A manual on standards affecting school personnel in the United States.* Washington, D. C.: National Education Association, 1974.

Stock, J. R., Newbord, J., Wnek, L. L., Schenck, E. A., Gabel, J. R., Spurgeon, M. S., & Ray, H. W. *Evaluation of Handicapped Children's Early Education Program (HCEEP). Final report.* Contract # OEC-0-74-0402. Columbus, Ohio: Battelle Center for Improved Education, 1976.

Strauss, S. Guidelines for analysis of research reports. *Journal of Educational Research,* 1969, *63,* 165-169.

Sutherland, J. H. *The learning disabilities label as a biasing factor in the complex visual-motor integration performance of normal fourth grade children.* Unpublished doctoral dissertation, The Pennsylvania State University, 1976.

Swan, W. W. The handicapped children's early education program. *Exceptional Children,* 1980, *47,* 12-16.

Swanson, W. L. Optometric vision therapy—How successful is it in the treatment of learning disorders? *Journal of Learning Disabilities,* 1972, *5,* 37-42.

Swartwout, W. J. Visual abilities and academic success. *Optometric Weekly,* 1972, *63,* 1229-1234.

Symond, P. M. A research checklist in educational psychology. *Journal of Educational Psychology,* 1956, *47,* 100-109.

Szasz, T. *Ideology and insanity.* Garden City, N.Y.: Anchor-Doubleday, 1970.

Tharp, R. G., & Wetzel, R. J. *Behavior modification in the natural environment.* New York: Academic Press, 1969.

Thomas, A. Personal communication: Letter of rejection to Bob Algozzine, 1979.

Thomas, A. Personal communication: Letter of rejection to James Ysseldyke, 1980.

Thomas, A. Personal communication: Letter of rejection to Bob Algozzine, 1981.

Thorndike, R. L. Concepts of culture-fairness. *Journal of Educational Measurement,* 1971, *8,* 63-70.

Thrasher, R. Florida's alternative education law stresses positive, not punitive, schooling. *Phi Delta Kappan,* 1981, *62,* 547.

Thurlow, M. L., & Ysseldyke, J. E. Current assessment and decision-making practices in model programs for the learning disabled. *Learning Disability Quarterly,* 1979, *2,* 15-24.

Thurlow, M., & Ysseldyke, J. E. Instructional planning: Information collected by school psychologists *v* information considered useful by teachers. *Journal of School Psychology,* in press.

Tittle, C. K. Women and educational testing. *Phi Delta Kappan,* 1973, *55,* 118–119.

Tobias, S., & Zibrin, M. Does blind reviewing make a difference? *Educational Researcher,* 1978, *7*(1), 14–16.

Tolor, A., & Brannigan, G. C. Sex differences reappraised: A rebuttal. *Journal of Genetic Psychology,* 1975, *127,* 319–321.

Tom, A. R. NCATE standards and program quality: You can't get there from here. *Phi Delta Kappan,* 1980, *62,* 113–117.

Torgesen, J. K., & Dice, C. Characteristics of research on learning disabilities. *Journal of Learning Disabilities,* 1980, *13*(9), 5–9.

Trachtman, G. M. *Evils of educational change.* Invited address at a joint conference of Council of School Superintendents & New York State Association of School District Administrators, Grossinger, N.Y., 1964. [Note 26 to 1981 paper]

Trachtman, G. On such a full sea. In J. Ysseldyke & R. Weinberg (Eds.), *The future of psychology in the schools: Proceedings of the Spring Hill Symposium. School Psychology Review, A Special Issue,* 1981, *2,* 138–181.

Tramonti, J. Visual perceptual training and the retarded school achiever. *Journal of the American Optometric Association,* 1963, *34,* 543–549.

Travers, R. M. W. *An introduction to educational research* (2nd ed.). New York: Macmillan, 1964.

Tucker, J. A. Ethnic proportions in classes for the learning disabled: Issues in non-biased assessment. *The Journal of Special Education,* 1980, *14,* 93–105.

Tuckman, B. W. *Conducting educational research.* New York: Harcourt Brace Jovanovich, 1979.

Turney, B., & Robb, G. *Research in education: An introduction.* Hinsdale, Ill.: Dryden Press, 1971.

Tyack, D. B. Ways of seeing: An essay on the history of compulsory schooling. *Harvard Educational Review,* 1976, *46,* 335–389.

Ullmann, L., & Krasner, L. *A socio-psychological approach to abnormal behavior.* Englewood Cliffs, N.J.: Prentice-Hall, 1969.

U. S. Department of Education. *To assure the free appropriate public education of all handicapped children: Second annual report to Congress on the implementation of Public Law 94–142: The Education for All Handicapped Children Act.* Washington, D. C.: Department of Education, 1980.

U. S. Department of Health, Education and Welfare. *Progress toward a free appropriate public education.* Washington, D. C.: Bureau of Education for the Handicapped, 1979.

U. S. Office of Education. Assistance to states for education of handicapped children: Procedures for evaluating specific learning disabilities. *Federal Register,* *42*(250), December 29, 1977. (a)

U. S. Office of Education. Education of handicapped children: Implementation of Part B of the Education of the Handicapped Act. *Federal Register, 42*(163), August 23, 1977. (b)

U. S. Senate, Report No. 94–168, *Education for All Handicapped Children Act,* June 2, 1975.

Vacc, N., & Kurst, N. Emotionally disturbed children and regular class teachers. *Elementary School Journal, 1977, 77,* 309–317.

Van Dalen, D. B. A research checklist in education. *Educational Administration and Supervision,* 1958, *44,* 174–178.

Van Sickle, J. H. Provision for exceptional children in the public schools. *Psychological Clinic.* 1908–1909, *2,* 102–111.

Vasquez, J. Measurement of intelligence and language differences. *Aztlan,* 1972, *3,* 155–163.

Vonnegut, K., Jr. *Breakfast of champions.* New York: Dell Pub. Co., Inc., 1973.

Walker, H. M. Methods of research. *Review of Educational Research,* 1956, *26,* 323–344.

Wallace, A. Schools in revolutionary and conservative societies. In F. Ianni & E. Story (Eds.), *Cultural relevance and education issues.* Boston: Little, Brown, 1973.

Wallen, J. E. W. *The mental health of the school child.* New Haven, Conn.: Yale University Press, 1914.

Ward, A. W., Hall, B. W., & Schramm, C. F. Evaluation of published educational research: A national survey. *American Educational Research Journal,* 1975, *12,* 109–128.

Washington Research Project, Children's Defense Fund. *Children out of school in America.* Washington, D. C.: Children's Defense Fund, 1974.

Weinberger, J. A., & Michael, J. A. Federal restrictions on educational research. *Educational Researcher,* 1976, *5*(11), 3–8.

Weiskopf, P. E. Burnout among teachers of exceptional children. *Exceptional Children,* 1980, *47,* 18–23.

Werry, J., & Quay, H. The prevalence of behavior symptoms in younger elementary school children. *American Journal of Orthopsychiatry,* 1971, *41,* 136–143.

Whiteman, M., & Deutsch, M. Social disadvantage as related to intellective and language development. In M. Deutsch, I. Katz, & A. Jensen. *Social class, race, and psychological development.* New York: Holt, Rinehart & Winston, 1968.

Winer, B. J. *Statistical principles in experimental design* (2nd ed.), New York: McGraw-Hill, 1974.

Woellner, E. H. *Requirements for certification, 1979–1980.* Chicago: University of Chicago Press, 1979.

Wolfensberger, W. Twenty predictions about the future of residential services in mental retardation. *Mental Retardation,* 1969, *7*(6), 51–54.

Wolfensberger, W. Will there always be an institution? II: The impact of new service models. *Mental Retardation,* 1971, *9*(6), 31–38.

Wolfensberger, W. *The principle of normalization in human services.* Toronto: National Institute on Mental Retardation, 1972.

Wolfensberger, W., & Kurtz, R. A. (Eds.), *Management of the family of the mentally retarded.* New York: Follett, 1969.

Yoshida, R. K., & Meyers, C. E. Effects of labeling an educable mentally retarded on teachers' expectancies for change in a student's performance. *Journal of Educational Psychology,* 1975, *67,* 521–527.

Ysseldyke, J. E. Diagnostic-prescriptive teaching: The search for aptitude-treatment interactions. In L. Mann & D. Sabatino (Eds.), *First review of special education.* New York: Grune & Stratton, 1973.

Ysseldyke, J. E. Assessment of retardation. In J. Neisworth & R. Smith, *Mental retardation: Issues, assessment and intervention.* New York: McGraw-Hill, 1978.

Ysseldyke, J. E. Issues in psychoeducational assessment. In G. D. Phye & D. Reschly, *School psychology: Perspectives and issues.* New York: Academic Press, 1979.

Ysseldyke, J. E., & Algozzine, B. Perspectives on assessment of learning disabled students. *Learning Disability Quarterly,* 1979, *2*(4), 3–13.

Ysseldyke, J. E., Algozzine, B., & Allen, D. Regular education teacher participation in special education team decision making. *Elementary School Journal,* in press.

Ysseldyke, J. E., Algozzine, B., & Mitchell, J. Special education team decision making: An analysis of current practice. *Personnel and Guidance Journal,* in press.

Ysseldyke, J. E., Algozzine, B., Regan, R., Potter, M., Richey, L., & Thurlow, M. *Psychoeducational assessment and decision making: A computer simulated investigation.* Research Report #32. Minneapolis: University of Minnesota Institute for Research on Learning Disabilities, 1980.

Ysseldyke, J. E., Algozzine, B., & Richey, L. S. How many students are handicapped? *Exceptional Children,* in press.

Ysseldyke, J. E., Algozzine, B., Richey, L. S., & Graden, J. Declaring students eligible for learning disability services: Why bother with the data? *Learning Disability Quarterly,* in press.

Ysseldyke, J. E., Algozzine, B., Rostollan, D., & Shinn, M. A content analysis of the data presented at special education placement team meetings. *Journal of Clinical Psychology,* in press.

Ysseldyke, J. E., Algozzine, B., Shinn, M., & McGue, M. Similarities and differences between low achievers and students labeled learning disabled. *The Journal of Special Education,* in press.

Ysseldyke, J. E., Algozzine, B., & Thurlow, M. L. *A naturalistic investigation of special education team meetings.* Research Report #40. Minneapolis: University of Minnesota Institute for Research on Learning Disabilities, 1980.

Ysseldyke, J. E., & Mirkin, P. K. The use of assessment information to plan instructional interventions: A review of the research. In C. Reynolds & T. Gutkin (Eds.), *A handbook for school psychology.* New York: John Wiley, 1981.

Ysseldyke, J. E., & Salvia, J. Diagnostic-prescriptive teaching: Two models. *Exceptional Children,* 1974, *41,* 181–186.

Ysseldyke, J. E., & Salvia, J. A. Methodological considerations in aptitude-treatment interaction research with intact groups. *Diagnostique,* 1980, *6,* 3–9.

Ysseldyke, J. E., & Shinn, M. R. Psychoeducational evaluation: Procedures, considerations, and limitations. In D. Hallahan & J. Kauffman (Eds.), *The handbook of special education.* Englewood Cliffs, N.J.: Prentice-Hall, 1981.

Ysseldyke, J., & Stevens, L. Specific learning disabilities: The learning disabled. In C. Reynolds & R. Brown (Eds.), *Psychological perspectives on childhood exceptionality.* New York: John Wiley, in press.

Ysseldyke, J. E., & Thurlow, M. L. *The special education assessment and decision-making process: Seven case studies.* Research Report #44. Minneapolis: University of Minnesota Institute for Research on Learning Disabilities, 1980.

Zabel, R. H., & Zabel, M. K. Burnout: A critical issue for educators. *Education Unlimited,* 1980, *2*(2), 23–25.

Zigler, E., & Baller, D. Impact of institutional experience on the behavior and development of retarded persons. *American Journal of Mental Deficiency,* 1977, *82,* 1–11.

Author/Source Index

Subject Index

Reader Response Form

Ysseldyke and Algozzine, *Critical Issues in Special and Remedial Education*

We would like your reactions to the material presented in this text. We will use the information you provide to improve subsequent editions of this book. Please take a few minutes and complete the items below. When you have finished, mail the form to:

College Marketing
Houghton Mifflin Company
One Beacon Street
Boston, MA 02107

Thanks.

1. Do you think there are chapters that we could have included to provide more complete coverage of the "issues"? If so, what are they?

2. Do you think any of the present chapters are unnecessary? If so, what are they?

3. Do you think the coverage in any chapter was insufficient? If so, indicate the chapter and material that should be added.

4. Do you think the coverage in any chapter was excessive? If so, indicate the chapter and material that should be deleted.

5. We attempted to present a fair, even-handed treatment of the issues we believe are important in special and remedial education. Please list any chapters or sections of chapters where, in your opinion, we accomplished this and/or did not accomplish it.

6. Please indicate your reaction to the following selected areas of the book:

	Disliked very much			Liked very much	
a. Chapter outlines	1	2	3	4	5
b. Extensiveness of citations	1	2	3	4	5
c. Writing style	1	2	3	4	5
d. Choice of vocabulary	1	2	3	4	5
e. Overall level of content coverage	1	2	3	4	5
f. Experiment I812 (frog story)	1	2	3	4	5
g. Legal and legislative review	1	2	3	4	5
h. The critical issue	1	2	3	4	5

7. What did you like most about the book?

8. What did you like least about the book?

9. Tell us about yourself (are you a graduate or undergraduate student, a professional; what is your major area; etc.).

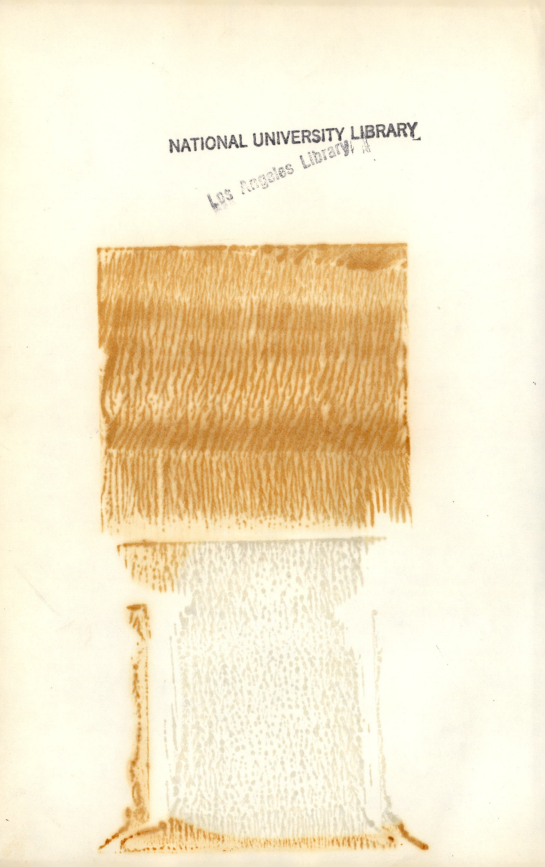